Nathan Matthews

The City Government of Boston

Nathan Matthews

The City Government of Boston

ISBN/EAN: 9783744791038

Printed in Europe, USA, Canada, Australia, Japan

Cover: Foto ©Suzi / pixelio.de

More available books at **www.hansebooks.com**

THE CITY GOVERNMENT OF BOSTON.

BY

NATHAN MATTHEWS, JR.,

MAYOR OF BOSTON, 1891–1895.

A VALEDICTORY ADDRESS TO THE MEMBERS OF THE
CITY COUNCIL, JANUARY 5, 1895.

BOSTON:
ROCKWELL AND CHURCHILL, CITY PRINTERS.
1895.

CITY OF BOSTON.

IN BOARD OF ALDERMEN, January 5, 1895.

Ordered, That His Honor Mayor Matthews be requested to cause fifteen hundred copies of his valedictory address to be printed and bound; the expense to be charged to the contingent fund of the Mayor's office.

Passed. Approved by the Mayor, January 5, 1895.

A true copy.

Attest:

J. M. GALVIN,
City Clerk.

TABLE OF CONTENTS.

	PAGE
INTRODUCTION	9, 10
CHAPTER 1. — ORGANIZATION OF THE CITY GOVERNMENT	11–16
Section 1. General Outline	11
" 2. The Executive Department	11
" 3. The Legislative Branch	13
" 4. The Board of Street Commissioners	14
" 5. The School Committee	14
" 6. The Board of Police	15
" 7. In General	15
CHAPTER 2. — ACCOUNTS AND REPORTS	17–27
Section 1. Department Reports	17
" 2. Financial Reports	18
" 3. Difficulties of Investigation	19
" 4. Changes effected	21
" 5. Estimates of Income	22
" 6. The Monthly Exhibits	24
" 7. Other Changes	24
CHAPTER 3. — EXPENDITURES AND REVENUES	28–40
Section 1. In General	28
" 2. Current Expenses and Annual Revenues	30
" 3. Additional Sources of Revenue	32
" 4. County Expenses	32
" 5. The Tax-limit	36
" 6. Valuations	37
CHAPTER 4. — INDEBTEDNESS	41–53
Section 1. Definitions	41
" 2. Increase since 1890	42
" 3. Special Reasons	43
" 4. Loans authorized, but not issued	44
" 5. Loans issued since January 1, 1891	47
" 6. Means of keeping the Debt down	48
" 7. Loans to be authorized in 1895	50
" 8. Analysis of City Loans since 1822	50
" 9. General Review of the City Debt	51
CHAPTER 5. — THE PUBLIC HEALTH	54–66
Section 1. Organization	55
" 2. Quarantine	56
" 3. Small-Pox	56
" 4. The City Hospital	57
" 5. Garbage	58
" 6. Street Cleaning	58
" 7. Street Watering	58
" 8. Sewers and Surface Drainage	59
" 9. Pest Holes and other Nuisances	64

CHAPTER 5. — *Continued.* PAGE
    Section 10. Water Supply 64
    " 11. Results 66
CHAPTER 6. — EDUCATIONAL FACILITIES 67–72
    Section 1. The Public Schools 67
    " 2. Public Libraries 71
CHAPTER 7. — BUILDING OPERATIONS 73–81
    Section 1. The Suffolk County Court House . . . 73
    " 2. The New Public Library 73
    " 3. Buildings in the Parks 75
    " 4. The Architect Department 75
    " 5. New City Hall 81
CHAPTER 8. — THE PUBLIC STREETS 82–96
    Section 1. Street Lines and Grades 82
    " 2. Construction, Maintenance, etc. 87
    " 3. Financial 89
    " 4. Bridges 92
    " 5. Grade Crossings 92
    " 6. Overhead Wires 93
    " 7. Compensation for the Use of Streets . . . 94
    " 8. Street Travel 95
CHAPTER 9. — STREET LIGHTING 97–101
CHAPTER 10. — PROTECTION AGAINST FIRE 102–103
    Section 1. Building Laws 102
    " 2. Fire Department 102
    " 3. Overhead Wires 103
CHAPTER 11. — RELIEF OF THE POOR 104–107
CHAPTER 12. — PAUPER AND PENAL INSTITUTIONS 108–111
CHAPTER 13. — PARKS 112–116
CHAPTER 14. — THE CIVIL SERVICE 117–120
CHAPTER 15. — LABOR MATTERS 121–125
CHAPTER 16. — STATE LEGISLATION 126–132
CHAPTER 17. — COMMERCIAL FACILITIES 133–137
    Section 1. Docks 133
    " 2. Railroad Terminals 136
CHAPTER 18. MUNICIPAL INVESTMENTS 138–163
    Section 1. The Public Lands 138
    " 2. The Quincy Market 140
    " 3. The Mystic Water-Works 140
    " 4. The Cochituate Water-Works 143
    " 5. The East Boston Ferries 153
    " 6. Summary of above undertakings . . . 160
    " 7. The Subway 161
CHAPTER 19. — THE CITY CHARTER 164–173
    Section 1. The Charter of 1822 164
    " 2. The Charter of 1854 167
    " 3. The Charter Amendments of 1885 . . . 168
CHAPTER 20. — THE PROBLEM OF CITY GOVERNMENT . . 174–185
CONCLUSION 186–188

LIST OF TABLES

IN THE APPENDIX AND THE TEXT.

I. General Tables.

APPENDIX: PAGE
No. 1. Polls, population, valuations, tax-rate, 1822 to 1894 . 190–191
" 2. Population by districts, 1638 to 1890 192
" 3. Area, population, polls, registered voters, and property-owning voters by wards 193

TEXT:
List of laws procured, 1891–1894 127–130
Comparative cost of work by contract and day labor, Coch. W.W. . 124
Street lamps and prices, 1891 and 1895 98
Price of gas to private consumers, 1891 and 1895 99
Increase in electric lights, 1882 to 1895 100
Electric lights by wards, January 1, 1895 100

II. Annual Revenues and Expenditures.

APPENDIX:
No. 4. Percentage of taxes collected, 1875 to 1895 194
" 5. Revenues applicable to the general appropriations, 1860 to 1894 195–209
" 6. Operation of the tax limit, 1885 to 1895 210
" 7. Tax calculations for the year 1894 211–212
" 8. Ordinary department expenditures, 1885 to 1894 . . 213–217
" 9. Salaries and wages paid, 1893-4 218–221
" 10. Payments for pensions, 1872 to 1894 222
" 11. War payments, 1861 to 1894 223
" 12. Surplus revenues, 1822 to 1894 224–225
" 13. Total expenditures, 1855 to 1894 226

TEXT:
Per capita expenditures, U.S. census of 1890 28
Current receipts and expenditures, 1891-2, 1892-3, and 1893–4 . . 20

III. Indebtedness.

APPENDIX:
No. 14. Loans issued, 1822 to 1894 227

LIST OF TABLES.

		PAGE
No. 15.	Sinking-fund receipts prior to April 30, 1871	228
" 16.	" " since " " "	229–231
	(Exclusive of water-debt sinking-funds.)	
" 17.	Total funded debt, gross and net, at close of each fiscal year, 1822 to 1894	232–233
" 18.	Total funded debt, gross and net, at close of each calendar year, 1855 to 1894	234
" 19.	Debt statement, December 31, 1894	235
" 20.	Borrowing capacity December 31, 1894, under St. 1885, ch. 178	236
" 21.	Borrowing capacity January 1, 1895, under St. 1885, ch. 178, and St. 1891, ch. 93	237–238
" 22.	Loans authorized outside of debt limit, 1885 to 1895	239
" 23.	Loans authorized but not issued, December 31, 1894	240
" 24.	Loans for the "Laying Out and Construction of Highways," December 31, 1894	241–242

TEXT:

Analysis of loans issued from 1822 to 1895	51
Loans issued between January 1, 1891, and December 31, 1894	47
Loan order approved January 5, 1895	53
Loans issued since January 1, 1891, for purposes to which the city had been committed prior to that date	43
Loans authorized but not issued December 31, 1894, for purposes to which the city has been committed since January 1, 1895	46

IV. Municipal Investments.

APPENDIX:

		PAGE
No. 25.	The "public lands," expenditures and receipts, 1822 to 1894,	243
" 26.	The Quincy market, payments, receipts, and net results, 1825 to 1894	244–249
" 27.	East Boston ferries, expenditures, 1858 to 1894	250
" 28.	" " receipts, 1858 to 1894	251
" 29.	" " net results, 1858 to 1894	252
" 30.	Mystic water-works, payments, 1863 to 1894	253
" 31.	" " receipts, 1863 to 1894	254
" 32.	" " net results, 1863 to 1894	255
" 33.	" " sinking-funds, 1874 to 1894	256
" 34.	" " debt, gross and net, 1862 to 1894	257
" 35.	Mystic and Cochituate water-works, payments from revenue for maintenance and extension of mains, 1885 to 1894	258
" 36.	Cochituate water-works, expenditures, 1844 to 1894, divided according to appropriations	259–264
" 37.	Cochituate water-works, expenditures, 1846 to 1894, divided according to sources from which the money was obtained	265

LIST OF TABLES.

					PAGE
No. 38.	Cochituate water-works,	receipts, 1846 to 1894			266
" 39.	" "	assessments, 1880 to 1894			267
" 40.	" "	department charges, 1854 to 1894,			268–271
" 41.	" "	hydrant charges, 1870 to 1894			272
" 42.	" "	net result of expenditures and receipts, 1846 to 1894			273
" 43.	" "	loans authorized and issued, 1846 to 1894			274–277
" 44.	" "	sinking-funds, 1871 to 1894			278
" 45.	" "	debt, gross and net, 1847 to 1894			279

TEXT:

Results of Quincy market undertaking 140
Decrease in the Cochituate water debt between January 1, 1891, and
December 31, 1894 49

V. Park Tables.

APPENDIX:

No. 46.	Park	appropriations, 1875 to 1895 .				280–283
" 47.	"	expenditures, 1875 to 1895 .				284–286
" 48.	"	statistics, December 31, 1894				287
" 49.	"	betterments, to January 31, 1894 .				288
" 50.	"	debt, gross and net, December 31, 1894				289

TEXT:

Cost of park lands, 1877 to 1894 38

ERRATA.

Page 24, note 2. — In first line, omit word "statement."
Page 45, table. — In last line but one, *for* " $50,000," *read* " $6,950,000." (See Table 23.)
Page 65, line 8. — *For* " December," *read* " January."
Page 112, note 1. — Substitute the following: " See St. 1870, ch. 283. The vote was taken at the State election of 1870, and resulted in 9,233 yeas to 5,916 nays."
Page 117, second paragraph, line 4. — *For* " or," *read* " for."
Page 150, note 1. — In third line from bottom, *for* "funded," *read* "unfunded."
   In second line from bottom, omit words "that year and."
Page 212, tenth line from bottom. — *For* " 1884," *read* " 1894."
Page 236, Table 20. — Water debt should be $1,000 more than stated, and other figures corrected accordingly. (See Table 21.)
Page 242, Table 24. — In fifth line from bottom, *for* " $147,162.91," *read* " $247,162.91."

VALEDICTORY ADDRESS.

To the Honorable the City Council:

GENTLEMEN : It has been customary for the mayors of this city, particularly for those who have held office during a succession of years, to close their connection with the City Government by a farewell message. These addresses have generally included a review of the administration of the outgoing Mayor, as well as recommendations for the improvement of the City Government suggested by his experience in office.

It has seemed to me that I ought not to leave the service of the city which has honored me with four successive elections without placing upon record a summary of the opinions which experience has caused me to form concerning the merits and defects of municipal government as administered to-day in Boston. This task necessarily involves a more or less detailed analysis of the management, past and present, of the various branches of the City Government; but I shall endeavor to execute it with as much brevity as the case permits. If frequent references are found to what has been done and to what has not been done during the years in which I have been personally connected with the City Government, I trust it will be understood that they were necessary and could not be avoided without losing sight of the true purpose of a valedictory address.

No general description of the City Government has been published since Quincy's Municipal History of the town and city from colonial days to 1830; and it is difficult to secure facts, figures, or dates relating to the work of the municipality as a whole, or to any particular part of it. It seemed, therefore, that this paper could be made not only appropriate to the occasion, but useful to the public, if prepared in the form of a short compendium of information concerning the several branches of municipal service; and it has accordingly been written with this object in view.

CHAPTER 1.

ORGANIZATION OF THE CITY GOVERNMENT.

SECTION 1. *General Outline.* The City Government as now organized consists of a Mayor and thirty-three executive departments under his control; of a legislative branch composed of a board of twelve Aldermen and a Common Council of seventy-five members; of a city clerk and city messenger elected by the city council; of a board of three Street Commissioners, elected by the people; of a School Committee consisting of twenty-four members elected by the people; of a Board of Police, consisting of three commissioners appointed by the Governor of the Commonwealth; of various county officers, including the judges of the Supreme Judicial, Superior and Probate Courts, the sheriff, clerks of court, register of probate, etc.; of certain attendants upon the legislative branch, namely, the clerk of committees, and the clerk of the Common Council; of a few temporary commissions, such as the Board of Survey and the Transit Commission; and of a host of minor officers, such as constables, weighers of coal, measurers of grain, inspectors, etc.

SECTION 2. *The Executive Department.* This consists of twelve boards or commissions, as follows: The Board of Assessors, the Board of Fire Commissioners, the Board of Health, the Boston City Hospital, the Board of Trustees of the Public Library, the Trustees of Mt. Hope Cemetery, the Board of Park Commissioners, the Board of Commissioners of Public Institutions, the Board of Registrars of Voters, the Overseers of the Poor in the City of Boston, the Board of Commissioners of Sinking-Funds, and the Boston Water Board; of twenty single heads of departments, — the City Architect, City Auditor, City Collector, City Engineer, Superintendent of Ferries, Superintendent of Public Buildings, Inspector of Milk and Vinegar, Inspector of Provisions, Superintendent of Lamps, Superintendent of Markets, Superintendent of Printing, Inspector of Buildings, Superintendent of Public Grounds, City Registrar, Sealer of Weights and Measures, Superintendent of Streets, City Surveyor, City Treasurer, Water Registrar, and Commissioner of Wires; and of a Law Department in joint charge of the Corporation Counsel and the City Solicitor. This makes a total of thirty-three departments, in charge of eighty-two persons, acting singly or as members of commissions, all of whom are appointed by the Mayor subject to confirmation by the Board of Aldermen, and all of whom are subject to removal by the Mayor for such cause as he may deem sufficient.

This organization is smaller by five departments than in 1890; the departments of Bridges, Cambridge Bridges, Sewers, and Sanitary Police having been consolidated with the Street Department under a single superintendent, and the Ancient Records Commission having been abolished and its work assigned to the City Registrar. The Board of Directors of East Boston Ferries was also abolished and the department placed in charge of a single superintendent. The Department for the Inspection of Wires, created in 1890, was abolished in 1891 as a separate department, and the work was placed in charge of the Board of Fire Commissioners; but a new department was created in 1894 to carry out the provisions of the law relating to overhead wires passed in that year.[1]

These reductions and consolidations have been productive of excellent results, and, as frequently suggested to the City Council, indicate the value of further changes tending to a simplification of the machinery of government and a concentration of responsibility. Among these changes are the substitution of single superintendents or commissioners for the Board of Commissioners of Public Institutions, the Board of Fire Commissioners, and the Boston Water Board. The work of the Fire Department is purely executive in

[1] St. 1894, chap. 454.

ORGANIZATION OF THE CITY GOVERNMENT. 13

character, that of the other two departments nearly so. The office of Water Registrar should either be made a subordinate division of the Department of Water Works, or consolidated with the Collecting Department. The Inspectors of Milk and Vinegar and of Provisions might be made subordinate officers of the Board of Health, which has general charge of all matters relating to the public health; and Mount Hope Cemetery could also be placed in charge of this Board.

As to the terms of office for the Mayor and his executive officers, it is my opinion that they should all be longer than at present. The Mayor should be elected for a term of two or three years; and the length of service of the heads of departments should be indeterminate. This is to a great extent the present practice, most of the heads of the more important departments having held office continuously under the various Democratic and Republican administrations of the recent past;[1] and it would, I believe, be well to change the statutes and ordinances so that the heads of departments as well as the subordinate officers of the Government shall hold office indefinitely until death, resignation or removal.

SECTION 3. *The Legislative Branch.* This, in my opinion, should be reconstructed by abolishing the present bicameral system and substituting a single legislative body. This body should be larger than the present Board of Aldermen, but not so large as to become unwieldy, and liable to degenerate into a debating society. The scheme which has seemed to me on the whole the most desirable, and which has been advocated on other occasions, is to establish a single legislature of twenty-four or twenty-seven men, elected at large, eight or nine each year, for a three-years term. If minority representation is desired, some system should be invented different from that in operation under the law of 1893.[2] This law is admitted on all hands to have

---

[1] For instance, no changes have been made since 1890, except those caused by death or resignation, in the heads of nineteen of the thirty-three executive departments, namely: Board of Assessors, Auditor, Collector, Engineer, Ferries, Fire, Hospital, Inspection of Buildings, Inspection of Milk and Vinegar, Inspection of Provisions, Printing, Markets, Public Buildings, Public Grounds, City Registrar, Sinking Funds, Surveyor, Treasurer, Board of Health.

[2] St. 1893, ch. 473, accepted by the people at the State election of 1893.

been a failure; and it is extremely doubtful whether any system of minority representation can be devised that will secure satisfactory results.

It would be foolish, indeed, to expect that this, or any, reconstruction of our municipal legislature will remove all the difficulties in the way of securing an economical and business-like government. The representatives of the citizens, howsoever elected, will continue to represent with more or less fidelity the wishes and principles of their constituents; and as long as the people at large, while in favor of economy as a general principle, yet desire appropriations for particular purposes on a scale that makes economy impossible, just so long will it be difficult to restrain the City Council, however constituted, from an improvident expenditure of the public funds. I believe, however, that some gain would follow from the change suggested; that a more responsible class of aspirants for positions in the City Council would appear, if the term of service were longer and the work of legislation restricted to a single body; and that in this way the difficulties of securing economy in expenditure would be diminished, though by no means removed.

SECTION 4. *The Board of Street Commissioners.* Why the Board of Street Commissioners should still be elected by the people, I have never been able to understand, except upon the theory that its members had sufficient influence to secure its omission from the scope of the charter amendments of 1885. The present system tends to create a division of responsibility, and the members of this board, like the other heads of departments, should, in my opinion, be appointed by the Mayor.

SECTION 5. *The School Committee.* The School Committee has been an unpaid elective body from the earliest times; but the business of the schools has outgrown the capacity of a board selected in this manner; and there is constant friction between the Mayor and City Council, who are responsible for the school appropriations, and the School

Committee, which has sole charge of expending them. Such friction is inevitable where the business in question is voluminous and complicated, and the responsibility for its proper conduct divided. I should recommend the passage of a law placing the public schools in charge of a superintendent, to be appointed in the usual way by the Mayor of the city.

SECTION 6. *Board of Police.* This department can never be managed to the satisfaction of the public so long as it remains in the charge of a State board [1] not responsible to the City Government, and composed necessarily of gentlemen who, whatever their personal qualifications, are yet regarded by a majority of the voters of this city with distrust. Besides the division of responsibility which the system entails, — the City Council being responsible within certain limits for the appropriations, and the Board of Police for their expenditure, — there are many special objections to the plan, such as the inability to secure the enforcement of the city ordinances. The Board of Police should be abolished; the police force should be restored to the control of the city, and placed in charge of a chief or superintendent appointed by the Mayor, and responsible through him to the people of the city; and the license-granting powers of the Board should then be vested in a special license board.

It will be said that this plan has already been tried, and that the present system has worked better. I cannot assent to this proposition as a statement of fact, for the department was never so mismanaged as between the years 1889 and 1893; but even if true, the transfer of a purely local concern, such as the police force of a city, to the control of the Commonwealth is a violation of the principle of local self-government and a constant source of irritation to the people. The gain in efficiency, if any, is not commensurate with the breach of principle involved.

SECT. 7. *In General.* Most of the changes urged in this chapter have been recommended on previous occasions.

---

[1] Established by St. 1885, ch. 323.

The question may arise, however, why these reforms, if reforms they be, have not been pressed with greater energy. The answer is, that the changes urged depend, with minor exceptions, upon the action of the State Legislature; that they are commonly regarded as political in character; and that I have intentionally and consistently refrained from urging any measure of a political character upon the committees of the General Court. I felt that the best work I could do was to administer the government as I found it, without wasting time in seeking radical organic changes, which the Legislature was not likely to grant at my request, and the advocacy of which was calculated to impair the influence that the Mayor properly possesses with committees of the General Court in respect to legislation affecting the financial interests of the city.[1]

[1] While I have no reason to complain of any partisan action on the part of the legislative committees of the past four years in matters relating to city finances and public improvements, yet my advocacy of a change, really political, or thought to be such, would have had very little weight with a Republican Legislature. The fate of the annual attempt to increase the term of office of the Mayor shows the impossibility of securing this reform from a Republican Legislature, so long as it was regarded by many as a scheme for the benefit of a Democratic administration. Now that the next Mayor is to be a Republican, there is more chance that the measure will pass.

CHAPTER 2.

ACCOUNTS AND REPORTS.

The current accounts of the city are accurately and intelligently kept by the Collector, Treasurer, and Auditor; and the method of paying out money is well calculated to prevent mistaken, illegal, and fraudulent payments.[1] The system is, or rather has been, defective in what might be termed the ledger part of it, that is in respect to capital, improvement, or investment accounts, and in the character of the reports printed for public information.

SECTION 1. *Department Reports.* The annual reports of the different departments I found to be much fuller than those published by most cities; but they were deficient in financial information. Statistics relating to the total cost or net results of the various public undertakings described in the reports were almost wholly lacking, and when given, generally inaccurate; while the few comparative statements of annual expenditures and receipts were incomplete and misleading.

Taking, for instance, the annual reports of the several departments for the year 1890,[2] we find that the City Architect has nothing to say about the cost of our school-houses and other public buildings except in respect to the payments during that particular year. The Board of Ferry Commissioners present a "statement" of the cost of the department from the purchase of the ferries, which is several hundred thousand dollars out of the way, and a "trial balance" worthy of the most advanced

---

[1] The drafts of the several departments, all countersigned by the Auditor, and approved by the Mayor, amounted to 1,652 during the fiscal year 1893-4, and involved the payment of $33,911,179.04. Practically every payment requires the written voucher of the head of a department, of the Auditor, of the Mayor, and of the Treasurer. The City Auditor's books are particularly well kept.

[2] Published in two volumes as Document 1 of the year 1891.

style of speculative railroad book-keeping.[1] The Trustees of the Public Library furnish a list of the Trustees and Examining Committees for thirty-nine years, as well as much other interesting information, but omit all mention of the millions of dollars in process of expenditure upon the new building on Dartmouth street.[2] The report of the Board of Park Commissioners contains no tables from which the amount expended in any one year, or the total cost of all the separate parks, can be ascertained. The report of the Water Board contains a short and insufficient if not inaccurate statement of the "cost of construction of the water works," but not a figure concerning total expenditures, total receipts, net cost, loans issued, changes in rates, department charges, and other facts necessary to a correct understanding of our water-works finances; nor is there anything to show the operation of the sinking-funds, or the steady increase in the debt. No figures are to be found in the entire two volumes showing the cost of our hospitals, cemeteries, markets, public institutions, school-houses, public grounds, or public buildings.

It may be said of the department reports, as a whole, that they contained little information of the kind described; and that such information as they did contain was always insufficient, generally inaccurate, and sometimes purposely misleading.

SECTION 2. *Financial Reports.* The annual reports of the City Auditor were also defective. Of the two hundred pages devoted to the payments for the year, a large proportion was occupied by the names of the different contractors, material-men, and teamsters, with the amounts paid to each on each separate job. Such lists were of little

---
[1] See chapter 18, § 5, and Appendix, Tables 27 to 29.

[2] Reference is, however, made to the semi-annual report of the Trustees upon the condition of this building. This report — Doc. 9, of 1891 — contains what purports to be a statement of the cost of the building to date, but is not, by reason of omitting all payments, amounting to $91,440.57, made prior to the month of May, 1888. The cost of the land, $203,925.00, was also omitted, and the accounts are otherwise incomplete. See Doc. 186, of the year 1892, for a proper set of estimates and accounts.

value without still fuller information, and were otherwise out of place in a general account of the financial operations of a great corporation. On the other hand, the few summarized statements of cost, notably those relating to the water-works and ferries, were inaccurate or insufficient, and there was practically nothing in the volume from which the citizens could learn what the city had expended on its various undertakings, what its annual average receipts were, or what had been the comparative cost from year to year of maintaining the different branches of municipal service.

The annual calculation of "ways and means," and the methods ostensibly followed in making up the annual tax-levy and appropriation order, were represented to be the same as before the passage of the tax-limit law of 1885; but if a totally different method had not in fact been used, a deficit would have annually resulted, or an illegal tax-rate, or both.[1]

The monthly exhibits or reports of the Auditor, Treasurer, and Collector were also deficient in the amount of information furnished; and no statement at all was published of the expenditures for the last month of the fiscal year.[2]

Then the period covered by the annual reports of the Auditor, Treasurer, Collector, and Sinking-Funds Commissioners was the fiscal year, which began on May 1 and ended on April 30; while the period covered by the annual reports of the other departments was the calendar year, from January 1 to December 31.

SECTION 3. *Difficulties of Investigation.* This condition of affairs made it impossible for any citizen to secure, without a most laborious investigation, accurate and complete information concerning the original cost

---
[1] The real way in which the appropriation orders have been made up since 1885 is shown in Appendix, Table 6; also in the inaugural addresses or messages accompanying the annual estimates submitted by the various Mayors.

[2] The payments during the month of April could only be discovered by subtracting each item in the statement for April 1 from the corresponding item in the Auditor's Annual Report — not printed, perhaps, for months — of the entire payments for the fiscal year.

of our various public undertakings, the annual cost of the various branches of municipal service, and the probable annual revenues. This information was peculiarly essential to the members of a City Government which was limited by law in the amount of money it could raise by taxation and from loans; and I am inclined to attribute the fact that it was so frequently thought necessary between 1885 and 1891 to borrow money for current expenses to the difficulty of estimating with accuracy the probable expenditures and receipts of the city. That the city can, as a matter of fact, live within its income as limited by the law of 1885 — that is, that it need not borrow money for the current expenses of administration — has been shown by the experience of the last four years; but the expenditures must, of necessity, very nearly equal the income,[1] and the departments can only be prevented from exceeding it by means of a sharp monthly watch upon every item of income and expenditure, and by monthly comparisons with the corresponding items for previous years.[2]

Called to the chief magistracy of the city without previous service in the Government, and believing that the first

[1] The current receipts and expenditures during the last three fiscal years have been as follows:

	Receipts.	Expenditures.	Surplus.
1891-92	$13,465,035 37	$13,381,001 27	$84,034 10
1892-93	14,612,771 22	14,212,233 56	400,537 66
1893-94	14,677,286 28	14,587,095 00	89,201 28

The surplus for 1894-95 will probably be about $100,000.

The receipts include the entire income of the city available for the general appropriations of the year. The expenditures include all unexpended appropriations from revenue for particular purposes, if any such there were at the close of the year. Such items are carried forward on the books of the new year, as credited to these special purposes; all other unexpended balances of appropriations, if any, — that is, all general department balances, — are allowed to lapse and figure in the surplus for the year.

[2] Blank forms were prepared for this purpose in 1892, and have proved of great assistance in the difficult task of keeping the department expenditures within the income of the city.

duty of a public officer charged with the disbursement of millions of dollars of the public money was to search the printed reports of the City Government for accounts that would show the cost from year to year of equipping and maintaining the various departments of municipal service, I was amazed to discover that practically there were none. I have in consequence been obliged to devote an inordinate amount of time to the work of securing this information, and of arranging it in convenient form for use. The time thus spent, amounting often to several hours a day for weeks at a stretch, has of course left so much less for the direction of the executive business of the city; but a correct and perspicuous system of accessible accounts is the only safe foundation for a successful administration of that business; and if my successors in office and all other inquiring citizens shall hereafter be able to investigate the financial operations of the city and its various departments with reasonable rapidity, I shall feel amply compensated for the time and labor bestowed upon this branch of the public business.

SECTION 4. *Changes Effected.* Some of the results of these labors can be seen by comparing the annual department reports for 1893–4 — particularly those of the Auditor, Architect, Board of Assessors, Board of Park Commissioners, and Street Department — with the corresponding documents for 1890; and by reference to the Appendix, which contains the tables that have been found the most useful in practice. These include eleven tables relating to the city debt and sinking-funds; ten relating to current revenues, expenses, and taxes; twenty-one relating to the water-works and other municipal investments; and eight relating to other matters. Still others will be found scatte red throughthe text of this message.[1]

Some of these tables have been submitted to the City Council in special messages; some were ordered to be printed in the department reports; some are now for the first time published.

---

[1] See Table of Contents, pp. 5 to 7.

The change in the fiscal year, effected in 1891,[1] and the order of December 5, 1891,[2] providing that the reports of all departments should be made for the fiscal year, have tended to simplify the book-keeping of the city, and to promote a correct understanding of our municipal finances.

A new system of book-keeping has been introduced into the Architect and Street Departments, so that it will be possible in these, the chief construction departments of the City Government, to compare the cost of future work with that executed during the past four years.[3]

SECTION 5. *Estimates of Income.* The method of estimating the income of the city available for the general expenditures of the year has been changed. This income consists of:

(*a*) Unappropriated cash in the treasury at the beginning of the year, being the surplus of receipts over expenditures for the previous year.

(*b*) Receipts from taxes for the current year.

(*c*) Receipts from unpaid taxes of prior years.

(*d*) Receipts from liquor licenses.

(*e*) The city's part of the tax on corporations collected by the Commonwealth.

(*f*) The miscellaneous receipts of the various departments.

For some years prior to 1893 it had been the custom to estimate so much revenue from liquor licenses, so much

---

[1] From 1822 to 1825, inclusive, the fiscal year ran from June 1 to May 31; from 1826 to 1891, inclusive, the fiscal year began May 1 and ended April 30; the fiscal year 1891-2 began May 1, 1891, and ended Jan. 31, 1892; and since then the fiscal year has begun February 1 and ends January 31. See ordinance approved March 21, 1891. This reform, so essential to that concentration of responsibility which the present charter seeks to secure, was for years blocked by the opposition of the heads of departments, notwithstanding its advocacy by every living ex-Mayor, as well as by the press, and in spite of the fact that Boston was the only city in the State in which the fiscal and political or municipal years were not coincident or nearly so. (See the reports of the Citizens' Association for 1888, 1889, 1890, and 1891, and various debates in the City Council, particularly that of July 1, 1889.)

[2] See also Rev. Ord. of 1892, chap. 3, sect. 22.

[3] Prior to 1891 the books and accounts of the Street Department were kept in such a manner that it was impossible to ascertain the comparative cost of the different items of work. See the Reports of the Citizens' Association for 1889 and 1890.

from the corporation tax, so much from the departments, so much cash, so much from back taxes, and the *entire amount* of the tax levy for the year. Now, as taxes are never paid in full during the year of levy, this way of figuring out the annual receipts of the city would obviously result in a deficit, unless the other items of income were purposely underestimated. This I found to be the case; the danger of appropriating too much money being averted by a systematic underestimation of the income from licenses, corporations, departments, etc. Why this fiction should have been resorted to I never could find out, and concluded that it was time that the revenues of a great city should be officially estimated according to the facts of the case, and not upon the theory that we could safely appropriate for the expenditures of the current year not only the uncollected taxes of prior years, but all the taxes of the current year. The calculation could be changed so as to conform to facts in one of two ways: either by deducting an arbitrary percentage from the taxes of the current year to cover the amount that would not come in before its expiration; or by leaving out of the calculation the receipts from the unpaid taxes of prior years, on the theory that the amount of these would be about the same from year to year; the other sources of income being, in either case, given at approximately the real figures. The latter course was selected for adoption, and for the last two years the several items of the city income have been estimated on the basis of what they were likely to be, the certain deficit in the item of taxes for the current year due to the non-payment of part of them until after the close of the fiscal year being assumed to be offset by receipts, not included in the estimate, from taxes of previous years unpaid at the beginning of the current year.[1]

A certain margin of safety must still, of course, be allowed, to guard against any unexpected shrinkage in taxes and

---
[1] Compare the estimates of revenue contained in the message on the annual estimates for 1890–1 (Doc. 49 of 1890), and for 1891–2 (Doc. 27 of 1891), with the estimates for 1894–5. (Inaugural Address, 1894, Appendix A.)

other receipts, and to cover the expenditures of those departments which are not under the control of the Executive.[1]

SECTION 6. *The Monthly Exhibits.* The monthly reports of the City Auditor have been amplified by the addition of a debt statement, of a list of loans authorized but not issued, and of a calculation of the borrowing capacity of the city, as well as amended in other particulars; and a special statement is now published showing the payments during the last month of the fiscal year (January).

The Collector's monthly statements of receipts formerly contained only the receipts of the month; those now issued include the receipts for the month, and also the receipts for the entire fiscal year to the date of the report.

The Treasurer's monthly statements contain a statement of the amount of cash in the treasury derived from loans, income and trust funds respectively, whereas formerly the receipts from all sources were lumped together, and were used (apparently) without distinction to pay drafts of all kinds.

SECTION 7. *Other Changes.* Numerous other minor changes in our municipal accounts and reports have been introduced, with the object of facilitating inquiry. I feel confident that the changes and additions as a whole have removed the first difficulty in the way of a successful administration of our municipal finances, — the difficulty of getting at the facts. It would be presumptuous, however, to assume that the opportunities for improvement have been exhausted. On the contrary, much remains to be accomplished,[2] in the

---

[1] County, schools, and, to some extent, police.

[2] For instance: according to the calculation of "ways and means" statement at the end of the Auditor's Annual Report, the amount of the tax levy is reached by deducting the estimated income of the city, from other sources than taxes, from the appropriations voted by the City Council. This is, of course, the way in which a city with unlimited powers of taxation proceeds; it was the way in which the tax levy for this city was calculated prior to 1885; it would be the way since the tax-limit law of that year if the city appropriated less than the amount allowed; but inasmuch as the practice has been to appropriate every dollar that the law allows, the theory on which this calculation of the "ways and means" is ostensibly based is an absurdity.

The real way in which the appropriation and tax orders are now made up is first

ACCOUNTS AND REPORTS. 25

way of simplifying and systematizing the financial records of the city; and as the business grows, new methods of accounting will from time to time be found necessary.[1]

to find out what the nine-dollar law allows the city to raise by taxes, and then to add to it the amounts for county expenditures and debt requirements exempted from the operation of the law; the result is the tax warrant for city and county purposes. The appropriation order is then reached by adding to the total tax warrant the amount of the estimated income of the city from other sources. See Appendix, Table 6.

In other words, the actual process is almost the exact reverse of that shown in the statement of "ways and means," which in the future should be reformed so as to fit the facts of the case. It has always been correctly shown in the Auditor's statement accompanying the annual estimates.

[1] This criticism of the system of municipal accounts and reports existing prior to 1892 might be carried much further, but no one who ever made a serious effort to get exact figures at the City Hall will dispute its accuracy. Those who have not had occasion to make such investigation, and who may be inclined to think the strictures in the text too severe, may be referred to the following extracts from the annual reports of the "Citizens' Association:"

From the report for 1889:

"The advisability of changing the fiscal year of the city so as to make it correspond with the municipal year was carefully considered by the committees of this Association last year, as will appear by reference to the last annual report."

. . . .

"Your committee addressed a communication to the City Council early in the year, setting forth the advantages of the proposed change, and requesting that the few amendments should be made in the ordinances which are required to effect the change. The matter was referred to the Committee on Ordinances, who gave a number of hearings."

. . . .

"The City Treasurer and City Auditor appeared before the committee to oppose the change, but your committee could not see that the grounds of their opposition had any substantial basis."

From the report for 1890:

"The confusion caused by the multiplicity of our independent departments, the difference between the municipal and financial year, and the unsatisfactory method in which the books and reports of the several street departments are made up, all cause such hopeless confusion that it is entirely impossible for any one to know how our city work is really carried on, or how much it is costing, so that anything like careful and intelligent scrutiny and criticism on the part of citizens is quite out of the question. It is needless to argue that this is all wrong."

From the report for 1891:

"One of the serious troubles with our municipal system, as was pointed out in our last report (see pages 35–41), has been the faulty book-keeping and accounting in the executive departments. The reports were confused and unintelligible, giving very little information that was of any importance, and no two were arranged on the same plan. It was impossible to find out in any satisfactory manner what work had been done or the cost of any work, excepting by taking the lump sum of money expended; and the trouble was increased by the fact that the department reports covered the calendar year, while the figures relating to the several departments in the Auditor's report covered the fiscal year from May to May."

(*Opinion of Mr. E. W. Bowditch.*)

" If it is fair to assume that taxpayers have a right to know, in reasonable detail, how the city spends its income, then it is proper to assert that the usual methods of making up the printed reports for each department fall so far short of what they should, that their publication and circulation are, to the ordinary taxpayer, of comparatively little value.

" Their general arrangement is not such as admits of making either fair comparisons or even reasonable deductions. For a professional man there is little information conveyed, except the total expenditures. Obscurity is unnecessary, and their form should be so remodelled, and results so tabulated, that any citizen can tell the cost of any public work without difficulty. Moreover, reports that are not clearly stated are apt to cause distrust on the part of the reading public, usually unfounded, but frequently sufficient to raise the question of honesty of purpose of the authors."

. . . .

" Moreover, no two departments, as far as noticed, make the reports up in the same way, nor do they appear to carry on the business of the office in the same manner.

" All reports should be made up, so far as possible, on one general scheme or skeleton, amplifying where necessary, in order to secure clearness for readers. If this is expecting too much, there is no objection to retaining the present form, except the bulk; but, in addition, some scheme of tabulation for the expenditures should be adopted that would enable any one to understand without difficulty not only the total expenditures each year, but what is more important, what the payments are for, and at what rates per unit of measure."

" The folly of continuing a fiscal year that does not coincide with the calendar year is very apparent if the attempt be made to check any series of expenditures given in the department reports with figures given in the auditor's report. The former are for the calendar year, and the latter are for the fiscal year, which has ended the last day of April.

" The change recently authorized of having the fiscal year begin February 1, instead of May 1, does not cure the difficulty complained of, though the apparent differences between the expenditures, as shown by the department reports and those shown in the auditor's reports, will be very much less than heretofore."

(*Opinion of Messrs. Joseph Davis and J. Herbert Shedd.*)

" We also consider it desirable to provide for a uniform system of keeping accounts, and we believe that these accounts should be published in the annual reports in a tabulated form, so that each citizen can easily ascertain the cost of any particular public work."

These gentlemen, Messrs. Bowditch, Davis, and Shedd, were commissioned in 1890 by the Citizens' Association to make an investigation into the conduct of city business. The reasons for this investigation are given in the report of the Association for 1890:

" The impossibility of ascertaining the amount and cost of the work done by our several departments which has just been described, the knowledge that our expenditures *per capita* are nearly double those of any other large city in the country, without, it is thought, any corresponding benefit to our citizens, and the general feeling of distrust in regard to the way in which our city work has been done for many years, have all created a strong desire on the part of the Executive Committee to make a thorough and careful examination of our leading departments, in order that it might be ascertained how the work is really carried on, as such knowledge must be first obtained before any intelligent attempt can be made to improve our system."

CHAPTER 3.

EXPENDITURES AND REVENUES.

SECTION 1. *In General.* The expenditures of the city of Boston for many years past have probably been greater than those of any other large city in the country. As early as the year 1849, Mayor Bigelow publicly asserted this fact, and in 1850 repeated the statement, saying that he had "reason to believe that there was no other city in the world the affairs of which, in proportion to its size, were administered at so great an expense as ours." Mayor Gaston, in 1871, called attention to the fact that the federal census of 1870 showed that the people of Boston paid larger taxes *per capita* than those of any other large city in the country. Mayor Prince, in 1879, expressed an opinion to the same effect; and according to the federal census of 1890 Boston led all the large cities of this country in *per capita* expenditure for schools, libraries, fire protection, street lighting, and works of charity; while the expenditure for police was greater in one other city only. The exact figures are given in the following table, compiled from Census Bulletin No. 82 :

Cities.	Population.	Libraries.	Schools.	Fire.	Lighting.	Police.	Charity.	Total Ord. Exp.	Ord. Taxes.
Baltimore	434,439	.132	2.26	.649	.717	.179	.499	17.91	11.62
Boston	448,477	.363	4.28	1.945	1.321	2.64	2.283	35.94	23.13
Brooklyn	806,343	. . .	1.91	.163	.597	.157	.091	20.88	13.79
Buffalo	255,664	.015	2.92	1.185	1.018	1.46	.307	26.41	15.55
Chicago	1,099,850	.076	2.94	.90	.836	1.37	.019	16.73	6.73
Cincinnati	296,908	. . .	.166	1.113	.749	1.58	.878	21.74	9.07
Cleveland	261,353	. . .	. . .	.969	.629	1.13	.318	11.06	7.46
Detroit	205,876	.115	1.55	1.565	.533	1.22	.155	14.95	9.66
New Orleans	242,039	. . .	.075	.975	.763	.631	.002	11.69	10.11
New York	1,515,301	.016	2.69	7.333	.470	3.04	1.57	32.30	19.66
Philadelphia	1,046,964	. . .	2.53	.639	.368	1.84	.462	18.95	11.55
Pittsburg	238,617	. . .	2.58	.930	.525	1.26	.329	12.93	11.25
St. Louis	451,770	. . .	. . .	1.066	.694	1.23	.784	13.74	7.23
San Francisco	298,997	.103	3.32	1.548	.964	1.81	.291	18.86	10.11

The current expenses of the city — that is, the money spent annually by the several departments for running expenses, maintenance, and repairs — are thus relatively larger than elsewhere. This is due principally to the desire of the people of this city for more and better service from the municipality than is required in other cities; — a fact particularly noticeable in everything that relates to water supply, schools, streets, libraries, collection of garbage, public lighting, and similar municipal conveniences. Special reasons for the relatively high rate of expenditure may also be found in the great length of streets compared with the population of the city; in the low water-rates and ferry-tolls established by the authorities in response to popular demand; in the high salaries paid to school teachers, police officers, and firemen; in the relatively large amount of work done by day labor; in the obligations from year to year imposed upon the city by the Legislature, such as extra sessions of the courts and experimental "drunk laws;" in the insistence by the Legislature on the taxation of municipal bonds;[1] and in its refusal to allow the municipality to obtain a revenue from the corporations using the public streets.

Further reasons for a comparatively large expenditure are to be found in the necessarily excessive cost in this city for a water supply, for drainage facilities, and for widening and straightening out the streets of the city proper. For reasons more fully explained below[2] the expenditures for these purposes have been relatively very heavy. The water-works have cost over $20,000,000, while nearly $40,000,000 has been expended for street widenings and changes of grade, and $20,000,000 more for sewers and improvements connected with the problem of drainage.

If, however, we compare the expenditures of twenty years ago with those of to-day, we do not find any extraordinary

---

[1] The exemption of our bonds hereafter issued from taxation for municipal or county purposes would save the city from one-fourth to one-half of one per cent. in the rate of interest paid on future loans.
[2] See chap. 5, §§ 8 and 10, and chap. 8.

increase. The actual expenditures — understanding by that phrase all payments on account of the city of Boston, including county expenses and State tax, except for debt redeemed — were $18,552,612.48 in 1873–4, and $15,388,-632.28 in 1874–5; while in 1892–3 they amounted to $21,300,665.04, and in 1893–4 to $21,696,999.35. The average amount expended during the five fiscal years from 1872–3 to 1876–7 was $15,761,661.47, while the present rate of expenditure is between twenty-one and twenty-two millions.[1] The net debt of the city has increased from $27,812,935.23 on December 31, 1874, to $36,493,864.42 on December 31, 1894.

Thus although the expenditures of the city are still large, and probably larger relatively than those of most other cities in the country, it is satisfactory to discover that while the population has increased 46 per cent. in twenty years, the actual expenditures have increased only 36 per cent. and the net debt 31 per cent.; and that the tax rate has fallen from an average of $14.06 per thousand for the ten years from 1874 to 1884 to an average of $12.96 per thousand for the ten years from 1884 to 1894.

SECTION 2. *Current Expenses and Annual Revenues.* The large appropriation order of 1884 — $10,284,019 for department purposes, or only $281,667 less than the department appropriations for 1894–5 — and the consequent high tax rate, induced the Legislature of 1885[2] to limit the amount of taxation for municipal purposes to nine dollars on the thousand of the average valuations for the preceding five years, less abatements to December 31 preceding. The interest and debt requirements were excepted; and in 1887[3] an additional amount of $425,000 was allowed for county purposes.

This law caused an immediate reduction in the annual appropriation order, and the tax rate fell from $17 in 1884 to $12.80 in 1885; since which time it has fluctuated between

---

[1] See Appendix, Table 13.
[2] St. 1885, chap. 178.
[3] St. 1887, chap. 281.

$12.60 and $13.40, the average having been, as already stated, $12.96.[1]

Notwithstanding this curtailment of income, in 1887 the salaries of the policemen and firemen were increased by an amount equivalent to $187,000 per annum, on the basis of the number at present employed, and the ferry-tolls were reduced to the lowest possible point. The task of keeping the departments within the limited appropriations allowed by law was a difficult one under any circumstances, and the difficulty was not diminished by the increase in salaries and reduction in revenue referred to. It is not, therefore, surprising that the practice of borrowing money for current expenses should have been revived, and recourse had to this expedient in three of the fiscal years that have since elapsed.[2]

During the past four years the city has lived strictly within its income, no money having been borrowed for the current expenses of the Government.

There has been an increase during these four years in the revenue from the water-works,[3] in the amount received from liquor licenses,[4] and in the product of the $9 law;[5] and there has been a decrease in the cost of gas, electric lights, telephone charges, and in a few other particulars.

On the other hand, there has been an increase in expenditure due to establishment of the new street-cleaning and street-watering services; and the School Committee and other departments generally have received a regular annual increase in appropriations.

---

[1] See Appendix, Table 1. The tax rate during the past ten years has been as follows:

1885	$12.80	1890	$13.30
1886	12.70	1891	12.60
1887	13.40	1892	12.90
1888	13.40	1893	12.80
1889	12.90	1894	12.80

[2] 1888–9, 1889–90, and 1890–91; also in 1885–6. See p. 49.

[3] Which has indirectly been of assistance to the other departments in permitting a large reduction in the charges for fire hydrants, and thus releasing for general municipal purposes money previously taken from the tax levy for the maintenance of the water-works.

[4] Owing to an increase in the number granted, based on the growth of population.

[5] Due to increase in valuations.

Some saving in expenditure can, perhaps, be effected in the various departments, but it is not likely that a great or permanent gain to the city treasury will be realized in this way.

The revenues of the coming year, 1895–6, available for department expenditures are estimated at $10,914,814, which is about three hundred and fifty thousand dollars in excess of the department appropriations for 1894–5. The departments of Parks, Schools, Police, Hospital, Library, and County will need more money than in 1894; while smaller appropriations than those of last year will, I think, be sufficient for the departments of Public Grounds, City Clerk, Mt. Hope Cemetery, and Streets, On the whole it should be easier in 1895–6 than in any year since the limitation of the tax rate to keep the expenditures of the city within its income.

SECTION 3. *Additional Sources of Revenue.* Besides the probable growth of revenue from the ordinary sources noted in the preceding section, it would be possible to increase the income of the city very much if the Legislature would impose a direct tax on legacies, or otherwise relieve the city from the burden of sustaining an undue share of the cost of the State courts; or if it would authorize the collection of annual fees from the various corporations and private persons to whom privileges to use the streets are granted. The Board of Police has the power to add $500,000 to the annual revenues of the city by increasing the fees for liquor licenses; and the Legislature can accomplish the same result by abolishing the limitation in the number issued. Eventually, there should be a revenue from the subway. The substitution of the assessment plan for the system so long in vogue for building streets and sewers out of the public treasury would save at least half a million dollars yearly in the net payments from income and borrowed money for street improvements.

SECTION 4. *County Expenses.* The expenses of the county of Suffolk, all of which are borne by the city of Boston, but over which the city authorities have practically no control, are increasing much more rapidly than the department expenditures of the city proper. The expenditures for the county of Suffolk in the fiscal year 1885-6 were $416,970.03, while the appropriation for the current year 1894-5 was $570,000, which will be exceeded by about $50,000, making a total expenditure for the year of about $620,000; an increase of about $203,000, or 48.8 per cent., in nine years. The expenditures of the other departments have increased from $7,648,952.94 in 1885-6 to $9,935,686 originally appropriated for 1894-5, which will be exceeded[1] by about $200,000, making a total department expenditure on account of the city during the current fiscal year of about $10,135,000, an increase of $2,486,000, or 32.5 per cent. Nor is this all, for during the ensuing fiscal year the expenditures for the county of Suffolk are likely to exceed materially the amount expended this year.

The reason for this excessive rate of increase in the county expenses is to be found in the fact that the business transacted by the Supreme Judicial and Superior Courts in this city is increasing at a rate out of all proportion to the growth of population, which, roughly speaking, is the measure of the necessary increase in the general department expenditures of the city.[2] New sessions are being continually ordered by the Legislature or established by the courts; and I am informed by the Chief Justice of the Supreme Judicial Court and the Chief Justice of the Superior Court that in their opinion fully one-half of the judicial business of the Commonwealth is now transacted in this city. This concentration of litigation in Boston is due to the law governing the venue of transitory actions, which enables attorneys all over the Commonwealth to take advantage of the greater facilities for transacting business, of the more constant presence of the judges, and of the larger verdicts which are returned by Suffolk County juries, to bring their actions in this county.

---

[1] Owing to transfers from surplus revenue.
[2] The estimated present population of the city is 500,000, an increase of 110,000, or 28 per cent., over the result obtained in the State census of 1885.

The new court house, covering four times the area occupied by the buildings formerly used for court purposes, is already crowded, a result largely due to the unexpected increase in business. The expense of maintaining the new building in proper repair will also be considerably more than the amount expended on the old buildings for this purpose.

The tax limiting legislation of 1885 prohibited the city of Boston from raising by taxation for municipal purposes (exclusive of requirements on account of the city debt and the State tax) a sum greater than nine dollars on the thousand of the average valuations for the preceding five years, less abatements; while other cities were allowed to raise by annual taxation for municipal purposes a sum equivalent to twelve dollars on every thousand of the average valuations for the preceding three years, less abatements, and were in addition permitted to raise the requirements on account of their city debt and State and *county* taxes.[1] Inasmuch as the expenditures of the county of Suffolk were municipal expenditures of the city of Boston within the meaning of this law, the limit of taxation allowed in Boston was in reality less than that allowed for other cities, not only to the extent of the difference between nine dollars and twelve dollars on the thousand, but also to the extent of the expenditures for county purposes.

This inequality was partly removed in 1887 by a law which permitted the city of Boston to raise for county expenses a sum not exceeding $425,000 a year in addition to the amount permitted under the statute of 1885.[2]

The law still discriminated between Boston and the other cities of the Commonwealth, as in the case of this city the amount that could be added to the general taxes for county purposes was limited to $425,000, while other cities and towns were permitted to add the actual amount of the expenditure for county purposes. This discrimination is understood to have been based upon the fear that the city authorities of Boston, who themselves had the power to levy the county

---

[1] Stat. 1885, chap. 178.   [2] Stat. 1887, chap. 281.

tax, might make the annual appropriation for county purposes larger than necessary, transfer the surplus to the use of the municipal departments, and thus effectually evade the law limiting the rate of taxation. The limit was therefore fixed at $425,000, which was the appropriation for county expenses for the fiscal year 1886-7. This theory, however, omitted to take into account the inevitable increase from year to year in the expenditures for the county of Suffolk, which, for reasons stated, has been greater than anticipated.

Under these circumstances, attempts have frequently been made to induce the Legislature either to allow the city to assess in the annual tax the entire amount of the county expenditures, as well as the amount allowed by the law of 1885, or else, if it was still thought desirable to impose a limit on the county expenditures, to increase that limit above the $425,000 allowed by the Act of 1887. I have never believed, however, that these applications were wise, and have objected before committees of the Legislature to the passage of any law which, by increasing the amount to be taxed for county purposes, would indirectly increase the rate of taxation for current expenditures beyond the limits fixed by the Statutes of 1885 and 1887. It is possible, with economy and constant watchfulness, to administer the business of the city and county within the rate of taxation limited by these two laws; and that limit should not, in my opinion, be increased.

I do not, however, disagree with those who consider the present situation unfairly burdensome upon the city, which, through the operation of the laws relating to the venue of transitory actions, is obliged to pay an undue proportion of the expenses of litigation in Massachusetts; but the remedy for this condition of affairs, I conceive to be, not additional taxation of the citizens of Boston for the convenience of litigants from other parts of the State, but a readjustment of the judicial expenditures of the Commonwealth upon some basis which shall not impose upon the people of this city the cost of trying cases in which they are not concerned.

The recent decision of the Supreme Judicial Court confirming the constitutionality of the law of 1891[1] imposing a tax upon legacies and successions, and the large financial results which have accrued to the State of New York through the imposition of a tax upon direct as well as collateral inheritances and bequests, point out a way by which the burden of our judicial expenditures can be diminished in amount as well as distributed more equally than at present without any increase in the amount of annual taxation. The law of 1891 should be amended upon the lines of the New York statute[2] by including direct inheritances, devises, and bequests within its operation; and the taxes thus collected should either be paid directly to the treasurers of the several counties having jurisdiction over the estates, or to the Commonwealth. In the former case, the city of Boston would get the full benefit of the tax upon the estates of persons resident within its limits; and in the latter case the Commonwealth itself should assume the judicial expenditures of all the county courts, defraying them so far as possible from the tax on legacies and successions. If the latter plan is adopted, the city of Boston will no longer be forced to contribute an undue proportion of the judicial expenses of the Commonwealth, and on either plan the burden of taxation for county purposes to the people as a whole will be materially lightened.

SECTION 5. *The Tax Limit.* The tax limit imposed in 1885 permits the city, with the additional $425,000 allowed in 1887, to raise all the money needed for the current expenses of the Government, if administered with economy and vigilance. I have seen no reason to alter the opinion expressed to the Legislature in 1890,[3] and frequently since, that no change should be made in the tax limit. Much can be said in favor of abolishing the limit altogether, but nothing at all, in my judgment, in support of a higher one. An increase of a dollar or a dollar and a half in the

---

[1] St. 1891, ch. 425.
[2] I have at various times petitioned the Legislature for the passage of such a law, but the opposition to it has hitherto been sufficient to defeat the application.
[3] In an argument before the Committee on Cities February 27, 1890.

thousand would give the city from $800,000 to $1,200,000 per annum more to expend than can now be raised; but there is no real necessity for the increase in municipal service that such a sum would pay for, and there is every reason to fear that most of it would be frittered away on increases in the number and salaries of the city employees, or on unnecessary local improvements, and that in the end no benefit would be received commensurate with the increase in taxation.

Something might be said in favor of adding a dollar to the tax rate for the purpose of increasing the sinking-fund for loans outside the debt limit, or for the purpose of borrowing so much less; but no good reason can, in my opinion, be assigned for increasing the present burden of annual taxation for general municipal purposes.

SECTION 6. *Valuations.* The valuation of real estate for purposes of taxation is one of the most important duties of the municipality, and is in charge of a board of nine principal assessors, supported by seventy-two assistants. This work is judicial in its character, and therefore removed from the control of the Mayor, who would not be justified in forcing upon the assessors his personal views of the manner in which they should perform their statutory duties.

I am of the opinion, frequently expressed, that there is a systematic undervaluation of suburban and vacant lands, which results in a higher tax rate than ought to be declared, and in an inequitable distribution of the burdens of taxation.

Real estate in the business portions of the city, in the older residential parts, on the Back Bay, at the South End, and in Charlestown is assessed at from 60 to 90 per cent. of its value, while vacant, unimproved estates in the suburbs are assessed at from 25 to 60 per cent. of their market value. This, of course, is an opinion merely; but it is an opinion founded on special opportunities, both private and official, for drawing a correct conclusion.

And not only are suburban valuations low in comparison with those placed on other real estate, but they are relatively lower to-day than in the past; that is, there is a greater difference between the assessed and real values of this class of property than there was fifteen or even ten years ago.

The amounts paid for our park lands between 1877 and 1884 exceeded the assessors' valuation by $18\frac{2}{3}$ per cent.; the amounts paid between 1885 and 1890 exceeded the valuation by $66\frac{2}{3}$ per cent.; and the excess for the last five years (1890-1894) has been $88\frac{22}{100}$ per cent.[1] Lands recently purchased by the New York, New Haven, & Hartford Railroad Company have cost 77 per cent. above the assessors' valuations. Nine estates near each other were offered to the city in 1893, in response to advertisements for the department of Public Grounds, at from 47 to 497 per cent. above the assessed values; and the recent attempt to procure a site for a trade school has brought forth a similar result. A like experience constantly attends the efforts of the School Committee and other departments to obtain suburban sites.

It should be borne in mind that since 1890 the taxpayer has been protected against overvaluations by chapter 127 of the acts of that year, providing for appeals from the assessors of taxes to the Superior Court. Prior to the passage of this law the property owner had no redress from the assessors' figures, except an appeal to the County Commissioners, or, in the case of Boston, to the Board of Street Commissioners. He has now an appeal to the courts of law, with all that that implies. It is a significant fact that no such appeals have ever been taken from the valuations of our assessors. This is proof that they are not excessive; and

[1] The exact figures are:

Period.	Assessed value.	Amounts paid without interest or costs.
1877-1884	$1,387,588 50	$1,646,629 67
1884-1890	591,576 39	996,568 65
1890-1894	1,113,357 65	2,094,505 41

the figures given tend to show that assessed values are, in fact, much lower than they should be — particularly in the case of vacant suburban lands.

The question is not so much one of absolute or total valuations, — for a low valuation and a high tax rate are the same thing in the end as a high valuation and a low tax rate, provided all property is valued on the same basis. The real question is equality of valuation, and in this respect it is submitted that the owners of undeveloped suburban property in this city enjoy an unfair advantage over the rest of the community.

The discrimination in favor of vacant unimproved land works injustice to all who pay taxes on improved real estate or personalty, and also to those who are assessed a poll-tax only, for they pay substantially in full. Farms and country estates should be assessed as available for building lots if they have in fact a market value for that purpose. To value such lands solely with reference to their present use is a violation of the sworn duty of the assessors to make "a fair cash valuation of all the estate, real and personal, subject to taxation."[1]

The last man in the community whom the tax-gatherer should favor is the owner of vacant land who makes no improvements at his own expense, but allows his property to lie idle, preventing all the while its development by others, in the hope of reaping in the end an increment in value unearned by him and due exclusively to the enterprise and activity of others, and the growth of population. The speculator in vacant lands is everywhere a hindrance to prosperity, but he is the special curse of this community, where he not only controls the course of legislation[2] and the action of the City Council, but also the assessment of taxes.

The general tax laws of the State are as injurious to the prosperity of the city to-day as Mayor Quincy considered them in 1828; the double taxation of many classes of personal estate is driving wealth and business away more rapidly

---

[1] Public Statutes, ch. 11, § 45.   [2] See chapter 8, § 3.

than ever; but the heaviest and most inequitable of all the burdens that the general taxpayer in this community has to bear are the obligation to pay the entire cost of streets laid out and built in the suburban sections principally for the benefit of individual land-owners, and the failure of the assessors to place a " fair cash valuation " upon suburban land.

CHAPTER 4.

INDEBTEDNESS.

SECTION 1. *Definitions.* The expressions "debt," "gross debt," and "net debt" are not used in the same sense in all systems of municipal book-keeping. Sometimes temporary loans issued in anticipation of taxes and payable within the year are included, and sometimes not. In some systems loans authorized but not negotiated are included, and in other systems they are excluded. Sometimes all the cash in the city treasury is taken into account, and sometimes even unliquidated assets, such as real estate, is deducted at its estimated value in figuring out the net indebtedness. By the expression "net debt" is generally meant, however, the balance obtained by subtracting from the gross debt all liquidated assets of the city applicable to its redemption.

The system in use in Boston from an early period is to include in the gross debt all outstanding loans, notes, scrip, and other negotiable or registered obligations, not issued in anticipation of the taxes and payable within the year, and to include in the means of redemption all liquidated assets or property which is pledged to the redemption of the debt; the net debt being found by subtracting these means of redemption from the gross debt.[1]

---

[1] The "net debt" of towns and cities, defined by St. 1883, chap. 127, is arrived at by taking the gross debt of the city, deducting the amount issued for water purposes and also the amount of the sinking-funds. The "net indebtedness" of the city of Boston used as a basis for determining the borrowing capacity is reached by deducting from the gross debt all water loans, all loans authorized outside of the debt limit of 1885, and also the moneys and investments in the hands of the Commissioners of Sinking-Funds applicable to loans inside the debt limit. It is obvious that neither of these two kinds of "net debt" has anything to do with the real net debt of the city, as both of them leave out of account all water scrip and bonds, and one of them omits all loans issued outside of the debt limit. Moreover, neither of them include in the means of redemption anything beyond the moneys and investments actually in the hands of the Sinking-Funds Commissioners; whereas, as a matter of fact, securities in the hands of the City Collector of Boston

In the means of redemption are thus included the cash in the hands of the Sinking-Funds Commissioners, and the other investments of the sinking-funds, as well as notes, bonds, mortgages, betterments, assessments, and other liquidated obligations in the hands of the Collector, which are applicable or pledged to the payment of debt, and are to be handed over to the Commissioners of Sinking-Funds when converted into cash.

SECTION 2. *Increase since 1890.* While the exact net debt of the city at any given date is therefore easy to compute, a comparison of the real increase of indebtedness in one administration with the increase in another is not an easy matter. Such a comparison is complicated by various conditions: the amount of cash on hand derived from loans; the amount of loans authorized but not negotiated; the amount of the expenditures rendered necessary by the acts of previous administrations, but for which no money had been provided; the amount of expenditure necessitated by the acts of the administration in question, for which money must be borrowed in the future; and the amount of State loans, the interest and sinking-fund requirements of which are paid by the city.[1]

On December 31, 1890, the gross debt of the city was $55,440,561.06, the means of redemption $24,381,864.08, and the net debt $31,053,496.98.

During 1891 there was no increase in the city debt — meaning net debt — for the reason that the change in the fiscal year effected that year enabled the city to procure from the tax levy a large surplus above the amount needed for the current expenses of 1891–2; and this surplus was used for certain per-

---

are, generally speaking, as certain of collection and application to the redemption of the debt as the investments of the Sinking-Funds Commissioners.

The real net debt of the city has from the earliest times been held to be the gross debt, less all cash and other liquidated assets applicable to the redemption of the debt held by any committee, city official, or Board of Sinking-Funds Commissioners; and the statements of net debt have been made up upon this basis at the close of each calendar and fiscal year.

[1] The annual assessments on account of these loans are included in the State tax, and represent moneys borrowed by the Commonwealth for local armories, for the Metropolitan Sewerage system, for the Metropolitan parks, and to secure the abolition of certain grade crossings.

manent improvements for which money would otherwise have been borrowed. During 1892 there was also no increase in the debt, a result partly due to the fact that the City Council of that year attempted to use the borrowing capacity of the city for purposes which did not meet with executive approval,[1] and partly to the fact that the new buildings for the City Hospital and Public Institutions, to which a large part of the loans authorized that year related, could not be so pushed as to require much money until 1893. In 1893 and 1894 a considerable increase in the debt took place, the principal causes having been a change of policy respecting the completion of the park system, some unexpected opportunities for street widenings, the failure to sell the old Public Library building,[2] and the interference of the Legislature with the street-construction law of 1891.

The gross debt of the city on December 31, 1894, was $58,654,211.56; the means of redemption, $22,160,347.14; and the net debt, $36,493,864.42; an increase in four years of $5,440,367.44.

SECTION 3. *Special Reasons for the Increase.* A special reason might be assigned for this increase in the large sums of money which had to be borrowed during the past four years to meet what may be called the legacies of prior administrations, handed down in the shape of work to the execution of which the city was committed, but for which no money had been provided. These items [3] would

---
[1] See veto message of May 24, 1892.
[2] This property was supposed to be worth $1,000,000, and has been in the market for nearly a year. Its proceeds are pledged to the sinking-fund for the debt created to build the new Public Library on Dartmouth street.
[3] As follows:

Object.	Year in which the city was committed to the work.	Money borrowed between Jan. 1, 1891, and Dec. 31, 1894.
Cochituate Water-Works	1846	$1,575,000
Parks	1875	4,600,000
Improved Sewerage	1877	300,000
New Library Building	1886	989,000
Roxbury High School	1887	87,000
Stony Brook	1887	68,000
Commonwealth Avenue	1887	660,000
New Court House	1887	521,000
Department deficiencies for the fiscal year	1890–91	340,000
Total		$9,140,000

The amount charged to parks does not include the sums borrowed on account of the North End park taken in 1893 ($150,000), and on account of the Brighton playground taken in 1894 ($25,000).

account for $9,140,000, or almost double the entire increase.

All such arguments are, however, more or less fallacious, for the reason that every administration inherits a certain amount of borrowed money, leaves behind it a certain amount, has or ought to have a certain amount of property to sell, is obliged to finish up a great deal of work to which the city has been committed in previous years, and itself leaves uncompleted projects behind for which no money has been raised.

SECTION 4. *Loans authorized, but not issued.* It is particularly misleading to include in the net debt all unnegotiated loans.[1] Every administration ought to leave ample authority to borrow money behind it; and the money should not be borrowed in advance of the necessity for it, as the city has to pay about three and a half per cent. per annum for interest, and receives only about two per cent. on its bank deposits. If, as must be the case, public works are authorized, the construction of which will take a number of years, it is better to obtain the authority to borrow all the money needed, and only issue the loans from time to time, as required, than to borrow it all at once, or fail to procure the right to issue enough bonds to complete the work.

A special effort has been made by this administration to secure from the Legislature and the City Council the

---

[1] As was done by Mayor Cobb, who in his valedictory address figured out that the debt had been reduced during the three years of his administration by over $500,000. The fact, however, is that during those three years the actual net debt of the city rose from $21,176,398.13, on December 31, 1873, to $28,277,032.96, on December 31, 1876, an increase of $7,100,634.83. Deducting from this figure the increase in the net debt due to the annexations on January 4, 1874, we have still an increase of $3,972,994.23 in the three years. The fallacy of taking into account the loans authorized but not negotiated, at the beginning and end of the period in question, while leaving out of account the cost of works begun without providing the money to complete them, is further shown by the fact that during these three years the city was practically committed to a system of public parks, to the construction of the main drainage works, and to the extension of our water-works along the Sudbury river; enterprises which have since cost $25,000,000 more than the amounts provided for them prior to December 31, 1876.

power to issue from time to time as required all the loans needed for the completion of the public works to which the city is committed. The loans authorized and not negotiated December 31, 1894, were as follows:

Date of Order.	Object.	Inside of Debt Limit.	Outside of Debt Limit.
Oct. 24, 1891,	Library building, Dartmouth st..		$200,000 00
April 26, 1893,	Additional supply of water		1,800,000 00
May 17, 1893,	Public park, Wards 6 and 7	$150,000 00	
Feb'y 1, 1894,	New buildings, City Hospital ...	300,000 00	
Feb'y 12, 1894,	Charlestown bridge	740,000 00	
June 8, 1894,	Public parks		1,000,000 00
June 25, 1894,	Laying out and construction of highways		1,000,000 00
July 12, 1894,	Columbus-avenue extension.....	300,000 00	
St. 1894, ch. 548	Rapid transit		50,000 00
		$1,490,000 00	$10,950,000 00

The City Council can also authorize a further loan under St. 1891, chap. 323, for the laying out and construction of highways, of $747,162.91; while the borrowing capacity of the city under St. 1885, chap. 178, and St. 1891, chap. 93 was on January 1, 1895, $2,509,074. On that date loans amounting altogether to $15,696,236.91 could be issued without further action of the Legislature.

If any one deems it proper,[1] in calculating the increase in the net debt during a given period, to include loans author-

---

[1] No regular statements were printed of loans authorized but not issued until recently, when, for the convenience of the Mayor and other financial officers of the city and for the information of the public, such a statement was incorporated in the monthly exhibit of the Auditor, first appearing in that for December 31, 1892. These statements have been thought by some persons to indicate a change of system, and the suggestion has been put forth that it was something altogether

ized but not issued on the theory that money must be borrowed for work begun during the period in question, it is necessary, of course, to omit all loans intended to pay for work which has not yet been ordered, and which may therefore not be undertaken, and to deduct all moneys borrowed during the period to complete works begun before it. If such a calculation were made at the present time, we should begin with an actual increase in the net debt of $5,440,367.44; add to it the amount of loans not yet negotiated needed to defray the cost of work to which the city is actually committed through the acts of this administration, namely, $7,440,000,[1] and deduct the $9,140,000 borrowed on account of work previously ordered. This calculation would result in an apparent increase in the net debt of $3,740,367.44.

A still more complicated calculation might be made by taking into account the cash on hand derived from loans at the beginning and end of the period in question.[2]

But these calculations are unending, and, to a great extent, misleading. The important point is the actual increase or decrease in the net debt as it appears upon the Auditor's books; and if further considerations are to be taken into account, it would appear to be sufficient to scrutinize the purposes for which bonds have been issued during the period

---

new to refrain from borrowing money as soon as authorized. This, however, is not the case, as probably no date could be picked out for many years on which the city did not have the right to borrow a large amount of money on account of loans not then negotiated. Thus, the amount of loans authorized but not issued, on December 31, 1872, was $4,077,000, without counting the loan of $20,000,000 to rebuild the burnt district, which was subsequently declared void by the courts; $4,086,000 on December 31, 1877; $3,298,500 on December 31, 1882; $789,000 on December 31, 1890; and so on.

[1] North End park $150,000
Hospital 300,000
Bridge 740,000
Subway 4,950,000
Columbus avenue, etc. 1,300,000

$7,440,000

[2] The cash on hand derived from loans December 31, 1890, was $3,480,401.38, and on December 31, 1894, $2,029,084.52.

in question, and to consider the character of those unexecuted projects to which the city has been committed by the acts of the administration in question.

SECTION 5. *Loans issued since January 1, 1891.* The use made of the city's credit during these four years is shown in the following table, which gives the purposes for which bonds were issued between December 31, 1890, and December 31, 1894:

LOANS ISSUED BY THE CITY OF BOSTON BETWEEN JANUARY 1, 1891, AND DECEMBER 31, 1894.

(*Exclusive of temporary loans in anticipation of taxes repaid during the fiscal year.*)

Cochituate Water-Works		$1,575,000
Sewers		457,860
Improved Sewerage		300,000
Stony Brook		68,000
Paving, Street Construction, etc.		1,957,910
Street Widenings, Extensions, and Changes of Grade		882,500
"Laying Out and Construction of Highways"		1,500,000
Bridges and Tunnels		343,300
Rapid Transit and Charlestown Bridge		60,000
Parks		4,775,000
Public Grounds		100,000
Public Buildings and Sites:		
Suffolk County Court House	$521,000	
School-houses and Sites	1,773,025	
Fire Department	175,000	
Police Department	25,000	
Public Institutions	804,500	
City Hospital	778,500	
Board of Health	50,000	
Public Libraries	1,044,000	
		5,171,025
Ferries		53,000
Quincy Market		10,000
Department Deficiencies of the fiscal year 1890–1		340,000
Tug-boat for Sewer Division		25,000
Total		$17,618,625

SECTION 6. *Means of keeping the Debt down.* In view of the steady increase in the city debt, it should be the aim of every administration to keep it from expansion except for absolutely necessary purposes, and to adopt every proper method of reducing it.

A vigorous and fearless use of the veto power is necessary. During the past four years 241 loans or items in loan bills, involving an aggregate expenditure of $2,683,375, have met with executive disapproval.

Applications to borrow money outside of the debt limit, whether emanating from the City Council or members of the Legislature, have been consistently and successfully resisted, if the effect of granting them would have been to increase the real burden of indebtedness; except in the case of the Park, Library, and Court House Loans. The loans for these purposes had from the beginning almost been authorized outside of the debt limit. The street construction law of 1891 also authorized the issue of bonds outside of the debt limit; but as that act was originally drawn, no increase in the net debt could arise from its operations. Whatever increase has taken place [1] in the net debt due to the issue of loans for the "laying out and construction of highways" is the result of the action of subsequent Legislatures in amending, against my protest, the financial provisions of the original law. These provisions ought to be restored, and no more suburban streets should be built at public expense. A large loan outside of the debt limit has also been authorized for the construction of the subway; but if this project is properly carried out, it should not result in a permanent increase in the city debt or in any permanent burden upon the taxpayers. It ought to be a self-supporting investment. Water loans have also been issued outside the debt limit; but the water-works are now upon a self-supporting basis, and the net water debt is less than four years ago.

I see no reason for requesting or authorizing any further loans outside the debt limit.

---

[1] $894,163.77. See Appendix, Table 24.

INDEBTEDNESS. 49

No loans have been issued for current expenses during the last four fiscal years.[1]

The use of the city's credit for trivial or perishable objects has been discouraged; the object consistently kept in view in the exercise of the borrowing power of the municipality having been to restrict its use to objects of permanent, admitted, and general utility.

The net debt of the water-works (Cochituate and Mystic) has been reduced by $967,988.06;[2] and if the present theory of management is adhered to, there is no reason why there should not be a very material reduction in the water debt during the next ten years, notwithstanding the necessary construction of expensive storage-basins on the Sudbury water-shed.[3]

All proceeds of sales of land should be turned into the sinking-funds, or devoted to purposes for which otherwise money would be borrowed. Since 1890, $430,022.21 has been realized from the sales of land, of which $140,833.88 was paid to the Commissioners of Sinking-Funds; $144,977.97

---

[1] LOANS FOR CURRENT EXPENSES.

Such loans have been frequent in the history of the city. See Mayors' inaugurals in 1835 and 1855. The aggregate amount of the department deficiency loans since 1822 is $3,284,133.53, besides which a large part of the loans entered simply as "miscellaneous," amounting to $3,763,355.97, were probably issued for the running expenses of the government. Of the deficiency department loans, $1,628,439.30 was issued between the limitation of the tax rate in 1885 and the commencement of the fiscal year 1891-2. It should be noted, however, that these last-mentioned loans were not all for strictly current expenses, and it is quite likely that the loans entered in the earlier reports as miscellaneous or deficiency loans were partly for permanent improvements. Since the limitation of the tax rate in 1885, out of the total amount of money borrowed to make up department deficiencies, — namely, $1,628,439.30, — only $1,344,632.10 was really for the current expenses of the government, the rest having been used to make good transfers from department appropriations for buildings and other permanent improvements.

The law of 1891 (chap. 206), prohibiting the borrowing of money for current expenses without the certificate of the Mayor that the loan is in his opinion necessary, has been a great help in preventing the City Government from issuing such loans. No occasion has arisen since the passage of this law which, in the opinion of the Executive, called for a certificate that a loan of this character was necessary.

	Dec. 31, 1890.	Dec. 31, 1894.
[2] Net Cochituate debt	$10,391,743 77	$9,443,032 90
" Mystic "	19,277 19	
Total	$10,411,020 96	$9,443,032 90

[3] See chapter 18, §§ 3 and 4.

was used for school-house sites, buildings, and furniture; and $144,210.36 was treated as general revenue. Since early in 1893, all proceeds of sales of land have gone into the sinking-funds. Down to 1870 it was provided by ordinance that all such moneys should be used to pay the debt; but from that year to 1893 they were subject to the order of the City Council. In 1893-4 and 1894-5 the general appropriation order provided that such receipts should be credited to general revenue or paid over to the sinking-funds, as the Mayor and Auditor should determine in the last two months of the fiscal year. In these two years they have in fact been covered into the sinking-funds.

Besides the act prohibiting loans for current expenses,[1] the Legislature has contributed to a sounder administration in respect to the use of borrowed money by authorizing the Treasurer to keep a general loan account,[2] and by prohibiting the City Council from making transfers from one department to another, except upon the recommendation of the Executive.[3]

SECTION 7. *Loans to be authorized in 1895.* Besides the special loans already authorized but not issued, the city has a general borrowing capacity of $2,509,074,[4] of which use can be made during the coming year to provide reasonable additions to the school accommodations of the city, to furnish a few more buildings for the Department of Public Institutions, to enable the City Hospital to procure the rest of the land between Massachusetts avenue and the building for out-patients, and to complete certain features of the park system.

A further loan of $747,162.91 can also be authorized for street improvements and sewers, under St. 1891, chap. 323, and amendments.[5]

SECTION 8. *Analysis of City Loans.* The loans issued by the city of Boston have been analyzed and tabulated, with the following result:

---

[1] St. 1891, chap. 206. [2] St. 1893, chap. 192. [3] St. 1893, chap. 261.
[4] As of January 1, 1895; reduced to $2,337,074 by the loan order approved January 5, 1895.
[5] See Appendix, Table 24.

INDEBTEDNESS.   51

The total amount of obligations issued between May 1,
1822, and December 31, 1894, exclusive of debts assumed
on annexations, renewals of matured loans, and notes issued
in anticipation of taxes and paid off within the fiscal year,
has been $110,715,431.18.

Cochituate Water-Works	$20,146,711 11
Mystic Water-Works	222,000 00
Public Lands, etc., including Church-st. district and similar improvements	6,464,302 81
Drainage	8,947,860 00
Street Improvements	30,065,477 68
Laying Out and Construction of Highways,	1,500,000 00
Bridges	2,037,700 00
Parks	10,448,000 00
Public Buildings	19,730,001 83
Public Grounds	504,700 00
Markets	709,335 25
Ferries	720,000 00
Mount Hope Cemetery	42,000 00
Harbor	8,000 00
War Expenses	2,013,850 00
Rapid Transit	60,000 00
Department Deficiencies	3,284,133 53
Miscellaneous	3,813,358 97
Total	$110,715,431 18

SECTION 9. *General Review of the City Debt.* At the
incorporation of the city in 1822 there was no public debt
except the sum of $100,000 issued on account of the prisons
and court house recently erected by the town of Boston.
During the next thirty years there was a gradual increase of
indebtedness, which by 1850 had arisen to $5,000,000. By
1860 it was $7,500,000. At the close of the war it was
about $9,000,000, and remained at about that figure until
1870. During the next seven years a great increase took
place; the net debt on December 31, 1869, having been
$9,085,686.36, while on December 31, 1876, it was $28,-

277,032.96. This increase of over nineteen million dollars was due partly to the annexation of the surrounding towns, but principally to the extraordinary expenditures for street widenings, over twenty-two million dollars having been spent for that purpose between 1868 and 1875. The Legislature of 1875 [1] restricted the amount of indebtedness that the city could incur to three per cent. of the last valuation; and the ten years between 1876 and 1886 was a period of reduction, the net debt having fallen by December 31, 1885, to $24,700,014.29. In 1885 the Legislature (St. 1885, chap. 178) interposed another barrier by limiting the debt that might be incurred, except for water supply, to two per cent. of the average valuations of the preceding five years, less abatements to December 31 preceding. At about this time, however, certain undertakings involving a great outlay were begun, under special acts authorizing loans outside the debt limit. The cost of the new court house and the new public library, as also most of the money spent upon the parks, has been met by loans issued during the past ten years outside the debt limit; and the debt has in consequence risen from about twenty-five million dollars in 1885 to about thirty-six and a half millions in 1895.[2]

With the completion of these three undertakings, — the court house, the public library, and the parks, — which together have involved the issue since May 1, 1885, of loans amounting to $14,079,000, there is no reason why we should not again enter upon a period of reduction, if it were not for the contemplated construction of the subway. This enterprise, if carried out, will preclude all possibility of reducing the debt during the next few years; but apart from the loans for the subway, which ought to be self-supporting, the debt of the city should be less in 1900 than 1895.

There has been an increase in the city debt of nearly $12,000,000 in ten years; but if we take a longer period, —

St. 1875, ch. 209. Water debts are excluded from the computation.
The loans authorized by the Legislature outside the debt limit of 1885 amount to $24,406,000, of which $14,681,000 have been issued. See Appendix, Table 22.

say, twenty years, — we find that the increase has been but
$8,000,000; that the ratio of increase has been less than the
rate of increase in population; and that the debt is less *per
capita* to-day than twenty years ago.[1]

There would seem, therefore, upon the whole, to be cause
for congratulation rather than alarm in the fluctuations of the
city debt during the past twenty years; and if the debt is
still larger than that of most cities, estimated *per capita*, it
should be remembered that the cost of rendering this locality
fit for the habitation of great numbers of people has necessarily been more than if Boston had, like other places, been
favored with natural advantages for the inexpensive acquisition of drainage facilities, water supply, and broad thoroughfares for travel.

The credit of the city never stood higher than at present, the
four per cent. loans issued in November, 1894, having been
placed at a lower rate of interest to the purchaser than ever
before. The premium realized was 13.55 per cent. for thirty-
year bonds, a figure equivalent to a net rate of $3\frac{28}{100}$ per
cent., which is less than the interest paid on any other loan
of equal size ever offered by the city to the public.[2]

---

[1] Taking the net debt as it stood December 31, 1874, — namely, $27,812,935.23, —
and the population as given by the State census of 1875, we have a *per capita* debt of
$81.34; while on the assumption that there are now 500,000 people in the city, the
debt *per capita*, December 31, 1894, was only $72.93.

[2] The figures given in this paper are brought down to December 31, 1894, unless
otherwise stated. Between that date and to-day (January 5, 1895), the million-dollar
park loan authorized by the Legislature of 1894, to be issued on or subsequent to
January 1, 1895, has been negotiated on a basis of 3.28 per cent. A loan order has
also passed the City Council for $177,000, divided as follows:

New school-house, Ward 15, in vicinity of Boston and Harvest streets	$70,000
Primary school-house, North and West Ends	45,000
Cudworth-street School-house, East Boston, additional land in rear of	5,000
New school-house, Aberdeen District	30,000
New ward-room, Ward 22	5,000
Eustis-street School-house, grading grounds	7,000
Moulton-street Primary School-house, additional land for	5,000
Street Department, Gold-street bridge	10,000
	$177,000

All of the items in this order have this day been approved, except that of $5,000 for
a new ward-room in Ward 22. As the ward lines are to be changed this year, it would
seem best to postpone all further expenditure for ward-rooms until the city is redis-
tricted.

CHAPTER 5.

THE PUBLIC HEALTH.

Believing that the first business of a great city was to protect the health of its inhabitants, I have deemed it my duty to pay special attention to the possibility of improving its sanitary condition.

The death rate of the city of Boston, due to preventable causes, has shown a marked decrease during the past twenty years, the average percentage of deaths from these causes during the last ten years having been 18.45 per cent. of the total number of deaths, while during the ten years next preceding the percentage was 26.78, and the city can no longer be officially described as "one of the most unhealthy of large cities;"[1] but it is nevertheless a fact that the percentage of deaths in this city from preventable causes is still greater than in London, Paris, and some other cities, and therefore greater than it should be.[2] As the cause of the reduction in the relative mortality from preventable causes during the past twenty years could fairly be assigned to the improvements in drainage and sewage disposal effected during that period, so I found it to be the opinion of the health experts of the city that a still further reduction could be effected through the action of the public authorities, and the expenditure of public money; and it was in particular the opinion of the Board of Health that although the percentage of deaths from diphtheria, scarlet fever, and other zymotic diseases was lower in Boston than in any other large city in this country, the excessive

---
[1] See inaugural address of Mayor Prince, 1877.
[2] The percentage of deaths in this city, due to preventable causes, during the past ten years has been 18.45 per cent. of the total number of deaths. The figure for 1893 was 17.43 per cent. The average during the past ten years in London has been 17.2 per cent.; in Paris, 17 per cent.; in New York, 23 per cent.; and in four other large American cities, about 20 per cent.

rate in this city as compared with London and Paris was due to the superior hospital accommodations of the latter cities for the isolation and treatment of contagious diseases.

SECTION 1. *Organization.* The general powers of the city relating to the public health, vested in the City Council by the general laws of the Commonwealth, by the charters of 1822 and 1854, and by various special laws, were in 1872 transferred by the City Council to a Board of Health.[1]

This Board has charge, by virtue of the city ordinances,[2] of the quarantine, the small-pox hospital, the public bath-houses, and the public cemeteries, except Mount Hope Cemetery. It also attends to the abatement of nuisances, to the licensing of undertakers, to the authorization of stables, and to many other less important matters. Its chief function is to prevent the introduction and spread of contagious diseases, and for this purpose maintains a large corps of physicians and inspectors. Public vaccination is furnished when necessary, and a system of medical inspection of the public schools has recently been established.[3] The Board has also been endowed by special statutes with special powers over certain kinds of nuisances, such as defective plumbing, obnoxious vaults, stagnant flats, etc.

Acute diseases (other than small-pox and cholera) and surgical cases are treated in the City Hospital, an institution established in 1861, and governed by a board of five trustees, constituting a corporation known as The Boston City Hospital. This board has charge of the City Hospital on Harrison avenue, and of the Convalescent Home in Dorchester.

The Inspector of Milk and Vinegar and the Inspector of Provisions are officers appointed to discharge the duties imposed upon the city by the statutes relating to the sale of milk, vinegar, and provisions.[4]

The Superintendent of Streets has charge of all matters

See Stat. 1821, chap. 110, sect. 17; Stat. 1854, chap. 448, sect. 40; and the Ordinance of December 2, 1872. For a short time at the commencement of the City Government a Board of Health existed, but it was abolished in 1824.

[2] Rev. Ord. of 1892, chap. 15.
[3] November 1, 1894.
[4] P.S., ch. 57, § 1, ch. 58, § 1, and ch. 60, § 71.

relating to the collection of garbage; to the cleaning and watering of the streets; to the construction and maintenance of the public sewers; and to surface drainage, except the Back Bay Fens and Muddy River improvement, which are in charge of the Park Commission.

The water supply of the city is in charge of the Boston Water Board.

SECTION 2. *Quarantine.* Gallop's Island, containing about sixteen acres, was purchased for a quarantine station in 1860 at a cost of $6,600. Down to the threatened invasion of cholera in 1892, $45,304.41 had been expended for improvements, consisting of a wharf and a few wooden buildings.

In that year additions were made, consisting of four new buildings, and a separate disinfecting plant was established upon the mainland near Swett street. These improvements, costing $56,702.18,[1] have given to the city a quarantine and epidemic plant which, in connection with the other islands in the harbor, render Boston as well protected a city as any in the country against attacks of cholera and yellow fever.

The buildings can also be used in case of epidemics of other diseases.

SECTION 3. *Small-pox, Diphtheria, etc.* The present small-pox hospital is situated on Canterbury street, in Ward 24, on a lot containing about four acres, purchased in 1877.[2] The cost of land and buildings has been $31,388.72.[3]

Diphtheria and scarlet fever have hitherto been treated in private houses or at the City Hospital; but the accommodations of the latter institution have long been felt to be insufficient, and the isolation of patients to be very imperfect. Accordingly, in 1892, it was determined to erect new wards for the treatment of contagious diseases on the land then occupied by the Department of Public Grounds on the south side of West Chester Park (now Massachusetts avenue) and

---

[1] $22,638.99 at Gallop's Island, and $34,063.19 at Swett street.
[2] Prior to this purchase a building on Swett street had been used as a small-pox hospital. It was destroyed by fire in 1872.
[3] Land, $9,034.00; buildings, $22,354.72.

immediately opposite the City Hospital. This plant, consisting of seven buildings[1] with accommodations for 210 patients, is now practically complete and ready for occupation. The cost will be about $500,000; and the buildings are considered to be the best built and best arranged of the kind to be found in any American city.

SECTION 4. *The City Hospital.* This institution was begun in 1861, opened in 1864, and occupied in 1890 an area of about eight acres, between Harrison avenue and Albany street. The original cost of the land and buildings was about $400,000, and the total appropriations for the entire plant, consisting of twenty-one buildings, from 1861 to 1891, were $873,627.15.

Since January 1, 1891, appropriations amounting to $1,096,320.29[2] have been voted, and out of them the seven buildings for the contagious wards already mentioned have been built; also an ambulance stable and a new boiler-house; and several other buildings are now in process of construction for surgical and pathological purposes.

The land appropriated to the use of the hospital has been increased by about six acres.

If further appropriations are made, sufficient to secure the rest of the land between Massachusetts avenue and what was formerly Springfield street, and to erect thereon a nurses' home and two or three additional wards, the city will not only have one of the finest municipal hospitals in the world, but will have as large an institution as can easily be handled by a single administrative force. If a further development of this great charity is then deemed wise, it should take the direction of cottage or special hospitals in the different sections of the city.

---

[1] An entrance lodge, an administration building, a domestic building, a nurses' building, a laundry building, and two ward buildings; the whole surrounded by a brick wall.

[2] The appropriation of $100,000 for land and buildings for the Department of Public Grounds, rendered necessary by the transfer of the nursery grounds on West Chester park to the City Hospital, should be added to the amount specifically assigned to the Hospital Department. This makes in reality a total of nearly $1,200,000 appropriated in the last four years for improvements at the City Hospital.

SECTION 5. *Garbage.* House offal is collected by the employees of the Sanitary Division of the Street Department, and carted to various central stations, whence it is sold to farmers or taken out to sea. This method of garbage disposal has long been criticised, and after much investigation an experimental contract for a small plant in the Dorchester district has this year been given to a corporation exploiting a patented system of reduction. If the system proves a success, it can be introduced in other sections of the city, unless some better and cheaper invention is presented. If it proves in any respect a nuisance to the neighborhood, the contract provides that it shall be removed at the request of the Board of Health.[1]

SECTION 6. *Street Cleaning.* It seems unnecessary to refer to the condition of the streets prior to the concentration of the different branches of street service in the hands of the late superintendent, or to the elaborate system of street cleaning introduced by him and its results. These results are recognized upon all hands; and the chief improvement now possible would seem to depend upon the citizens themselves, who, by abstaining from throwing paper and other refuse matter into the streets, would greatly facilitate the task of cleaning them. The present city ordinances forbid such conduct; but the Board of Police has either been unable or unwilling to enforce them.

SECTION 7. *Street Watering.* After various futile attempts to formulate and introduce a street-watering system upon the assessment plan, it was determined in 1892 to make a systematic effort to water the streets of the city at public expense. A special street-watering service was established by the Superintendent of Streets; the amount of money annually devoted to the purpose was doubled; paved streets were entirely excluded from the work of the department; and the macadamized streets were divided up into sections, the watering of them being either let out to contractors or done by teams hired by the department. This

---

[1] See Document 148, of 1894.

system involved a complete change in the method of watering the residential sections of the city on the Back Bay and at the South End, whence had come the principal complaint about dust. Since the introduction of the new methods, practically no complaints have been received at the City Hall of dusty streets, and the physicians and other citizens who were the chief promoters of the change appear to be entirely satisfied with the results accomplished.[1]

SECTION 8. *Sewers and Surface Drainage.* For obvious topographical reasons Boston is a difficult and expensive city to drain. Without the benefit enjoyed by New York, Philadelphia, London, and other cities, of powerful river or tidal currents, and consisting in great part of filled land rising a few feet only above tide water, and in great part of rock, the soil can only be made fit for the occupation of a dense population by the most elaborate and expensive arrangements for the disposal of sewage and surface drainage.

The colonial system of "common sewers," built, owned, and managed by private citizens under public regulation, which was established at an early date in the history of the town, — probably prior to 1700, — lasted until 1823, when it was superseded by a system of public sewers, built, owned, and controlled by the city.

For the next fifty years the principal question connected with the drainage of this city was how to recover that portion of the cost of sewer construction that ought to be paid by the individuals immediately benefited; it being the aim of the authorities to collect a reasonable percentage of the cost of the public sewers in assessments on abutting or neighboring estates, in order that the individuals specially benefited should contribute to the cost of the work, and that the public appropriations available for the purpose should go as far as possible. It would have

---

See Stat. 1890, chap. 365; Stat. 1891, chap. 179; inaugural address, January, 1892; City Document 44, of 1892; and the annual reports of the Street Department for 1892–3 and 1893–4.

been much better to assess the entire cost, as is done in most of the large cities of the country; but the public funds of this city have always been regarded as held partly in trust for the development of real estate, and no administration has ever succeeded in getting rid of this radical vice in our financial system.

A great variety of assessment plans have been tried under various ordinances of the City Council and various acts of the Legislature: the principal ones being the ordinance of July 7, 1823; the general sewer law of 1841, chap. 115, accepted by the city April 7, 1841; chap. 232 of the Acts of 1878; chap. 456 of the Acts of 1889; chap. 346 of the Acts of 1890; and chap. 402 of the Acts of 1892. Under the ordinance of 1823 such sum could be assessed as the Mayor and Aldermen should deem just and reasonable; but from that year to 1837 only 21 per cent. of the cost of the sewers was in fact collected by assessments. In 1837 an attempt was made to assess the entire cost; but this idea seems to have been abandoned almost as soon as conceived, and the scheme was adopted of charging to the abutters three-quarters of the cost of the sewers, paying the remaining quarter out of the city treasury. This system lasted until 1889, but it did not result in the collection of the 75 per cent. theoretically assessed; the amount received under the Act of 1878, chap. 232 (which was the best of these 75 per cent. laws), down to 1889, having been only 38 per cent. In 1889 an entirely new plan was adopted, and modified the next year; the result of the two acts being that only 21 per cent. of the cost of construction was returned by the abutters in assessments. This was felt to be an imposition upon the taxpayers of the city, and the Legislature of 1892 was petitioned for a law which would authorize a larger assessment. The Sewer Act of 1892 was expected to produce the 75 per cent. which had for years been theoretically conceded to be a fair assessment; but up to February 1, 1894, the assessments amounted to only 59.9 per cent. of the amount spent for construction. The

Legislature of 1894 relaxed some of the provisions of this law, against the protest of the city; and the result is that, taking into account all the money spent for sewer construction under the law of 1892 to December 31, 1894, I find that only 58.8 per cent. has been covered by assessments. This percentage may be increased somewhat when the sewers now in process of construction are finished and assessed; but the present sewer law, though fairer for the city than its predecessors, is still unduly favorable to the abutters.

In view of the fact that the community has had to pay the entire cost of the Improved Sewerage and Metropolitan Sewerage systems, and of the Stony Brook, Muddy River, and Back Bay Fens improvements, and that it also defrays the whole expense of maintaining and keeping in repair the ordinary sewers, it seems only fair that at least 75 to 85 per cent. of the total first cost of the latter should be collected from the estates for the special benefit of which the sewers are built. The law should be amended in this sense, and the entire cost up to $7 or $8 a running foot should be assessed, instead of only $4 as at present.[1]

While the question of assessment was, is, and will continue to be of great importance, it was entirely superseded in urgency by the necessity, which became apparent about twenty years ago, of supplementing the system of public sewers, then all draining by various connections into the tide waters about the city, by entirely new and different methods of disposal. There being in most parts of the city no great fall towards the shore, and nowhere a tidal flow sufficient to sweep the sewage out to sea, the flats surrounding the city were gradually converted into permanent sewage deposits, their offensiveness became more and more apparent, the increase in the annual death rate was a cause of legitimate alarm, and the community became convinced of

---

[1] As some of our sewers cost from $10 to $75 a foot, the proposed change would still leave ample room for public contribution. The sum originally advocated before the committee on cities of the Legislature of 1892 was six dollars, but the real-estate owners induced the committee to fix it at four.

the necessity of adopting an entirely different system of sewerage disposal.

Accordingly, in 1876, after an agitation lasting some years, the Legislature authorized the city to establish main sewers and drainage works from and through the different sections of the city proper to discharging works at Moon Island.[1] The preliminary surveys for this system were made in 1876, the act of the Legislature was accepted in 1877, and the work was begun in that year. It was sufficiently advanced to be ready for use in 1884, — up to which time it had cost about four million dollars, — and has been in successful operation ever since. Since then about two million dollars more has been spent in improvements and extensions, bringing the total cost to December 31, 1894, up to $6,304,068.09.[2]

The next important drainage work undertaken by the city was the care of Stony Brook, the principal natural channel for the surface drainage of Roxbury, West Roxbury, and the westerly part of Dorchester. This stream had given much trouble since 1850, and a good deal of money had been spent by Roxbury and West Roxbury, and, since annexation, by the city of Boston, in unsuccessful efforts to restrain its waters in times of flood. An elaborate improvement of the system was undertaken in 1880, and completed in 1884, at a cost of about $400,000. This work was proved to be a failure by the flood of 1886, and a still more elaborate and expensive scheme was thereupon adopted. The work was begun in October, 1887, and completed in December, 1888. The cost of the conduit was about $650,000, and about $375,000 more has been expended for land and damages. Stony Brook, as a whole, has cost the city of Boston up to December 31, 1894, the sum of $1,470,317.58.[3]

The next large work undertaken for the purpose of controlling the surface drainage was the creation of the basin

---
[1] St. 1876, ch. 136.
[2] Of which $631,231.33 has been expended since the 1st of January, 1891.
[3] Of which $95,330.15 has been spent since January 1, 1891.

known as the Back Bay Fens, into which Stony Brook and Muddy River have their outlets. This improvement was undertaken in connection with the park system, authorized by popular vote in 1875. The first appropriation for the Fens was made in 1877, and the improvement has cost to date $2,614,303.93,[1] part of which is properly chargeable to the park which has been built upon its borders, and part to its purpose as a storage basin for the surface waters brought down by Stony Brook and Muddy River.

Muddy River, draining portions of Brookline and West Roxbury, has been improved and its shores utilized for park purposes at an expense to date of $1,452,050.97, all of which but $226,617.01 has been expended during the past four years.

In addition to these improvements, undertaken on municipal account, the Commonwealth has built a metropolitan system of drainage for portions of the city and the neighboring towns. This system is divided into two parts: the Charles River Valley, or south part, — covering Brighton, part of the city proper, Newton, Watertown, Waltham, and Brookline, — which was completed in 1892, and enters the main drainage system of the city of Boston at a point on Huntington avenue; and the north part, which is to take care of the sewage of East Boston, Charlestown, and the towns and cities on the north bank of the Charles river. This work is nearly completed, and will be ready for use early in the coming year. The cost of the Metropolitan system (both parts) will be about $5,500,000, of which Boston will pay between 20 and 25 per cent., in the form of annual assessments included in the State tax.[2]

With the completion of the Metropolitan Sewerage System there is no reason why the people of this city should not be congratulated upon having as complete and successful arrangements for the disposal of surface drainage and sewage

---

[1] Of this amount $442,617.33 has been expended since January 1, 1891.

[2] The city's share of the Charles-river part of the system is 23.02 per cent. of the cost of construction and 25.05 per cent. of the cost of maintenance. Its share of the north part of the system is 20.45 per cent. of the cost of construction and 22.65 per cent. of the cost of maintenance.

as can be furnished under the adverse topographical conditions of the case.

The expense to the city,[1] since 1873, of ordinary sewers, the main drainage system, the Back Bay Fens, and the Stony Brook and Muddy River improvements, has been about $12,500,000, while the Commonwealth has disbursed, as already stated, $5,500,000 in addition. The cost has been enormous; but the work is done and paid for, and the decrease in the death-rate during the past twenty years is evidence of the wisdom of the expenditure.

SECTION 9. *Pest-holes and other Nuisances.* Notwithstanding the removal of the main cause of the pollution of the tidal flats surrounding the city, these still continued to be offensive in many cases, — particularly where cut off by the construction of parks, roads, or other embankments from the daily access of the tide. After struggling for years with the owners of these flats to induce them to put their property in a proper sanitary condition, the Legislature was appealed to; and in 1893 a law was passed,[2] after much opposition from interested parties, giving to the Board of Health the power to compel the abatement of these nuisances by proceedings in equity. Under the operation of this law almost all the flats and marsh surrounding the Back Bay Fens have been filled with gravel and other clean material, and the odors formerly proceeding from these lands have entirely ceased.

Other laws increasing the powers of the Board of Health in the abatement of nuisances have been urged and secured.[3]

SECTION 10. *Water Supply.* If it has been difficult to drain the city properly, it is a still more difficult task to supply it with a sufficient amount of pure water. No rivers, lakes, or other natural source of water supply, adequate to the needs of a large population, exist in this part of New

---
[1] For construction merely: maintenance and repairs excluded.
[2] Stat. 1893, chap. 342.
[3] Particularly Stat. 1893, chap. 460; 1894, chap. 119.

England; and it has been necessary, therefore, to create the supply by means of storage or impounding basins. Besides Lake Cochituate, the original source of the supply procured by the city in 1846, there have since been built five large basins along the upper reaches of the Sudbury river. A sixth is now in process of construction. This work is enormously expensive, the net cost of the Cochituate Water-Works having been $19,615,810.16, to December 31, 1894; and the limit of capacity of the Sudbury river system will before many years have been reached. It will then be necessary to go much farther away in search of water; and believing that a similar necessity would be felt by some of the surrounding communities, and that the whole question of our future water supply was therefore a proper matter for investigation by the Commonwealth, I petitioned the Legislature of 1893 to appoint a State commission to investigate the subject. The matter was referred by the Legislature to the State Board of Health, which is now engaged in an elaborate inquiry, the results of which are soon to be made public.

No expense is spared to improve the quality of the Cochituate water and its color; and although the latter is what is technically known as "high," — that is to say, the water is not as white as that of many other cities, — yet its quality is believed to be of the best. The defect of our water system is its inadequacy in quantity; and this defect can only be met by the expenditure of great sums of money in the future, as in the past, for additional sources of supply.

The Mystic Water Works, obtained by the city by the annexation of Charlestown, have been a much more advantageous investment from a pecuniary standpoint; but the supply is wholly inadequate to the needs of the communities now dependent on it, and very much remains to be done to protect the upper waters of the Mystic system from pollution. In the meantime the quality of the water is poor. After two years of negotiation, arrangements have been completed, awaiting only the favorable action of the City

Council, by which the shores of Mystic Lake and the Abbajona River as far as Walnut street in Winchester, can become public property, through the joint action of the town of Winchester, the Metropolitan Park Commission, and the Boston Water Board. The acquisition of this land will remove the principal source of pollution; but if we are to continue to use the Mystic waters, it will be necessary to expend large sums in adding to the supply and in protecting the shores of the stream from pollution above the point named.

SECTION 11. *Results.* The results, from the standpoint of the public health, of this activity and expenditure — the amounts expended since January 1, 1891, for the improvements mentioned in this section having been about $8,000,000, or nearly half the total amount of money borrowed by the city during the past four years — remain, of course, to be seen; but I have the utmost confidence that these results will be appreciated by the community, and that among them will in the near future be found a reduction in the death rate of this city from preventable diseases to a point as low as that of any large city in the world.

CHAPTER 6.

EDUCATIONAL FACILITIES.

SECTION 1. *The Public Schools.* The public schools of this city have always been a source of civic pride, and the special concern of the City Council, which has ever been solicitous to provide the money needed to establish and maintain them upon the most liberal basis. The current expenses of the school department have risen during the past sixty years from about one-ninth of the total annual expenditures of the city to about one-sixth; and the annual expense per pupil from $8 to $28. The salaries of the school teachers are higher than anywhere else, and it is believed that in this as in other items more liberal appropriations are made by this city for the purposes of public education than by any other in the world.

While many persons entertain grave doubts as to the tendency of the present methods of popular education, believing that in too many cases the practical result is rather to unfit than to fit the youth of the community for their subsequent work in life, it is not disputed, I think, that the schools of Boston are most ably conducted for the purposes kept in view by the committee. The main criticism that is heard concerns the theory itself, and very many citizens, among whom I count myself, would prefer to see more attention paid to industrial education in its different branches, and less to the more advanced and ornamental work to which so much of the activity of our school system is now directed.

With this idea in mind, it was a special source of gratification that after many years of agitation the City Council of 1891 was induced to appropriate a liberal sum for the establishment of a Mechanic Arts High School. This building was occupied in 1893, and has been crowded with pupils from its opening day.

A further and still more practical step in the direction of industrial training was taken in 1893 by the trustees of the Franklin Fund, who determined to devote the sum then available from that fund, viz., $328,940, to the purpose of building and maintaining technical or trade schools. If schools of this character can be established and conducted as successfully as in some other cities of this country, it will be possible for the children of Boston mechanics to learn a trade — a difficult thing under existing industrial conditions.

The chief function of the Mayor and City Council in reference to the schools is to furnish the money needed to maintain them, and to provide the additional buildings required from year to year. Owing to the limited means at the disposal of the city during the years immediately succeeding the passage of the tax law of 1885, it was difficult to obtain the money needed for new school-houses; and from that time to 1890 no new primary schools were provided and but two grammar schools. This resulted in a serious deficiency in school accommodations, and in February, 1889, the School Committee addressed a request to the City Council for a large number of new grammar and primary school-houses. During that year land was purchased, under appropriations voted by the City Council, for nine new grammar and primary school buildings; but all efforts to obtain an appropriation for the buildings themselves failed until late in the year 1890, when the School Committee again called the attention of the City Council to the necessity of these new buildings.[1] In this communication the committee state that the nine new schoolhouses requested "represent the accumulated necessities of three or four years, and provide only for what may be called the arrearages;" and they estimate the cost of the additional accommodations due to growth, and shifting of population, and necessary renewals, at from $200,000 to $300,000 per annum; which would give one new

---

[1] School Document 18 of 1890.

grammar school and two new primaries each year. The money to build four of the nine school-houses needed to make up the "arrearages" was obtained that year, the loan order of October 17, 1890, containing an item of $340,000 for two grammar schools and two primaries. In March, 1891, the School Committee asked for an appropriation of $375,000 for four additional grammar schools and four additional primaries, as well as $48,157.20 for new sites, and also for an appropriation for a Mechanic Arts High School. During that year (1891) over $700,000 — a larger sum than in any previous year in the history of the city — was appropriated for school-houses, sites, and furnishings, including three grammar school buildings, seven primaries, a Mechanic Arts High School, and several sites for future buildings. Large sums have also been raised in 1892, 1893, and 1894 for school-house purposes, partly from revenue, but principally from loans. The total appropriations for these purposes made between January 1, 1891, and December 31, 1894, have been $1,958,111.22, which has permitted the construction of fourteen primaries, three grammar schools, and one Mechanic Arts High School; while one primary, three grammar schools, and one high school are under construction.

It should seem that these new buildings, exceeding the number estimated as necessary by the School Committees of 1890 and 1891, ought to provide sufficient accommodations for all children desiring to attend the public schools; but a number of the school-houses are still overcrowded, and probably will be even when the buildings now under construction are finished. I am at a loss to assign a cause for this condition of affairs, except that, according to information gathered from members of the School Committee, the most judicious selection of sites is not made by the committee. The entire matter of locating the new buildings is in charge of the School Committee, the City Council uniformly granting the requests of the committee to the extent of the money at their disposal; and the committee seems to apportion the new buildings among the different sections of the city rather with a view to pleasing the members from those districts and their constituents than with reference to the real necessities of the case. It has frequently happened that after the City Council has voted an appropriation for a certain school and the order has been duly approved by me, members of the committee have come to the office to say that they regretted that this particular school had been ordered, as school-houses in other parts of the city were really more needed than the one in question. The difficulty seems to be that requests to the City Council for school-houses are log-rolled through the School Committee in much the same way that paving and other appropriations for local purposes are log-rolled through the City Council itself. A mistake may also have been made by the committee in recommending a large number of small primaries rather than a smaller number of larger ones. In view of the fact that nearly two million dollars has been spent during the last four years for new sites and buildings, of the fact that the twenty-one primary and grammar school-houses provided since Jan. 1, 1891, accommodate 9,022 pupils, and of the fact that the increase of school accommodations during the past five years has been as much as during the fifteen years preceding these five, I am unable to account for the present insufficiency of school-houses except in the manner suggested.

It is now proposed to spend $2,500,000 more upon additional school-houses; and to borrow the money outside the debt limit. Such a loan would result in an unnecessary increase in the debt and in the cost of maintaining the School Department. If the School Committee of 1890 and 1891, which comprised among its members men particularly well versed in the needs of our school system, could after long consideration reach the conclusion that an annual expenditure of $200,000 to $300,000, in addition to an immediate appropriation of $550,000 to make up the "arrears," was sufficient to meet the current needs of the city in the matter

EDUCATIONAL FACILITIES. 71

of new school-houses, there can be no real necessity, after nearly $2,500,000 has been appropriated in five years, for an immediate expenditure of $2,500,000 more. The reasonable annual needs of the School Department in the matter of new buildings, whether they are from $200,000 to $300,000, as estimated by the School Committees of 1890 and 1891, or even greater, can readily be met by appropriations within the debt limit. The first thing for the School Committee to do is to scrutinize more carefully the local demands for new school-houses, and to recommend only those which are really needed; the last thing is to petition the Legislature for authority to borrow money outside of the debt limit for any ordinary municipal purpose such as the construction and equipment of school-houses; and the Legislature of 1895 will do well to follow the example of that of 1890 and refuse the application. The present borrowing capacity is $2,509,074.35; and from two to two and a half million dollars can be borrowed every year within the debt limit.

SECTION 2. *Public Libraries.* Of these there are eleven: the original building upon Boylston street, built in 1855-7, at a cost, including land, of about $365,000; nine branches in different parts of the city, namely, Brighton, Charlestown, Dorchester, East Boston, Jamaica Plain, North End, Roxbury, South Boston, and the South End; and a building recently purchased upon Cambridge street for a West End branch.[1] There are also thirteen suburban delivery stations.

The building on Dartmouth street, which is soon to replace that upon Boylston street, is nearly completed; it has cost more than double the original estimate; and the accommodations afforded by it are not considered by the best judges to be commensurate with its size and cost. It is rather a palace for books than a working library for the people. Upon entering office in 1891, I found,

---
[1] The Old West Church, bought in 1894, at a cost of $35,000.

however, that the building had progressed so far in all its structural features as to be incapable of radical change; and the only thing to do was to see that it was built within the additional appropriation voted that year. This, I think, will be accomplished.[1]

---

[1] See pp. 73–74.

CHAPTER 7.

BUILDING OPERATIONS.

The building operations of the city, as conducted in January, 1891, consisted of the Suffolk County Court House, in charge of a special commission; of the new Public Library on Dartmouth street, which was being constructed by the Trustees of the Public Library; and of certain buildings upon the parks, in charge of the Board of Park Commissioners; while the remaining buildings then under construction were in charge of the City Architect.

SECTION 1. *The Suffolk County Court House.* This building, begun in 1887, has been finished, occupied, and turned over to the Justices of the Supreme Judicial Court, under the provisions of a special law.[1] The cost of the building, including site and furnishings, has been $3,828,601.80, all procured by loans.[2] The new building covers 87,000 square feet, or over four times the space covered by the buildings which it was intended to supersede. Notwithstanding this enormous increase in area and the great sum of money spent upon the building, it is already crowded, and at some not distant day additional accommodations will be necessary.

SECTION 2. *The New Public Library.* This building was begun in 1886 on land partly given by the State and in part purchased by the city. After some money had been spent in the execution of plans prepared by the then City Architect, the Trustees decided to discontinue the work and to secure the services of one of the leading architectural firms in the country. Begun again in May, 1888, under plans furnished by the new architects, the work had progressed

---
[1] Stat. 1894, chap. 453.
[2] Of this amount, $521,000 has been borrowed since January 1, 1891.

so far by 1891 that all the structural parts of the building were practically complete and many of its decorative features fixed by contract.

It was apparent, however, that the building would cost very much more than the original estimates, and more than the amounts appropriated by the City Council, which up to January 1, 1891, aggregated $1,654,000.[1] An act was accordingly procured from the Legislature of 1891,[2] and accepted by the City Council, authorizing the city to borrow an additional million dollars outside of the debt limit for the completion of the building.[3]

Before any further contracts were let under the new appropriation, it seemed prudent to call a halt and ascertain, with as much accuracy as possible, exactly what it would cost to finish the building, and also to see that it was completed in the manner provided for the construction of public works by the contract law of 1890; that is, by means of a few large contracts, let by competition. This investigation covered a period of several months, and resulted, late in 1892, in the signing of contracts for the essential completion of the building for about $200,000 less than the appropriation. This surplus has since been utilized for paintings and other decorative features, which could never have been procured if the former methods had been permitted to continue, without still further appropriations.[4]

The building is now nearly completed; the books are being removed to it from the old library; and the Trustees expect that it will be thrown open for public use in a few weeks. There still remains to the credit of the building an unexpended appropriation of $303,590.49, which ought to be sufficient to complete it.

The result of this undertaking as a whole will be that at a cost for land and building, including the abortive construc-

---

[1] Of which $1,000,000 had been borrowed outside the debt limit.
[2] St. 1891, ch. 324.
[3] Of which $800,000 has been borrowed since January 1, 1891, and $200,000 remains still to be issued. Total loans issued for the library since January 1, 1891, $989,000
[4] For a fuller account of this matter, see Doc. 186, of 1892.

tion of 1886, of about $2,650,000, the city will have a public library the conveniences of which will be much greater than those of the present building, — though much less than could have been secured from a different and wiser planning, — and which is conceded to be in some respects one of the finest examples of modern public architecture in the country.

SECTION 3. *Buildings on the Parks.* The practice of the Board of Park Commissioners has generally been to employ private architects to prepare, at the usual professional rates, plans and specifications for, and superintend the construction of, the various buildings erected on the parks. Two buildings were under construction on January 1, 1891, and have since been finished; nine others have been begun and completed during the past four years; and two more are now in process of construction.

This completes the list of buildings actually needed for the popular use of the park system, and when those now under construction are completed the city will have upon its parks thirteen buildings, which will have cost about $375,000.

SECTION 4. *The Architect Department.* —This department has charge of the general building operations of the city, including school-houses and buildings for the fire, police, and other departments. It was established in 1874, prior to which time private architects had been employed by the various committees having charge of the buildings.

On the first of January, 1891, the work of the department was in the following condition: The Roxbury High School, begun in 1887, was still uncompleted and the appropriation exhausted. The sum of $87,000 was contained in the loan order of January 26, 1891; and with this appropriation the building was finished and turned over to the School Committee on October 1, 1892. Two grammar school-houses (the Henry L. Pierce school-house, in Dorchester, and the Bowditch school-house, in Jamaica Plain) and two primary school-houses (the Prince school-house, on St. Botolph street, and the Adams school-house, in East Boston) had been contracted out during the last few weeks of the City Government of 1890, on the credit of appropriations furnished that year. These buildings were finished and turned over to the School Committee during the year 1892.

Several buildings were also under construction for the Fire Department, all of which were finished during the year 1891; namely, Engine-house Nos. 38 and 39, on Congress street; Ladder-house No. 17, on Harrison avenue; Engine-house No. 9, in East Boston; Engine-house No. 44, at Allston; and Engine-house No. 22, at Egleston square. The money for these buildings had been appropriated prior to 1891. There was also an appropriation of $165,000 for a building for the Fire Department headquarters, for which no site had been procured.

On March 30, 1891, the City Architect was removed, and a new appointment made. For the reasons necessitating a complete reorganization of this department, and for an account of the results accomplished, reference is made to the proceedings of the Board of Aldermen of March 30, 1891; to a special message, dated September 24, 1891, concerning certain changes in the Architect Department (Doc. 136 of that year); to a special message, dated October 31, 1892, on the past and present management of the Architect Department (Doc. 181 of that year); and to the annual reports of the department for the years 1891, 1892, and 1893.

During the four years commencing January 1, 1891, besides the buildings just enumerated, finished, with the exception of the Roxbury High School, out of appropriations voted by preceding City Councils, appropriations for new buildings, aggregating nearly four and a half million dollars, have been made, partly from taxes, but principally from loans, as follows: $1,958,111.22 for school-houses and sites; $1,096,320.29 for the new buildings of the City Hospital; $100,000 for the city nurseries; $56,-702.18 for the quarantine hospital and disinfecting plant of the Board of Health; $907,500 for land and buildings for the Department of Public Institutions; $205,511.97 for land and buildings for the Fire Department; $72,092.78 for land

BUILDING OPERATIONS. 77

and buildings for the Police Department; and $83,000 for land and buildings for the Ferry Department.

With these appropriations the following work has been accomplished: eleven primary school-houses of brick, accommodating 3,976 pupils, three wooden primaries, accommodating 672 pupils, and three grammar schoolhouses, accommodating 1,568 pupils, have been finished; a grammar school-house, accommodating 672 pupils, is still under construction; and work is soon to be begun upon a primary school-house accommodating 504 pupils, and two grammar school-houses, accommodating 1,680 pupils. The fifteen primary schools will accommodate 5,152 pupils, while the six grammar schools will accommodate 3,920 pupils. A mechanic arts high school has also been built, and a new high school is under construction. For the City Hospital, an ambulance stable and a boiler-house have been built; a separate hospital for contagious diseases has been substantially completed, and will be ready for occupation during the month of March, 1895; a group of buildings for pathological purposes, consisting of a two-story laboratory, a chapel, and a morgue, are now being plastered; and a new surgical ward and a practically new operating building have been begun; making a total of fourteen buildings provided for the City Hospital. For the Board of Health, four buildings have been erected on Gallop's Island, and two on Swett street. For the Department of Public Institutions, a combination chapel, dining-hall, and domestic building, a combination boiler-house and laundry, and three dormitories accommodating 203 patients, have been erected at Austin Farm; a domestic building and two dormitories accommodating 178 patients have been erected at Pierce Farm; a boiler-house, barn, women's dormitory accommodating 320 inmates, and a hospital consisting of three buildings or wards accommodating 300 patients, have been erected at Long Island; 312 new cells have been added to the House of Industry, at Deer Island; a boiler-house and domestic building and a dormitory accommodating 52 boys have been erected for the Parental School, in West Roxbury; making a total of about 15 new buildings for this department. For the Fire Department there has been constructed upon a lot purchased on Bristol street a building for a department headquarters, fire-alarm service, water-tower, practice tower, and a boiler-house; an engine and ladder-house at Andrew square, South Boston; an engine-house at Ashmont; and a ladder-house on Friend street; besides which Hose-house No. 7 has been completely remodelled; and Engine-house No. 27 is being rebuilt. For the Police Department a station and court-house has been built at Brighton, and an annex for court and patrol-wagon has been made to Station 13, Ward 23. For the Park Department a pier head-house at Marine Park and an athletic house on the Charlesbank are being built.

The total amount expended upon the buildings in charge of the City Architect between May 1, 1891, and December 31, 1894, has been $2,999,898.47. The expenses of the department, including all sums charged to the special appropriations for the several buildings for inspectors, watchmen, experts, etc., have been $93,420.25, which is $3\frac{1}{8}$ per cent. upon the expenditures for construction. This percentage may be contrasted with the corresponding figures for previous periods in the history of the department; the cost of the department from 1874 to 1889 having been $6\frac{3}{4}$ per cent., and for 1889 and 1890, $10\frac{3}{8}$ per cent., of the expenditures for construction.[1]

In respect to methods of construction, more substantial and less easily combustible buildings have been necessitated by the new building law; the cubic contents of each school-room have been increased; special attention has been paid to heating and ventilation; and many novel methods have been adopted, in some cases invented, particularly in the hospitals at Long Island and Austin and Pierce Farms.

As to the relative cost of the new buildings, a comparison is difficult, except in the matter of school-houses, which in a

---

[1] See Doc. 136 of 1891.

general way furnish a substantially accurate basis. The twelve brick primaries provided during the last four years accommodate 4,480 pupils, and have cost $134 per pupil and $3.21 per square foot of finished floor area; while the seven primaries built during the period immediately preceding the present administration — that is, between 1881 and 1891 — accommodate 3,472 pupils, and cost $119 per pupil and $3.20 per square foot of finished floor area. As to the grammar school-houses, the six constructed under the plans of the present City Architect will accommodate 3,920 pupils, and will have cost about $137 per pupil and $2.83 per foot of finished floor area; while the last six grammar school-houses built under the former system, — namely, the Martin, Minot, O'Brien, Thomas N. Hart, Henry L. Pierce, and Bowditch grammar school-houses, — erected between 1885 and 1891, accommodate 4,032 pupils, and cost $158 per pupil and $3.08 per foot of finished floor area. The Brighton High School-house will cost about $130,000, or $2.79 per finished foot of floor area, while the next preceding high school built in this city — namely, the Roxbury High — cost $4.61 per finished foot of floor area. The twelve brick primaries provided during the last four years give an average of 618 cubic feet per pupil at a cost of 21 cents per cubic foot; while the seven brick primaries built in the period preceding gave 575 cubic feet per pupil at a cost of 21 cents per cubic foot. The three wooden primaries of the latter period, when compared with the seven wooden primaries of the earlier period, result as follows : for each pupil 672 cubic feet to 445 cubic feet, at a cost of 15 cents to 13 cents per cubic foot. The six grammar school-houses of the present Architect give to each pupil 702 cubic feet, at a cost of 17 cents per cubic foot; while the last six built, prior to 1891, gave to each pupil 710 cubic feet, at a cost of 19 cents per cubic foot. The cost of the Brighton High School will not exceed 18 cents per cubic foot, while the cost per cubic foot of the Roxbury High was 26 cents.

In interpreting these comparisons account must be taken

of the vastly more substantial construction of the new buildings and of the more elaborate arrangements for heating and ventilation.

A completely new system of contract forms has been adopted in this department (as also in the Street Department and the City Engineer's office), and has proved a great protection to the city in its works of construction.

The results obtained by this department have been secured at probably less cost than in private work. This is due not simply to the saving of about two per cent. in the professional expenses involved, but to the fact that by a fair and inflexible treatment of the business of the office the most responsible bidders have been induced to compete for the contracts advertised by the department. The city enjoys in some respects an advantage over private owners in its building operations, as no private citizen, however wealthy, keeps a daily bank balance amounting to millions of dollars; and a city contractor knows that as soon as his payments are certified, the money can be had without any of the delays which, under the most favorable circumstances, are incident to private work. Moreover, in work for the city, the contractor has practically only one man to deal with, — the City Architect, — while in private work there is the owner as well. Finally, the city is protected as, under the decisions of the courts, no private owner can be, against extortionate and fraudulent claims for extras. The contract law of 1890[1] practically prohibits all claims against the city for extras or work of any kind, unless evidenced by a written instrument signed by the City Architect, or the head of some other department, and approved by the Mayor. I consider this one of the most valuable laws ever placed upon the statute books of the Commonwealth; and to it, as well as to the other considerations here suggested, — particularly to the scrupulous fairness with which the business of the office has been administered, — I attribute the fact that

---

[1] St. 1890, ch. 418, §§ 4 to 6.

during the past four years our municipal building operations have been carried on in this department at actually less cost than would have been the case in private work.

It may fairly be claimed, I think, that this department, as at present managed, has demonstrated the possibility of the erection by municipal corporations of substantial, beautiful, and inexpensive public buildings. So long as such a management can be perpetuated it would be a mistake to abolish the department, as suggested in my first inaugural address; but the salary should be raised to a sum proportionate to the responsibility and labor of the office.

SECTION 5. *A New City Hall.* Such a building is needed, and ought to be built, either on the Public Garden, or next to the State House, before many years go by. Plans were prepared by the City Architect in 1892, and have been very generally commended; but in view of the more pressing necessity for other expenditures, particularly for rapid transit purposes, it seemed wise to postpone the erection of a new City Hall for some years at least. In the meantime the old Court House has been fitted up for the use of several departments.

CHAPTER 8.

THE PUBLIC STREETS.

The plotting of suburban streets in advance of laying out or construction is in charge of the Board of Survey, created in 1891. The laying out, widening, and extending of streets, and all matters relating to changes of grade, are in charge of the Board of Street Commissioners, created by St. 1870, ch. 337, subject in certain cases to approval by the City Council, and in all cases since the passage of St. 1892, ch. 418, to the approval of the Mayor. Everything that relates to the maintenance, watering, and cleaning of streets, and the construction of most streets, is in charge of the Superintendent of Streets. The City Engineer has charge of constructing some streets, and both he and the City Surveyor devote a large part of their time to the work of the Board of Street Commissioners and of the Street Department.

Other matters relating to the streets which have recently received the attention of the City Government are the bridges across the tide-waters surrounding the city; the grade crossings of the various street railroad companies; the presence of overhead wires in and across the streets; the compensation to be paid for the use of the streets by the private citizens and corporations having privileges therein; and the relief of the business streets of the city from overcrowding.

SECTION 1. *Street Lines and Grades.* The topographical conditions of the original town were ill-adapted to good street lines, and the resulting narrow and crooked highways have been a subject of criticism and regret for over 200 years.[1] Nothing could be done with the lanes

---

[1] As early as 1665 a royal commission described the streets as " crooked with little decency or uniformity;" and the necessity for constant widenings was recognized in the building act of 1692. A readjustment of street lines has been attempted after nearly every large fire, beginning with that of 1676.

of the old town except to widen and extend them at enormous expense;[1] but when the original limits of the town were enlarged by annexation and by the filling of the tidal flats on either side of Boston Neck, efforts were made to see that in the new territory thus acquired the mistakes of the old town were not repeated. South Boston, annexed in 1803, was laid out upon a systematic, rectangular plan, under the provisions of a special act of the Legislature.[2] The "Neck Lands," being that portion of the public lands on either side of Boston Neck, redeemed by filling for building purposes, were laid out by the City Government with broad, rectangular streets; and the same plan was adopted for the development of the land acquired by the filling of portions of the South Bay. When the Back Bay was filled, this portion of the city was also laid out upon a systematic, rectangular plan, through the coöperation of the Commonwealth, the city, and the private owners of the flats.

After the annexation of Roxbury in 1868, and Dorchester in 1870, it became apparent that the streets previously laid out in the suburban territory thus acquired were nearly as tortuous and narrow as those of the city proper, and that unless something was done the people would suffer a repetition in these portions of the city of the evils so plainly felt in the older part. It was therefore determined to secure the laying out of new streets in Roxbury and Dorchester upon public lines, and various plans were devised for the accomplishment of this purpose, the practical result being the creation of the Board of Street Commissioners in 1870. This Board had, however, no power to lay down street lines in advance of the actual taking for highway purposes, and before many years it became evident that its work was largely confined to an acceptance or rejection, as public streets, of private ways laid out haphazard for the benefit, and according to the personal ideas, of the individual

---
[1] Since 1822 nearly forty millions of dollars have been spent for street widenings, extensions, and changes of grade — mostly in the city proper. See Auditor's Annual Report for 1893-4, pp. 202-208.
[2] St. 1803, ch. 111.

land-owners, without reference to the general needs of the travelling public or to the growth of the community. It thus appeared — especially after the amount of suburban territory within the city limits had been more than doubled by the annexation, in 1874, of West Roxbury and Brighton — that there was need of more systematic methods of street plotting; and a demand arose for the adoption of methods similar to those in force in New York, Brooklyn, Chicago, and the newer Western cities, for the development of streets upon a comprehensive, public plan. The result of this agitation, lasting twenty years, was the passage, in 1891, of the act creating the Board of Survey.[1]

The theory of this law,[2] in so far as it relates to street plotting, is that the city, through the Board of Survey, shall prescribe the lines to which all future streets must conform. The owner is entitled to compensation, as under the former system, when the land shown upon the Board of Survey plans as appropriated to street purposes is actually laid out as a highway by the Board of Street Commissioners, providing he can prove damage and insists upon compensation. The duration of the Board was limited to three years from the first of May, 1891, in the belief that its work could be accomplished within that period; but so many difficulties were encountered and so much delay was caused by accidental circumstances, — such as the necessity of waiting until certain grade-crossing problems had been solved, — that when the first of May, 1894, was reached only about one-fourth of the work contemplated by the original act had been completed. The existence of the Board was therefore extended[3] to May 1, 1897. I can see no reason why the entire work, as originally contemplated, should not be finished by that date.

---

[1] See inaugural addresses of Mayor Shurtleff, Mayor Cobb, Mayor Martin, Mayor O'Brien, and Mayor Hart, as well as the inaugural address of January 5, 1891; also report of the commission appointed in 1884 to prepare a revision of the city charter, Doc. 120, of 1884.

[2] St. 1891, ch. 323. [3] By St. 1894, ch. 335.

It was inevitable that such a radical change in the method of laying out public streets in this city, as was contemplated by the law of 1891 and its amendments, should create hostility on the part of land-owners, — particularly those of the speculative kind, who not only desire to develop their own property without regard to the rest of the community, but insist on having it done at public expense; but on the whole there has been less opposition to the Board of Survey than was expected. Its assistance has been eagerly sought by most of the more responsible land-owners and builders; the plans hitherto filed have met with general approval; and I believe that when the work is done, the public will welcome it as a great reform, and oppose all efforts to undo it. One hundred and eighty-four plans have been filed to date, covering 3,391 acres, and showing 91.27 miles of prospective streets laid out, widened, or extended.

While the work of the Board of Survey will take care of the new streets in the still undeveloped suburban sections of the city, the streets of the business portion of the city cannot be improved by any such means, but only through the expenditure of great sums of money for widenings and extensions, at public expense, or by the adoption of hitherto untried methods. One such method is the duplication of the capacity of the streets by constructing subways beneath them, — a plan about to be tried by the Boston Transit Commission under the authority of ch. 548 of the Acts of 1894. Another method would be to give the Board of Street Commissioners power to widen streets by arcading.[1] Another is to establish building lines.[2]

With some of the principal streets of the business section of the city duplicated by the construction of subways, with others widened by arcading, and still others widened or

---

[1] I petitioned for such a law in 1894, but there was opposition from real-estate owners; and this opposition, together with the difficulty of drafting a satisfactory bill, was sufficient to cause the rejection of the petition.

[2] See St. 1893, ch. 462, accepted by the City Council October 28, 1893, and St. 1894, ch. 439. These laws were passed at the instance of the Executive Department; and under the authority of them building lines have been established on Beacon street and Boylston-street extension.

extended by the establishment of building lines, or upon the old plan of paying for all the land taken; with the streets of the suburban districts plotted upon proper lines by the Board of Survey; there yet remained another class of streets, which has needed and received the attention of the City Government. I refer to radial thoroughfares leading from the city proper to the different suburban sections. Of the possible improvements of this character the more important have been provided for, in part or in whole, during the past four years: namely, the construction of Commonwealth avenue to Brighton; the extension of Boylston street beyond the Back Bay park; the widening of Huntington avenue and Tremont street to Brookline; the extension of Columbus avenue; the construction in connection therewith of a proper approach to Franklin park; the widening and extension of Blue Hill avenue; and better means of communication between the city proper and the towns and cities to the north *via* a new bridge to Charlestown.

The extension of Commonwealth avenue along the line of what was formerly Brighton avenue, and its construction to the width of 160 feet, was undertaken in 1887 upon an appropriation wholly insufficient for the purpose. During the past four years $843,671.05 have been appropriated from loans and revenue for this improvement, and it is now substantially completed, with the exception of a new bridge over the tracks of the Boston & Albany Railroad, to cover the cost of which an additional appropriation will be necessary. The avenue has lately been extended to connect with the new boulevard in Newton.

Boylston street has been extended to Brookline avenue, and its construction ordered under the provisions of a special law.

Huntington avenue and Tremont street have been widened so as to make an avenue 100 feet in width from Copley square to Francis street, and 80 feet in width from Francis street to the town of Brookline. Columbus avenue has been laid out from Northampton street to Franklin park.

The principle of the acts[1] under which Boylston street,

---
[1] St. 1894, ch. 416 and ch. 439.

Columbus avenue, and Huntington avenue have been laid out, is that the city shall pay the entire first cost of land and construction, and then assess the entire benefit or betterment upon all estates deriving benefit therefrom. These laws are similar to that under which Oliver street was widened in 1867, and differ from the general betterment law of the Commonwealth in providing that the whole instead of one-half the benefit may be assessed.

As to Blue Hill avenue, an order has been passed and approved widening this avenue to 120 feet from Warren street to the Neponset River at an estimated cost of $76,875. Construction will not be necessary for some years; but it was thought desirable to secure the widening while the land could be obtained at reasonable prices — particularly as the Metropolitan Park Commission has agreed to take as a parkway, and widen to 120 feet, Mattapan street in Milton, from the Neponset River to the Blue Hills reservation.

The first cost of these widenings and extensions is to be charged to the loans for "laying out and construction of highways;" and the loan of $1,000,000 authorized for this purpose, together with the $300,000 loan for Columbus avenue, is sufficient to provide the money required by the orders of the Board of Street Commissioners.

There is need of an avenue on the east side of the city from the business part, or at least from the South End, through Roxbury and Dorchester. The most available plan would probably be to widen Hampden street and extend it so as to connect with Blue Hill avenue. Columbia and Boston streets should also be widened, so as to make a proper connection between the Dorchester parkway and Franklin park. Brighton avenue and North Beacon street should also be widened.

In laying out these radial avenues, the Board of Street Commissioners can now set apart a special reservation for the street railway tracks;[1] and such reservations have been provided on Commonwealth avenue, Huntington avenue, and Blue Hill avenue.

---

[1] St. 1894, ch. 324, accepted by the City Council November 3, 1894.

SECTION 2. *Construction, Maintenance, etc.* The construction, paving, and repair of the public streets, as well as the cleaning and watering of them, is in charge of the Superintendent of Streets. The changes effected in the methods of cleaning and watering the streets have already been referred to.

The surface of the streets was in such poor condition four years ago as to be the cause of universal complaint, and it was necessary to expend large sums of money upon new and improved pavements. The liberal appropriations voted for this purpose by the City Councils of 1891 to 1894 have been expended with, it seems to me, excellent results in respect to both the character and the cost of the work. On January 1, 1891, there was in the entire city but one short piece of block stone pavement laid upon a concrete base; there were no brick pavements, only 1,453 sq. yds. of block asphalt, and 54,070 sq. yds. of sheet asphalt. During the past four years the area of sheet asphalt pavements has been increased to 107,074 sq. yds., and there are now 14,206 sq. yds. of block asphalt, 5,082 sq. yds. of brick pavements, and 54,404 sq. yds. of blockstone on concrete base.

As the business section of the city has been almost entirely repaved, and as the pavements of the residential section of the city have been very much improved, I do not think that large special appropriations for the Paving Division will be needed in the immediate future. The work of constructing the radial thoroughfares extending into the suburbs must be continued, probably by loan; but I see no necessity for borrowing any considerable sums during the next few years for pavements.

As to the relative cost of the work of the Paving Division during the past four years, comparisons with previous administrations are difficult, if not impossible, for the reason that prior to 1891 the books of the department were kept in such a manner as to make it extremely difficult to ascertain the exact cost of anything.[1] The entire book-keeping of the

---

[1] See Annual Reports of the Citizens' Association for 1890, pp. 36-41.

department, as well as the whole system of letting contracts and purchasing materials, was reorganized by the late Superintendent of Streets; and throughout his administration the books have been so kept as to make it possible, not only to ascertain the exact cost of every undertaking, but to facilitate comparisons with the work of succeeding administrations.

SECTION 3. *Financial.* The money for the laying out, widening, and extension of streets, the construction of them, and their maintenance, repair, etc., comes either from the annual appropriations out of the tax levy and other sources of annual income, or from special loans, or from the loans for the "laying out and construction of highways" authorized by chapter 323 of the Acts of 1891. The cost of maintenance and repairs, and everything that can fairly be termed current expenditures, must, under the provisions of chapter 206 of the Acts of 1891, be paid out of taxes and income; while everything in the nature of permanent improvements may, and under the present tax limit generally speaking must, be met by loan.

In this city the cost of street construction, like the cost of street widenings, sewers,[1] and other similar-improvements and conveniences, falls upon the general taxpayer to an extent that would not be tolerated in any other progressive community. Elsewhere, at least in all the larger cities of this country, substantially the entire cost of streets built for the development of real estate, including sewers, sidewalks, and other conveniences, is assessed upon the abutters. In some cities a small percentage is paid by the municipal corporation, but in most of the large cities of this country the entire cost falls upon the land-owners. This fact is of vital importance to a correct understanding of the problem of taxation in this city. Our taxes are admittedly high; but this is largely due to the fact that the city — that is, the general taxpayer — is compelled in Boston to pay for local improvements which in other communities are charged upon the land.

See chapter 5, § 8.

I shall not encumber the pages of this message with a repetition of the arguments so frequently addressed by me to the City Council, and to committees of the Legislature, in favor of a complete change in our methods of providing for street, sewer, and sidewalk construction, and of the substitution of the assessment plan, under which all the other great cities of this country have been so rapidly built up, for the taxation plan in operation here; except to state that every day's experience in the past four years has confirmed my belief in the wisdom and necessity of such a change.

It is not, as many persons are inclined to assume, a mere question of form; it is not true that it makes no difference to the taxpayer whether the burden of street construction falls upon him in his annual tax bill for general municipal purposes or in the form of special assessments; and it is fallacious to argue that the burden of taxation in Philadelphia, Brooklyn, or Chicago would be equal to that of Boston if the special assessments levied in the former cities were included in estimating the real amount of taxation. It is not a question of form, but of substance; the real issue being, not the amount of the special assessments, nor the amount of taxation including them, but rather how the burden of these assessments shall be distributed. The Boston system distributes the cost among the taxpayers at large, while under the other system the greater part, sometimes the whole, falls upon the estates particularly benefited, and those who own no such estates pay nothing. I believe the latter to be the correct theory; and I consider that the Boston plan is responsible, more than all other causes combined, for the relatively greater burden of taxation and debt in this city than in those communities which have been wise enough to adopt the assessment system.

The Legislature of 1891 was induced to take a great step in this much-needed reform; the act creating the Board of Survey also providing for the construction of streets in the suburban sections by assessment. This law had no sooner been passed, however, than it was violently attacked by the speculators in suburban real estate; and they had sufficient influence to induce the Legislature of 1892 to modify, and, in fact, to almost nullify, the financial provisions of the Act of 1891. In 1893 and 1894 still further retrograde action was taken; and the result up to date has been that the original purpose of the law has been thwarted, and that it no longer is, as was intended, an act for street construction on the credit of the city, with sinking-funds or assessments equal to the loan, but has been converted into an act for street construction at public expense, and has caused a considerable increase in the net debt of the city.[1]

The amendments to the law of 1891 were passed against as effective a protest as the City Solicitor and the Executive Department could prepare; and the success of the speculative element in the community in inducing the Legislature to overthrow the work of 1891 is indicative of the fact, which I have so frequently had occasion to deplore, that here to a greater extent than anywhere else in the world the real-estate speculator who desires to develop his land and increase its value at public expense seems to be in control of legislation.

The sewer law of 1892[2] has experienced a similar fate, having been so amended by succeeding Legislatures as to have lost its chief financial merits.[3]

The sidewalk law of 1892,[4] according to which the entire cost of sidewalk construction was assessed upon abutting estates, in conformity with the practice obtaining in other cities, met with a still worse fate. It was entirely repealed in 1893.[5]

The result of these attempted reforms in the financial methods of street construction has thus been unsatisfactory;[6]

---

[1] $894,163.77 up to December 31, 1894. See Appendix, Table 24.
[2] St. 1892, ch. 402.   [3] St. 1894, ch. 227 and 256.
[4] St. 1892, ch. 401.   [5] St. 1893, ch. 437.
[6] This experience is nothing new. As early as 1845 Mayor Quincy went to the Legislature in behalf of the city for a bill permitting street widenings by assessment, and the bill was lost by the votes of Boston members. Another unsuccessful application was made in 1856 by Mayor Rice. See also Inaugural Addresses of Mayor Smith in 1855 and Mayor Lincoln in 1866. The members of the Legislature most determined in their opposition to the construction law of 1891 have been the representatives from the suburban wards of Boston.

but some good has been accomplished. The proportion of cost assessed upon particular estates, and the corresponding benefit to the city treasury, is still greater than prior to 1891; and public attention has been directed to the subject in a manner which should prevent an entire relapse to former conditions.

It is discouraging to be obliged to chronicle the fact that the chief plunderers of the city treasury of Boston are not politicians or contractors, — for public opinion is always behind an Executive who stands up against the demands of such, — but the suburban speculators in real estate, who not only seek to secure a private and unjust advantage out of the public treasury, but, under the pretence of advocating public improvements, actually succeed. I believe that the greatest obstacle to the progress of this city and to its proper development as the metropolis of New England is the selfish owner of vacant lands, who makes no improvement at his own expense, but spends his time in agitating for the expenditure of the public funds upon local and private improvements which in other communities would be charged to him.

SECTION 4. *Bridges.* With the coöperation of the Commonwealth, a new bridge has been constructed over the Reserved Channel between Ward 13 and South Boston, connecting Congress street and the city proper with L street in South Boston; the old Dover-street bridge across Fort Point Channel has been entirely rebuilt; the bridge between North Brighton and Watertown has been rebuilt; the Chelsea-street bridge between East Boston and Chelsea, and the bridges between Charlestown and Chelsea, are being rebuilt; and loans have been authorized with which to construct a much-needed new bridge between the city proper and Charlestown.

SECTION 5. *Grade Crossings.* Those of the Boston & Albany Railroad at Cambridge and Everett streets, in Brighton, have been abolished. The crossing of the Boston & Maine Railroad at Causeway street has been discontinued, partly through the construction of the Union Station, and partly through the taking by the Transit

Commission of the terminal property of the Boston & Maine Railroad south of Causeway street; and the Boston & Maine crossings of Chelsea bridge are being abolished. On the system of the New York, New Haven, & Hartford Railroad, the grade crossings at West Fourth street and Codman street have been abolished, and arrangements have been made under special legislation for the abolition of all the grade crossings along the Providence Division, between Park square and Forest Hills. Negotiations are now in progress with this company for the abolition of the grade crossing at Dorchester avenue. The grade crossings in East Boston can best be dealt with by a complete change in the location of the railroad tracks in the manner suggested by the Rapid Transit Commission of 1891; but this cannot be done under the general grade-crossing act, and no agreement has yet been reached with the railroad companies. I have petitioned the Legislature of 1895 for relief in this matter. The question of abolishing the grade crossings of the Boston & Maine system in Charlestown and beyond abounds with difficulties; and these difficulties have been increased by the refusal of the railroad corporation to follow the advice of the Rapid Transit Commission, the Railroad Commissioners, and the City Government in respect to the manner of constructing its Union Station. The inconveniences of the plan adopted are already apparent, and the cost of abolishing the grade crossings in Charlestown, East Cambridge, and Somerville will be very much greater than if the Legislature of 1893 had not, at the instance of the corporation, rejected the bill prepared by the city and reported by the Legislative Committee on Transit.

SECTION 6. *Overhead Wires.* These are now being removed from the streets by the new Commissioner of Wires, under authority obtained from the Legislature of 1894, after a contest with the corporations interested lasting several years.

SECTION 7. *Compensation for the Use of Streets.* Of the various corporations and individuals using the public streets for either purely private or what may be termed semi-public purposes, only the gas and electric light companies can be said to pay any compensation for the valuation privileges they enjoy. The gas and electric light companies make special prices, less than those paid by the general consumer, to the city in respect to the public lights supplied by them. Thus the price paid by the city to the electric light companies, now thirty-five cents a night, is claimed to be about the actual cost to the companies, and is admittedly less than the companies charge private citizens for the same service. The gas companies make a price for the city which is less than the price for the general consumer as fixed by the Gas Commission; the annual difference or benefit to the city of the special prices for gas used upon the streets and in the public buildings amounting, at the present time, to $30,645 per annum.

With the exception of the gas and electric light companies, none of the persons or corporations using the streets pay anything for the privilege — a condition of things generally regarded as unfair to the city treasury, which has practically to pay the entire cost of maintaining the streets in good repair, and most of the original cost for land and construction. Efforts have been made by the City Governments of the past six years to procure from the Legislature authority to impose a special tax, or otherwise to exact compensation, for the use of the public ways by the various corporations and private citizens having privileges therein. As the streets of the city and their control belong, under the decisions of our courts, to the people of the Commonwealth, and not to the municipal corporation, the city authorities have no power to exact compensation for the use of the streets unless specially authorized to do so by the Legislature. The efforts to secure this authority have hitherto been unsuccessful, partly owing to a perhaps well-founded fear that the authority, if granted, would not be wisely exercised; but principally to the opposition of the special interests involved. With changes in the city charter and the constitution of the legislative branch of the City Government, such as have been suggested, the first difficulty would be removed or reduced to a minimum, and I should then hope that the Legislature would see fit to grant to the City Government the right enjoyed by municipal corporations in other parts of the world to secure full compensation for all privileges granted in the streets.[1]

SECTION 8. *Street Travel.* The streets of the business section of the city, never adequate for the demands of travel, have been completely diverted from their original and proper function as public highways and converted into locations for the benefit of the street-railway corporations and their patrons. After three years of agitation and discussion, in which I have felt it my duty to take an active part, the Legislature of 1894 adopted a plan,[2] subsequently ratified by popular vote,[3] for the relief of the streets from the congestion due to surface cars by placing the latter in subways constructed for the purpose. The work has been intrusted to a special commission, the members of which assure me that no financial or engineering difficulties have been discovered, and that construction will be commenced as soon as the season for work is at hand. The property of the Boston & Maine Railroad, between Haymarket square and Causeway street, has been taken for the northern terminal of the subway. This great undertaking will, I am convinced, if carried out in the spirit of the act granting the authority, relieve our streets of the congestion due to the presence of surface cars

---

[1] See Document 144 of 1890; inaugural addresses from 1891 to 1894; and the records of the State Legislature for the years 1891, 1892, 1893, and 1894, in regard to various petitions and bills presented by the Mayor, the City Solicitor, the Citizens' Association, and individual citizens. The foreign system of granting exclusive franchises for a term of years in return for a division with the city of all dividends declared above a certain percentage seems, on the whole, to be the most advantageous, and much preferable to the Massachusetts plan, under which the corporations get no exclusive or permanent rights and the public gets no rent. See the bill relating to street-railway franchises, presented to the Legislature of 1891 on behalf of the city, and the contract with the Brookline Gas Light Co. of February 27, 1893.

[2] St. 1894, chap. 548. [3] By 15,542 to 14,162 at a special election held July 24.

and tracks, and restore them to public use as highways for all classes of the people. The expenditure involved will be large, but should prove no permanent or real addition to our funded debt, as the rentals for the use of the subways ought to be sufficient to cover the interest and sinking-fund requirements on the forty-year loans issued for the purpose, and after the maturity of these loans to yield a clear profit to the city.[1]

The streets I found also to be encumbered by innumerable pedlers and other persons transacting private business upon the narrow sidewalks of the congested district, thus increasing the difficulties of travel. These nuisances have been to a great extent abolished; all pedlers having been excluded from the retail business section, and desks and other sidewalk obstructions prohibited.

Much remains that could be done to facilitate travel by regulating the use of the streets by teams. The interests concerned have, however, taken the not wholly unreasonable position that they should not be made the special object of regulation as long as the chief cause of congestion — the street-railway companies — are allowed locations everywhere; and this argument, together with others of less force, has hitherto sufficed to deter the Board of Aldermen from taking action. It seems now to be the opinion that the question of traffic regulations should be postponed until the street-car service has been permanently readjusted by the Transit Commission.

---

[1] See Chapter 18, § 7.

CHAPTER 9.

STREET LIGHTING.

The first attempt to light the streets by gas was made in 1834, prior to which time oil-lamps had been used, first put up in 1773 by subscription. Oil and gas were used for street lighting until 1882, when 113 electric lights were erected. Since then there has been a gradual diminution in the number of gas-lamps, and a gradual increase in the number of electric lights, and in 1891 naphtha was substituted for oil in the remoter suburban streets.

On the 1st of January, 1891, there were in use upon the public streets 9,282 gas-lamps, consisting of 9,247 four-foot burners and 35 large burners. There were also 2,957 oil-lamps, 99 naphtha-lamps, and 1,125 electric lights, each of 2,000 candle-power (commercial); making a total of 13,463 lights.

The prices charged by the gas companies ranged from $1 to $2 per thousand cubic feet; and the electric-light companies charged forty cents per lamp per night.

The contracts with the different gas companies expiring in 1893, an effort, with the details of which the citizens are familiar, was made to secure a reduction in the price. The final result of this movement was a series of contracts with the different companies at prices ranging from 70 cents to $1.50. These contracts expire in 1896 and 1897, at the option of the city, which has the right to insist indefinitely upon the maintenance of the present prices.

The number of gas-lamps and the respective prices for the same in use January 1, 1891, and January 1, 1895, are shown in the following table:

Price.	Number of Lamps at each price, Jan. 1, 1891.	Number of Lamps at each price, Jan. 1, 1895.
$2 00	3	
1 85	1,174	
1 60	665	
1 55	660	
1 50	3,930	998
1 00	2,815	163
1 35		439
1 25		1,032
1 17		1,886
90		671
70		2,251
	9,247	7,440

These reductions effected a saving to the city treasury of about $55,000 per annum in the prices paid to the various gas companies on account of the street lamps. An additional saving of about $10,000 was also brought about in the prices paid for lighting the public buildings, which were included in the special contracts with the gas companies.

All doubt concerning the validity of these contracts would seem to have been removed by a recent order of the Board of Aldermen, approved December 5, 1894.

Through competition between the different companies, appeals to the Gas Commission and the State Legislature, and the contracts referred to, a general reduction was also effected in the prices paid by private consumers for gas throughout the city amounting to about half a million dollars per annum.

The following table shows the reductions in detail:

Prices Paid by Private Consumers for Gas in the City of Boston.

Lamp Department, District.	Jan. 1, 1891.	Discount.	Jan. 1, 1895.	Discount.
City Proper, South part....	$1.30	$1.20 to large consumers only......	$1.00	
City Proper, North part....	1.30	$1.20 to large consumers only......	1.00	
Roxbury (Rox. Gas L. Co.) ..	1.70	20 cts. per M. off if paid in 12 days ...	1.00	
Roxbury (Brookline G. L. Co.),	......	....	1.00	
Dorchester	1.70	20 cts. per M. off if paid in 12 days ...	1.40	10 cts. per M. off if paid in 15 days.
South Boston...	1.70	Same as Dorchester,	1.40	Same as Dorchester.
Jamaica Plain ..	2.50	50 cts. off if paid in 15 days	1.80	15 cts. off if paid in 15 days.
Brighton	1.90	Net	1.50	10 cts. per M. off if paid in 12 days.
Charlestown	2.00	25 cts. per M. off if paid in 15 days . .	1.60	20 cts. per M. off if paid in 25 days.
East Boston	1.75	Net	1.60	10 cts. per M. off if paid in 15 days.

The controversies with the different gas companies having been adjusted during the year 1893, it remained to secure an improvement in the electric-light service of the city. During the year 1894 contracts have been made with the various electric-light companies, involving a reduction in price from 40 to 35 cents per light per night where overhead wires are strung and owned by the companies, and to 34 cents where the city owns the distributing plant. These reductions in the price of electric lights were predicated upon a certain increase in the number, as set forth in the several contracts, and the Superintendent of Lamps has accordingly erected during the past year 790 new electric lights, 520 of which are on the public streets, principally on the main thoroughfares leading from the city proper to the suburbs, and 270 upon the Common, Public Garden, and the parks.

The following table shows the annual increase in electric lights:

1882	113	1890		345
1883	222	1891		309
1884	55	1892		106
1885	48	1893		31
1886	56	1894		790
1887	80			
1888	119	Total		2,368
1889	94			

And the number on January 1, 1891, and January 1, 1895, are shown, by wards, in the following:

WARD.	January 1, 1891.	January 1, 1895.	WARD.	January 1, 1891.	January 1, 1895.
1	34	73	15	30	60
2	36	71	16	33	46
3	22	42	17	32	50
4	32	69	18	48	80
5	44	63	19	29	54
6	48	85	20	38	95
7	54	87	21	80	122
8	19	51	22	58	200
9	20	34	23	39	183
10	102	163	24	75	198
11	70	134	25	41	98
12	50	105			
13	53	88		1,132	2,368
14	40	117			

The electric lighting of the Common, Public Garden, and parks has been undertaken on the underground system; the city paying for and owning the distributing system, except the lamps, which are owned and cared for by the company, as in the case of overhead wiring.

The streets and parks of the city are now lighted by 2,368 electric arc lights, of 2,000 candle-power (commercial) each, by 7,440 gas-lamps, each supplied with four-foot burners, and by 2,761 naphtha-lamps; and the estimated cost of maintaining the department upon this basis, which involves twice the number of electric lights in use four years ago and a complete substitution of naphtha for oil, is only $12,165.57[1] more than was expended during the year 1890.[2]

---

[1] Expended in 1890, $557,492.63; estimate for 1895-6, $569,658.20.

[2] For the details and results of the contest for cheaper gas in 1893 see various messages sent to the City Council of that year, particularly those of January 1 (inaugural), January 30, February 13, February 27, March 1, May 18, and November 9, 1893; also printed testimony taken before the Legislative Committee on Investigation, the argument made on behalf of the city, reprinted separately, and chapter 474 of the Acts of 1893. The Commission appointed under the provisions of this act found the value of the property of the Bay State Gas Co. to be $1,500,000 in excess of the capital stock of $500,000. The company accepted the decision, issued $1,500,000 of new stock, and surrendered as cancelled the note of $4,500,000 by the date fixed in the act. In this way the nominal capitalization of the company was reduced from $5,000,000 to $2,000,000.

CHAPTER 10.

PROTECTION AGAINST FIRE.

SECTION 1. *Building Laws.* A new Building Law had long been considered a necessity, and radical changes were recommended by a special commission appointed in 1890, in a report submitted in 1891, too late for action that year. In 1892 the matter was taken up, and a law involving still more radical changes, drafted in coöperation with the Boston Board of Underwriters, was passed by the Legislature of that year. This law (Stat. 1892, chap. 419), which it has since been found necessary to amend only in minor details, marks an immense improvement upon all former Building Laws in operation in this city, both in respect to the character of the restrictions imposed to secure better construction, and to the manner of enforcing the law. The requirements of the Building Law of 1885, as well as those of its predecessors, were far behind the age, and resulted in the erection of a class of buildings which has literally created a conflagration district in this city. The law was also defective in omitting to provide any efficient means of enforcement. The new law has given, I think, general satisfaction, will need amendments only in minor particulars, and should in the course of time result in the rebuilding of this city according to sound methods of construction. The "Board of Appeal" established under the authority of the law of 1892 has been of great service in securing an intelligent and firm construction of the law.

SECTION 2. *Fire Department.* Associations have been formed for the purpose of securing from the State Legislature, by means of political influence and intimidation, those unreasonable privileges which the Commissioners have been unwilling to concede. The Fire Department has been the victim of political agitation both at the City Hall and at the State House, in the supposed interest of the firemen. The department is also extremely costly, and there appears to be no end to its demands for increased appropriations, both for current expenses and for buildings and equipment.

As already stated to the City Council, I believe that better results, financial and administrative, can be obtained by placing the Fire Department in the hands of a single commissioner, at an adequate salary.

SECTION 3. *Overhead Wires.* After failing for three successive years to induce the Legislature to give the city authority to compel the electric light and other companies maintaining wires in and across the public streets to put them underground, an appeal to the Legislature of 1894 was successful, and the authority given by chapter 454 of the acts of that year is now being exercised with good results by the new Commissioner of Wires.

CHAPTER 11.

RELIEF OF THE POOR.

This work, except so much of it as relates to paupers entitled to permanent support under the general settlement laws of the Commonwealth (see chapter 12), is in charge of the Overseers of the Poor in the City of Boston, consisting of twelve members, four of whom are appointed each year by the Mayor. This corporation has the right to receive trust funds, the income of which is applicable to the purposes designated by the several donors; and the amount of such funds now in its hands is about $375,000.

The Board also receives an annual appropriation from the City Government, averaging about $110,000, which is used for the relief of those entitled to public assistance under the statutes of the Commonwealth, who are not inmates of the Public Institutions.

The manner in which the duties of this Board — particularly during the serious crisis of the winter of 1893-4 — have been discharged by its members, who receive no compensation, and yet are obliged to devote a very large amount of time and labor to the duties of their office, deserves the highest commendation.

It is sometimes assumed that the city can expend any amount of money which it sees fit for the purpose of furnishing relief in the form of work or alms to the poor and destitute; but this is not the law. Municipal corporations in this Commonwealth are permitted only to expend the public moneys for the relief of such persons as are entitled to it under the provisions of the pauper statutes (P. S., ch. 84), and to the limited extent allowed by chapter 374 of the Acts of 1874. This latter statute authorizes the city to expend an amount not exceeding one fifteen-hundredth of one per cent. of the valuation for the year for such charitable purposes as the City Council may designate. The amount of the appropriation possible under this law is only about six thousand dollars; and while the city is not limited in the amount that can be appropriated for the use of the Overseers of the Poor, the appropriations can only be expended by that Board for the relief of those entitled to it by law. The appropriations granted to this Board cannot be used, any more than those given to other departments, in miscellaneous charity, or for the purpose of furnishing employment.

During the distress which prevailed in this city in the winter of 1893-4 efforts were made through appeals to the humanity and charitable disposition of the members of the City Government, by threats of personal violence, and by every species of political intimidation, to induce the city officials to strain the law or to connive at its evasion, and to disburse a part of the public funds raised by taxation or loan, either directly to those who stood in need of aid, or through the indirect process of creating work for the unemployed.

A considerable portion of my inaugural address last year was devoted to this subject and to the proper means of meeting an emergency which every charitable person was forced to recognize.[1] I stated my conviction that "the main reliance of every community in emergencies like the present must be the generosity and public spirit of its individual citizens," and that there was no doubt that the people of this city would respond then, as in the past, to all urgent and well-considered appeals in behalf of poverty and want. This confidence was not mistaken; the emergency was met and overcome; and what threatened to be a season of unusual hardship and severity happily passed away without the suffering and distress which so many of us were led to fear. This result was accomplished by the voluntary and individual action of the charitable people of this city, acting partly through their churches, partly through the various

---

[1] See also Inaugural Address of Mayor Cobb, 1875.

charitable societies, and partly through a citizens' relief committee specially organized for the purpose.[1] The action of the community in its corporate capacity was confined to the legitimate expenditures authorized by the statutes and to such coöperation in the way of accelerating the progress of the public works as seemed proper under the circumstances. An open winter favored the prosecution of these works, and it was possible for the first time in some years to continue work upon the parks and sewers throughout the year. No special appropriations were voted, not even under the law of 1874, and no public money was disbursed in this crisis that would not have been in any event expended, except that the Overseers of the Poor received a larger appropriation than usual in the annual appropriation order for 1894-5 for the purposes for which they are authorized by law to expend money.

At a time when State and municipal legislatures all over the country were besought to authorize the undertaking of public works for the sole purpose of furnishing occupation for the unemployed, and to resort to other methods of relief still more direct, it is cause for congratulation that the people of this city were able to meet the crisis and to avert the expected distress without recourse to illegal or unwise uses of the powers of government. Wherever a contrary policy was adopted, it failed, so far as my information goes. The Legislature of the State of New York passed an act authorizing the Park Department of the City of New York to expend $1,000,000 in park construction for relief purposes. It is notorious that this money was largely wasted, so far as its utility for park purposes was concerned, and that it was at the same time of little assistance in relieving the necessities of the poor. The result of the appeals made to the Legislature of this Commonwealth for the relief of the unemployed was the passage of an act authorizing the Metropolitan Park Commission to expend $500,000 in the construction of roadways. Not a dollar of this sum was expended

---

[1] The final report of the Citizens' Relief Committee is printed as Doc. 197 of 1894.

at the time, or has been since. Instances of the failure of the efforts made last winter to relieve the distress that then prevailed through the creation of work for the unemployed might be multiplied, if space permitted. The knowledge thus gained, taken in connection with the history of the experiments made during the past few years in London and other English towns to avoid the evils of pauperism through the establishment of public works, points to one of two conclusions: either that such efforts are after all unavailing to relieve distress, or that they operate to create the very evil they are intended to prevent.

CHAPTER 12.

PAUPER AND PENAL INSTITUTIONS.

These since early in 1889 have been in charge of the Board of Commissioners of Public Institutions, created by chap. 245 of the acts of that year, and consisted in 1891 of the House of Correction, in South Boston; the House of Industry, the House of Reformation, and the Truant School, at Deer Island; a lunatic hospital, partly in South Boston and partly at Austin Farm; a home for pauper children, on Marcella street in Roxbury; and three almshouses, on Long and Rainsford Islands and in Charlestown.

Disturbances, finally resulting in open riot, occurred at Deer Island in the latter part of 1891. A careful personal investigation satisfied me that those disturbances had been fomented by one of the commissioners and some of the subordinate officers at the island; and these officials were therefore removed, under circumstances more fully set forth in the messages to the City Council of February 5 and February 23, 1892. The ease with which discipline has been maintained among the prisoners from that day to the present seems to be proof conclusive that the right course was followed at the time.

Induced by this occurrence to investigate more carefully the general condition of our public institutions, I soon became convinced that they were one and all suffering from an utter inadequacy of accommodations, as well as from certain defects of management and system largely due to the lack of proper buildings.

The accommodations in the House of Industry at Deer Island were wholly insufficient for the average number of prisoners there, and the close proximity of this institution to the House of Reformation and Truant School for boys was objectionable in the highest degree. At Long Island there was but one building, constructed in 1885-8 without regard to modern methods of treatment and classification; and the building at Rainsford Island was still older, and wholly unadapted to the needs of a modern almshouse. The Lunatic Hospital at South Boston was unfit for the care of the insane in every respect, apart from its overcrowded condition. It was opened in 1839, and enlarged in 1846, since which time no money had been expended on it except for ordinary repairs. Some of the inmates were removed to Austin Farm in 1887, but that had furnished no permanent relief.

With the assistance of a Board of Visitors, composed of public-spirited citizens familiar with institutional work, appropriations have been made amounting to $907,500,[1] with which 376 additional cells have been provided at Deer Island; five new buildings for the insane have been erected at Austin Farm; 77½ acres of additional land have been purchased in the vicinity of Austin Farm, and three buildings for the insane erected thereon; a parental school for boys, consisting of two buildings, has been built on about 29 acres of land purchased in West Roxbury; and several hospitals and a new dormitory have been erected at Long Island.

These buildings are practically complete, and are either already occupied or will be within a few weeks. They will permit the department to concentrate at Long Island[2] all the paupers entitled under the laws of the Commonwealth to permanent support by the city; to transport all the truant boys to the beautiful home provided for them in West Roxbury; to devote Deer Island exclusively to the House of Industry and its prisoners; to remove the House of Reformation for boys to Rainsford Island; and to remove all the insane patients of the city, not boarded out in the State institutions, to Pierce and Austin Farms in Dorchester.

---

[1] Or more than the aggregate appropriations of the preceding twenty years for land and buildings for our public institutions.

[2] The Commissioners have been directed to place the new hospital at Long Island in charge of a corps of visiting physicians and surgeons, and thus assimilate, so far as possible, the management of this institution to that of the city hospital.

The new buildings will also permit the arrangement, separation, and classification of patients upon approved modern theories, and include larger and better hospital accommodations than can, I am satisfied, be found in similar institutions elsewhere in this country.

A large part of the time of the Board of Aldermen has been occupied during the year just closed with an investigation into abuses alleged to exist in these institutions. Investigations by a tribunal which has no power to compel the attendance of witnesses or to administer a binding oath, and to which the most reckless statements can be made without subjecting the witness to the penalties of perjury, are not apt to be fruitful in results.[1] The Board has listened with great patience to every one who had a complaint to bring against the management of the institutions, and has finally exonerated the commissioners from the charges brought against them. This result is, in my opinion, matter for public congratulation, as more vicious and undeserved attacks upon public officers than have at times been made in the course of this investigation have seldom been witnessed in the annals of municipal government.

I would not be understood, however, as condemning the opinions held by the Board of Visitors or by the public-spirited ladies and gentlemen who, if mistakenly, yet honestly, thought that the best way to secure the desired reforms was through a public investigation carried on in advance of the possibility of reform. The reports of the Board of Visitors in 1892 and 1894 contained many valuable suggestions which were promptly acted on by the department, others were found impracticable without additional legislation, and others were impossible of execution until the new buildings were completed. There was no possibility of intro-

---

[1] See message of February 23, 1892, for a fuller discussion of the difficulties surrounding such investigations. The chief practical result of the aldermanic investigation of 1894 has been to postpone for an entire year the filling of the vacancy caused by the resignation of the chairman of the Board, who desired, and in my opinion was entitled to, an opportunity to defend the management of the institutions from the charges brought.

ducing the more general reforms recommended by the Board so long as the inmates of our institutions were confined in the miserable, crowded quarters until recently existing. In other words, much of the criticism passed upon the commissioners was premature. Now that the new buildings are complete, administration upon the most approved modern institutional theory is for the first time possible. As it was unreasonable to expect a proper treatment according to modern methods of the pauper and criminal wards of the city in the public institutions as they existed four years ago, so now, with one of the most modern and elaborate plants to be found anywhere in the country, their mismanagement ought to be impossible.

CHAPTER 13.

PARKS.

The great benefit derived by the people of New York from the construction of Central Park induced the citizens of Boston to consider seriously the advisability of providing similar, or possibly better, park facilities for themselves. The attempt was made, in 1870, to commit the people at a special election to the creation of a park system, but the act provided that a two-thirds vote was necessary, and although a majority voted for it, the necessary two-thirds was not obtained.[1]

In 1874 a special commission was appointed to consider the subject, and in 1875 another act[2] was secured authorizing the city to establish a system of parks if the act were accepted by a simple majority vote. This act was accepted at a municipal election by 3,706 "yeas" to 2,311 "nays," and constitutes the basis of our present park system. A park commission was appointed under this act in 1875; and the first large appropriation was voted in 1877, being a loan of $450,000 for land for the Back Bay Fens. From that time to December 31, 1890, the work of constructing the various parks recommended by the commission and its landscape architects proceeded very slowly. There had been expended up to that date $6,537,616.33,[3] and with the exception of a portion of the Fens, a part of the Arboretum, a small park at the West End known as the Charlesbank, and parts of Franklin Park, there was practically nothing to show for this great outlay. That is to say, a great part of the work was still under construction and proceeding slowly; much of it had not been

---
[1] See St. 1870, ch. 283. A special election was held on November 8, 1870, at which 9,233 persons voted "yea" and 5,916 persons voted "nay."
[2] St. 1875, ch. 185.
[3] $3,028,068.94 for land, and $3,509,547.39 for construction.

begun at all; and the portions that were finished were inaccessible to the general public. The policy had been adopted — embodied in the Act of 1886 authorizing a loan of $2,500,000 — of expending only $500,000 a year for land and construction, on account of the main park system; and on January 1, 1891, there was but one instalment of this loan unissued. A new loan was evidently necessary, and accordingly the Legislature of 1891 authorized the borrowing of $3,500,000 in instalments of $700,000 per annum. As the work progressed I soon became convinced, however, that this rate of expenditure was too slow; that the present inhabitants of the city were deriving practically no benefit from the enormous expenditures on account of these parks; and that a wiser policy would be to finish all the absolutely necessary parts of the park system as rapidly as possible, so that the people of this day and generation could enjoy its benefits. Accordingly, in 1893, the prohibition against issuing more than $700,000 a year was remitted,[1] and the Park Commissioners immediately set about the completion of the system as rapidly as possible. This work has progressed so favorably that the Fens, the Muddy River Improvement, Jamaica Park, the Arboretum, and Franklin Park, as well as the connecting parkways, have been substantially completed and opened for public use during the year 1894. Much progress has also been made upon Marine Park; while the smaller parks, such as Wood Island and Charlestown Heights, have not been neglected.

It was expected that the loan of $3,500,000, authorized in 1891, would be sufficient to complete the system in all its essential features; but this expectation has not been fulfilled, owing principally to the unexpectedly heavy amounts which the city has been obliged to pay for land. Some additional expense has also been caused by the purchase of Franklin Field and Dorchester Park, but the main reason for the increase in the amount needed to complete the parks has been the large sums which have had to be paid to the

---
[1] St. 1893, ch. 211.

owners of land expropriated by the commission. An appropriation of $500,000 was made by the City Council of 1894 within the debt limit; a new park at the North End was bought, and is now being constructed under an appropriation of $300,000 within the debt limit; and the Legislature of 1894 authorized the city to borrow an additional million of dollars on or after the first of January, 1895. The whole of this loan will be needed to pay for the lands not yet settled for, to provide for the contracts now outstanding, and to finish up those parts of the main park system and Marine Park which seem reasonably necessary in order that the public may derive the full benefit of these parks, and the money which they have cost.

There has been expended from January 1, 1891, to December 31, 1894, the sum of $5,492,302.05, making a total expenditure for parks since 1875 of $12,029,918.38. The million of dollars to be issued the coming year[1] will bring the expenditures up to over $13,000,000, for which sum the park system as laid out by the first commissioners, with some few additions since, will be completed in all its essential features. Some of the details contemplated by the landscape architects, as well as the construction of the "strandway," will have to be omitted unless further appropriations are made. It seems to me that such appropriations should for the future be derived exclusively from loans within the debt limit, and that no application should be made to the Legislature for further loans for park purposes outside of the debt limit. An annual loan of a few hundred thousand dollars can easily be procured for park purposes within the borrowing capacity of the city under the statute of 1885, and such annual expenditure would seem to be about all the taxpayers should now be called upon to bear for the purpose of park construction.

The interest taken in the development and speedy completion of our park system has not been confined to parks within the limits of the city, and I have felt it desir-

---
[1] Issued January 4, 1895.

able that the city should lend its aid in every legitimate way to the scheme of metropolitan park improvements, authorized by the Legislature of 1893.[1] Under the authority of this act the Metropolitan Park Commission has secured about 6,225 acres of wild lands in the suburban towns, which, added to the municipal parks, public grounds, and water reservations, in Boston, Lynn, Malden, Cambridge, Newton, and other towns in the metropolitan district, make a total park area for this city and its suburbs of over 12,000 acres. To acquire the metropolitan reservations, and to connect them with boulevards or parkways, the commission has been authorized to expend $2,300,000, the larger part of which will fall upon the city of Boston. The Stony Brook reservation has been connected with the Arnold Arboretum by a parkway, part of which was taken by the Metropolitan Park Commission, and surrendered to the city, and the remainder of which was taken by the Boston Park Commissioners themselves. The Metropolitan Park Commission also proposes to connect the Blue Hill reservation with Blue Hill avenue, and thus with Franklin Park, by widening Mattapan street, in Milton, and to coöperate with the town of Winchester and the Boston Water Board in the preservation of the shores of Mystic Lake and the Abbajona River. Arrangements[2] have also been made with the President and Fellows of Harvard University for an addition of about 75 acres to the Arnold Arboretum.

The community now owns and can soon enjoy for purposes of public recreation park areas greater in extent and much more accessible in situation than are to be found within the limits of other large cities. That portion of the park system lying within the city limits and just completed has already commended itself to popular favor, and bids fair to revolutionize the appearance of the city, and to some extent the habits of its people. The great expenditure involved will, I am satisfied, prove one of the best investments that the city

---
[1] St. 1893, ch. 407.
[2] Awaiting the sanction of the Legislature.

has made, although not capable of earning a direct pecuniary profit; and the citizens may well congratulate themselves that the system was so judiciously laid out in the first place, and that the original plans have been so carefully adhered to by successive park commissioners.

CHAPTER 14.

THE CIVIL SERVICE.

Appointments of heads of departments and to some other offices are made by the Mayor, subject to confirmation by the Board of Aldermen. Subordinate appointments are made by the heads of departments, in some few cases the approval of the Mayor being also necessary. These subordinate appointees are all within the scope of the civil service rules, except the deputy superintendents, heads of divisions, and other persons charged with responsible executive duties, the employees of the City Treasurer, Collector, and Mayor, and some miscellaneous officers, such as messengers, deputy sealers of weights and measures, assistant assessors, etc.[1] With these exceptions, all the employees of the City Government, including the laborers, are within the scope of the rules laid down by the Civil Service Commission.

During the past four years these rules have been amended so as to include employees who up to that time had not been classified; and the rule permitting temporary employment or thirty days without drawing on the lists of the Civil Service Commission has been modified so as to allow such employment for a period of five days only.

The City Council of 1892 passed an ordinance forbidding city employees to serve upon political committees. An attempt to repeal this ordinance in 1893 was stopped by executive veto. A similar ordinance was passed by the City Council of Cambridge in 1892 and repealed the following year; and an attempt to induce the Legislature of 1893 to enact a similar law relating to State and county employees

---

[1] See St. 1884, ch. 320, and amendments, particularly St. 1893, ch. 95.

was defeated. The city of Boston thus remains the sole, as it was the first, public body in the country to prohibit office-holders from serving upon political committees or acting as delegates to political conventions. The object of this reform was to prevent the creation of a political machine consisting of office-holders; and this object has been successfully accomplished, as appears from the fact that since the passage of the ordinance, city officers and employees other than those elected by the people have not been permitted to serve upon the political committees of either party, or to act as delegates to nominating conventions.

Frequent requests are received for a statement of the general results of the application, through the State Civil Service Commission, of the merit system to the selection of municipal employees; and it may be proper to record here the opinions which the experience of the last four years has led me to form.

The system has not resulted in the elimination of politics from the City Government; for although little opportunity for political preference remains in respect to the original selection, yet as soon as appointed the employees form organizations for mutual protection and advancement. These organizations are political, though not partisan, in character; the laborers in the several departments organize in labor assemblies with the object of securing permanent employment, an increase in the number of holidays, higher wages, and, generally, an extension of the privileges accorded to this class of city employees; the firemen associate themselves together for the purpose of procuring more leisure, an increase in salaries, and otherwise to advance their interests; and the police officers work for pensions and other privileges. This activity among the civil service employees of the city is not political in character in the sense that it is exerted in favor of either the Democratic or Republican parties. It may rather be said to be antagonistic to the party for the time being in power. The movement is, however, distinctly political, as intended to secure special privileges from the City Government or the Legislature through political pressure. The adoption of the civil service principle has not eliminated political activity from the City Government; it has simply changed its form.

As to the fundamental question, whether better men are secured by this system than before, I am inclined to think that the advantage, while slight, is with the merit system. Theoretically, better men can be selected by the heads of departments than through any species of examination, oral or written; but practically, I think that better results are obtained in the long run through the merit system, making the exceptions stated at the beginning of this chapter. Some difficulty has been experienced in getting competent men from the civil service lists in certain classes of work, — particularly in stenography, — but with this exception I should say that the men sent down by the Civil Service Commission have been on the average superior to those likely to have been appointed by the departments, if allowed to select their employees at will — that is to say, under the pressure of political and personal considerations.

While, therefore, it cannot be said that the system has worked a radical improvement in the character and capacity of our city employees, and while it has wholly failed to eliminate politics, using that word in its broadest sense, from the public service, still it has one great advantage which in my opinion outweighs all inconveniences and shortcomings, and that is the protection it affords to the heads of departments against the pressure of individual office-seekers, politicians, and political committees. Without this protection, the difficulty of conducting the city business under the present charter, which concentrates all the executive business in the Mayor and heads of departments, would be increased to such an extent as to make the office of Mayor almost untenable; and it was a fortunate thing for the City Government that the civil service principle was introduced simultaneously with the charter amendments of 1885. On the whole, therefore, while the system has not worked in practice exactly as was predicted, still it has worked fairly well, and is an indispensable protection to the executive officers of the city.

Extreme partisanship in appointments to heads of departments has never obtained in this city, and while these officers are not within the scope of the civil service rules, it may not be out of place to record the fact that on January 1, 1891, there were among the salaried heads of departments twenty-seven Republicans. Of these, one was removed for cause, one resigned, one lost his place through a consolidation of departments, six were not reappointed at the expiration of their terms, and the remaining eighteen were either reappointed or transferred to some other department. Of the eighteen thus retained two have since died, one has resigned, and one has failed of reappointment.

CHAPTER 15.

LABOR MATTERS.

One of the chief difficulties in municipal government under democratic institutions is the treatment of the labor problem in its various aspects. The relations between the municipal corporation and its employees engaged in manual labor are everywhere the cause of unceasing agitation and discussion; and this is particularly the case in Boston, where from the earliest times a larger proportion of the public work has been done by day labor than in the other large cities of the country. The collection of garbage, at first let out to contractors, was intrusted to a department of the City Government to be handled directly by its employees, as early as 1824; and in the same year a street-cleaning service was inaugurated upon the day-labor plan. The lighting of the public lamps, which prior to 1868 had been done by the gas companies or other contractors, was at various times between that year and 1870 handed over to the lamp department, and has since been attended to by the employees of that department. Work upon the streets was done very largely by day labor as early as 1850; sewers have been built by day labor from an early period; the laying of pipes for our water-works has almost always been done by the day; since 1865 the construction of the great basins has frequently been attempted by day labor; and a large part of the work of park constructions since 1882 has been done by the day.

The present practice is to do all the work of maintenance, repairing, jobbing, pipe-laying, and all matters the proper execution of which is a question of opinion, and therefore difficult to secure through written specifications, by day labor employed directly by the city departments, and to let all works of large construction out by contract.

The day-labor system, even if excluded entirely from works of large construction, costs the city very much more than contract work, as, owing to the higher rate of wages paid, the smaller number of hours, and the large number of holidays and half-holidays without loss of pay, the city pays about sixty per cent. more than the market rate of wages.[1] A further loss is experienced through the necessity of furnishing, so far as practicable, permanent employment throughout the year, and also by the continued employment of men who have grown old in the service of the city.

On the other hand, a good deal of the city's work could not be done by contract without constant complaints from the citizens that it was not properly done. This applies to the collection of garbage, the cleaning of streets, the lighting of lamps, and other work of the sort, the proper execution of which is in the nature of things a matter of opinion and therefore incapable of accurate specification in a written contract. In the next place, work in the nature of jobbing — of which there is a great deal in the Street Department — probably costs no more under this system than if let out by contract, for the reason that the profits of the middleman in small jobs are necessarily large. Then there is a class of work difficult of inspection, such as the laying of water-pipes, which it is for the interest of the city to have done by day labor, even if it costs more, in order that the city authorities may be certain that it is well done.

Notwithstanding all that can be said against the execution of public works by day labor, I am satisfied that it is on the whole for the advantage of the city that work of the character mentioned should be done in this way; and as to the high rate of wages, shorter hours of work, and other privileges which swell the cost, it may be said that the wages paid to the city laborers have not been increased since 1882;[2] that

---

[1] The cost in the Street Department alone of holidays and half-holidays amounts to nearly $75,000 per annum. A city laborer (unskilled) receives about 24 cents per hour of actual work, while the contractors pay about 15 cents.

[2] When they were fixed by vote of the City Council at not less than two dollars per day.

the hours of labor are regulated by statute;[1] and that if the city is to employ day labor at all, it has been found practically necessary that the laborers should receive high wages, permanent employment so far as practicable, and generally a more liberal treatment than in private work. Whether city laborers work as faithfully as those employed by contractors depends on circumstances, principally on the discipline of the department and the energy of its foremen.

Passing now to the consideration of works of construction, we find wholly different conditions. Here the cost of the day-labor system is very much greater than contract work, and the results are in no respect more satisfactory.[2]

While there are opportunities for collusion and corruption in the contract system, still these opportunities can be and, so far as my experience goes, are avoided with comparative ease. Contracts for work of this character can be so drawn as to permit of accurate inspection, and with upright and watchful heads of departments there is no reason why public work of this sort cannot be carried on fully as cheaply and quickly as private work.

I have been at some pains to secure accurate comparisons of the cost of works of large construction done by day labor and by contract, and the following instances are given by way of illustration: At Lake Cochituate, in 1887, about 50,000 cubic feet of shallow flowage work was done by day labor, at a cost of $28,837.16; while the following year about 57,000 cubic yards of similar work was done by contract for $16,202.25. Stripping 54,000 cubic yards of loam from the bottom of Basin 6 cost by day labor 71 cents per cubic yard; while the average of five sections let out by contract, involving the removal of about 400,000 cubic yards, cost about 40½ cents a cubic yard. Rubble masonry was built on Basin 6 by day labor at a cost of $12.50 per cubic yard, and by contract for $7.50 per cubic yard.[3] The

---

[1] St. 1890, ch. 375, which went into effect January 1, 1891.

[2] See report of Citizens' Association for 1890, pages 17 and 18; and report for 1891, pages 97-99.

[3] On the other hand, the concrete work on the dam for Basin 6 cost the same by day labor as by contract.

work on Basin No. 5 (that now under construction, estimated to cost $2,500,000 for land and construction) is being done by contract; while the greater part of the work at Basin No. 6 was done by day labor; and the following table shows a comparsion of the results obtained :[1]

	DAM No. 5.	DAM No. 6.	
	Contract.	Contract.	City.
Stripping of Basin and Dam	0.24		0.57
Sodding embankment	0.28		0.90
Concrete core-wall	4.70		6.61
Plastering Portland cement	0.67		0.99
Delivering gravel on embankment	0.206 (est.)	0.206	
Spreading and rolling	0.119 (est.)		0.226
Stripping 496,207 cubic yards		0.405	0.64
Stripping 110,232 cubic yards			

The plan now being pressed by certain labor organizations (not composed of city employees) for the construction of public buildings by day labor employed directly by the

---

[1] The City Engineer, from whom these figures are obtained, makes the following explanation:

In the item of 496,007 cubic yards of stripping is included one section of 90,810 cubic yards, which was very difficult. Excluding that section, the average cost of stripping 405,197 cubic yards was 35½ cents per cubic yard. The city work necessarily costs more than that done by contract for the reason that the city pays in the country $2.00 for nine hours' work, gives one half-day per week during four months, all holidays, and two days for voting. The men work from eight to nine months per year. This makes the price paid for one hour of actual work about $0.24, while the contractor pays in ordinary years, in the country, $0.15 per hour.

The division of cost of building the dams is about as follows: Labor, 67 per cent.; teaming, 13 per cent.; tools, etc., 20 per cent.; and on this basis the city must pay 1.42 times as much as the contractor for the same effort. For stripping, the division of cost would be for labor, 75 per cent.; teaming, 20 per cent.; tools, etc., 5 per cent.; and the city must pay 1.49 times as much as the contractor.

city is too preposterous for discussion. The city has no opportunity to give constant employment to the skilled labor required in building operations, and would therefore be unable to secure the best workmen; it has no plant; the administration of such work would greatly enlarge the scope of political patronage; the cost may be safely set down as two or three times that of the present system; and all the advantages to be gained from competition under our present admirable contract law[1] would be lost.

Between the demands of the taxpayer for the execution of all public works by contract, and the demands of the labor organizations[2] that all public works should be done by the day, I believe that the safe, reasonable, and prudent course to follow in the public interest is the system now and for some time past in operation. According to this, all work of large construction is done by contract, through competition, except, perhaps, in certain special cases of peculiar difficulty; while jobbing, maintenance, repairs, and other work of the kind, including all that cannot be accurately specified and inspected, is done by day labor employed directly by the city departments upon liberal terms, in respect to wages, hours, holidays, and length of employment.

---

[1] St. 1890, ch. 418, sect. 4-6.

[2] There is no demand by the *city* employees for such a change in the methods of doing city work. It would obviously operate against their interests as tending to increase the number of persons on the labor rolls of the city without increasing the opportunities for permanent employment.

CHAPTER 16.

STATE LEGISLATION.

While the city is dependent upon the action of the State Legislature for permission to do a great many things that it desires to do, its financial concerns, on the other hand, are the subject of constant attack by individual members of the Legislature, both from this city and from other towns. The treasury of the city of Boston is regarded in many parts of the State as a fund to be drawn upon by compulsory legislation for the benefit of the smaller towns; and many of the representatives from this city make it their habitual concern to introduce and advocate bills for the transfer of portions of the city's money for the benefit of special interests and classes. The result is that during the annual sessions of the Legislature a large part of the work of governing this city must be transacted at the State House in the advocacy of needed reforms, and in defence of the city treasury against agrarian and class legislation.

I shall not encumber these pages with a detailed account of this work,[1] on the whole the most important that has devolved upon me during the past four years. It was inevitable, in the execution of this duty, that friction should be caused, enmities aroused, and misunderstandings created. Whoever undertakes such work in the public interest is sure to be accused of advocating measures which he has in fact opposed; of being hostile to measures which really received his hearty support; of going to the Legislature too often; of going too little; and generally

---

[1] Covering from fifty to a hundred appearances a year at committee hearings and conferences.

of interference with its work, or of neglecting it, according to the standpoint of the critic. Corporation lobbyists impugn his motives, real-estate speculators attack his character, and the horde of schemers who invade the Legislature with plans to plunder the taxpayers of this city become his personal enemies. On the other hand, the committees of the Legislature can generally be depended on to consider the municipal questions brought before them in a spirit devoid of partisan and personal motives.[1]

The following is a summary of the more important measures enacted during the last four sessions of the Legislature, and advocated by me either by petition, letter, or personal argument.

1891.

CHAPTER 93. An act to authorize the city to anticipate its authority to borrow money within the debt limit during the current municipal year, so that loans can be placed early in the year and their proceeds made available for expenditure during the working season.

CHAPTER 206. An act to prohibit the borrowing of money for current expenses.

CHAPTER 301. An act authorizing a loan of $3,500,000 for park purposes.

CHAPTER 321. An act amending the public statutes so that the ordinary loans issued by the city of Boston may be made payable, if desired, in twenty years, instead of ten.

CHAPTER 323. An act creating a Board of Survey, and providing for the construction of streets by assessment.

CHAPTER 324. An act authorizing the city of Boston to borrow $1,000,000 outside of the debt limit, to complete the new Public Library building.

CHAPTER 344. An act authorizing the extension of the Charlesbank from the West Boston bridge south.

---

[1] Except such questions as are, or are thought to be, political in character.

CHAPTER 365. An act creating a commission to consider the question of Rapid Transit.

CHAPTER 388. An act authorizing the construction of a bridge connecting L street and South Boston with Congress street and Ward 13.

CHAPTER 390. An act creating a special commission to consider the improvement of the Charles River.

1892.

CHAPTER 213. An act relating to the financial administration of our water-works, enabling the city to place its water-works, for the first time since their inception, upon a self-supporting basis.

CHAPTER 342. An act for the establishment of a commission to consider the advisability of establishing a system of metropolitan parks.

CHAPTER 371. An act authorizing the Board of Park Commissioners to acquire the property and franchises of the Jamaica Pond Aqueduct Company and the Jamaica Pond Ice Company.

CHAPTER 401. An act permitting the construction of sidewalks by assessment.

CHAPTER 402. An act relating to assessments for the construction of sewers.

CHAPTER 404. An act to provide an open space on the east side of the State House Extension.

CHAPTER 419. The new building law.

CHAPTER 433. An act providing for the abolition of grade crossings on the Boston & Providence Railroad by raising the tracks.

1893.

CHAPTERS 170 and 464, being amendments to the Building Law of 1892.

CHAPTER 192. An act relating to loans of the city of Boston, authorizing the City Treasurer to treat money derived from the various loans as a general fund for the purposes authorized.

CHAPTER 211. An act remitting the provision of the park loan act of 1891, that no more than $700,000 could be issued in a year.

CHAPTER 261. An act relating to transfers of appropriations.

CHAPTER 300, as amended by chapter 411. An act authorizing the Board of Park Commissioners to incorporate into our park system streets adjacent to or leading into the parks, upon the request of a majority of the abutters.

CHAPTER 339. An act for the extension of Boylston street.

CHAPTER 342. An act for the protection of the public health, giving courts of equity jurisdiction to enforce an order of the Board of Health for the filling of flats and marshes below grade 11.

CHAPTER 407. An act to establish a Metropolitan Park Commission.

CHAPTER 435. An act permitting the construction of an embankment in the rear of Beacon street.

CHAPTER 459. An act authorizing the State Board of Health to investigate the subject of an additional water-supply for the city of Boston and its suburbs.

CHAPTER 460. An act providing for the enforcement of all the orders of the Board of Health by decree, thus furnishing a more efficient remedy than had hitherto existed for the abatement of nuisances.

CHAPTER 462. An act authorizing the establishment of building lines on public ways.

CHAPTER 474. An act relating to the Bay State Gas

Company, the result of which was the cancellation of $3,000,000 of its nominal capital.

CHAPTER 475. An act authorizing the Board of Metropolitan Park Commissioners and the State Board of Health to consider the improvement of the Charles River.

CHAPTER 478. An act providing for the construction of a subway under Tremont street, subsequently accepted by the City Council.

1894.

CHAPTER 119. An act authorizing the Board of Health to compel the owners of private passageways to pave them.

CHAPTERS 257, 382, and 443. Amendments to the Building Law.

CHAPTER 288. An act authorizing the Metropolitan Park Commissioners to construct roadways and boulevards.

CHAPTER 324. An act authorizing the laying out of public ways with reservations for street railways, bridle paths, drains, sewers, electric wires, trees, grass, and planting.

CHAPTER 335. An act extending the term of the Board of Survey.

CHAPTER 416. An act providing for the construction of Columbus and Huntington avenues on the betterment plan.

CHAPTER 439. An act relating to the extension and construction of Boylston street and other adjacent streets, in the territory between the Back Bay Fens and Brookline avenue.

CHAPTER 454. An act providing for the putting of all electric wires underground.

CHAPTER 509. An act authorizing the Metropolitan Park Commission to acquire the shores of the Charles river above Cottage Farm.

CHAPTER 532. An act authorizing the taking of land on the east side of the State House for an open space.

CHAPTER 548. An act to promote rapid transit.

In addition to the laws embraced in the foregoing schedule, reference may be made to the anti-stock-watering laws of 1894, to the various acts for municipal lighting passed since 1890, to the law imposing a tax on legacies, to numerous acts for the abolition of grade crossings, to the investigation by a legislative committee into the capitalization of the Bay State Gas Company, and to the investigation by the Executive Council into the conduct of William M. Osborne, a member of the Board of Police; all matters to which I have been obliged to devote more or less time during the past four years.

Among the more important measures objected to and defeated may be mentioned the West End franchise bill of 1891; various measures annually introduced to drive foreign corporations out of the State by compelling a disclosure of the ownership of their stock; various other measures for increasing the burdens of double taxation; various amendments to the street construction law of 1891 offered for the purpose of compelling the city of Boston to construct streets for the benefit of private speculators; innumerable attempts to authorize the City Council to borrow money outside of the debt limit; the measure annually introduced into the Legislature for the ostensible purpose of securing a "redistribution" of the school fund, but really with the object of taking about $400,000 a year out of the city treasury of Boston and distributing it among the smaller towns and cities; bills to take away the fire department and other branches of municipal service from the control of the City Government; bills to compel the city to pay taxes upon the basins and other improvements built by it in the towns situated on the Sudbury-river water-shed; bills to increase the tax rate; bills to abolish the debt limit; bills to compel the city to use its money for improper purposes; and innumerable other measures in the interest of bad government.

On the other hand, unsuccessful appeals have been made to the legislatures of the last four years to extend still further the system of street and sewer construction by assessment; to exempt municipal bonds from taxation; to secure a tax on direct legacies and successions; to authorize the Mayor and Aldermen to exact compensation for the use of streets from corporations having franchises therein; to procure the right to manufacture light for municipal use in the streets, parks, and other public property of the city; and for other minor reforms.

CHAPTER 17.

COMMERCIAL FACILITIES.

SECTION 1. *Docks.* The early growth, prosperity, and wealth of Boston were due to foreign commerce, and its one permanent natural advantage is its harbor. During the past forty years, however, the commerce of this port has been declining in comparison with that of Philadelphia and Baltimore, cities less favored with harbor facilities than Boston. This is not the place to discuss the causes of this decline nor the remedy, in so far as this depends upon the individual enterprise of our business men and merchants; but there is a widespread belief that the community in its corporate capacity should take the problem up, and if it were certain that the decline in our commercial importance could be arrested or the foreign business of the city increased through the prudent and conservative action of the municipality, few would doubt the expediency of entering upon the work. The suggestion most frequently heard is that the city should undertake the construction of a great system of public docks in East Boston. Over seven hundred of our most prominent citizens and business firms have asked the City Government to petition the Legislature for such legislation as will permit the establishment of public docks in Boston harbor; and the City Council has requested me to send such a petition to the Legislature.

I have not been able to see my way clear to address such a petition to the General Court. The comprehensive scheme of public docks which has been presented in support of this request would involve the expenditure of millions of dollars; there is no consensus of opinion as to the best location for the docks; and it is altogether doubtful whether the establishment of them would in reality revive our languishing commerce. It should not be forgotten that the aid of the municipality was unnecessarily invoked for the establishment of railroads. Mayor Otis took the ground in 1829 that "the State and city must be up and doing, or the streams of our prosperity will seek new channels," and advocated the construction of railroads on public account, or by means of public contributions, "to save this State and city from insignificance and decay;" while the people voted on July 30, 1830, to request the Legislature to authorize the city to subscribe for $1,000,000 of railroad stock. And yet a railroad system was secured for Massachusetts without State or city aid; and the subsequent railroad speculations of the State proved very expensive and useless undertakings. So, in the matter of dock facilities, it is doubtful whether any more are needed, and it is possible that if needed they will be supplied at the expense of private capital.

For these reasons, and in view of the unfortunate results of some of our municipal undertakings of this character, I have been unwilling to officially endorse a vague and general petition for the establishment of public docks. Before any such scheme is entered on, there should, it seems to me, be a most careful and thorough investigation, not by committees of the City Government or the Legislature, but by a special body or commission of persons, competent through their experience and knowledge of commercial and municipal affairs to study the subject in all its practical and financial details. In advance of such an investigation, it seems to me that it would be folly to commit the city in any manner to the purchase, construction, ownership, or management of public docks upon the scale contemplated.

Moreover, if an addition to our dock facilities is really necessary, and can only be procured at public expense, ways exist to secure it without seeking legislative authority to establish municipal docks upon the scale suggested, and without an increase of the city debt beyond the limit now fixed by law. In the first place, the Commonwealth owns a large area of flats in Ward 13, which it is slowly filling and selling off for building purposes. If public docks are a necessity they can easily be obtained through the improvement by the Commonwealth of these flats for dock purposes, rather than for building lots. In the next place, the city of Boston owns large areas of flats on the other side of the harbor, which can be filled or developed either for building or commercial purposes without any special authority from the Commonwealth, except the right to change the harbor lines. The City Engineer has at my request prepared a modest scheme for the construction of two or more large docks upon the city flats known as Bird Island, off Jeffries Point, in East Boston. Docks or wharves could be built on this site of sufficient size to accommodate six or eight large ocean steamships at a time, at an estimated expenditure of less than $1,000,000. The city has from the beginning exercised the right to improve its land upon the harbor front for commercial purposes, and the only authority that would seem to be needed for the improvement of the Bird Island flats for this purpose would be the consent of the State and Federal authorities to the filling of the flats and to the construction of wharves beyond the present Harbor Commissioners' lines. The system of docks thus suggested would cost but comparatively little; the amount needed could be divided into two annual instalments of $500,000, a sum easily obtained within the present borrowing capacity of the city under the debt limit law; and the scheme, if successful, could be extended almost indefinitely in an easterly direction towards Governor's Island, or in a northerly direction, at right angles to the Governor's Island channel.[1] The city also has considerable property in South Boston, near the Reserved Channel, and a large area of flats in Dorchester Bay, which could be developed for dock purposes without any authority whatever from the Legislature or the Federal government.

If anything is to be done by the city of Boston in this

---
[1] See various plans and suggestions contained in the report of the Rapid Transit Commission of 1891, as well as the plans recently prepared by the City Surveyor and the City Engineer.

matter, it seems to me that it should be undertaken upon the modest and comparatively inexpensive plan here suggested, and substantially, if not exclusively, upon the property now owned by the city; and that it would be altogether unwise for the city to request or receive a general authority to purchase, develop, build, or maintain any grand scheme of public docks involving an expenditure of untold millions.

SECTION 2. *Railroad terminals.* Equally important with the improvement of the harbor is the necessity for an improvement in the terminal facilities of the different railroads entering Boston. This problem was exhaustively discussed by the Rapid Transit Commission of 1891, which made a number of recommendations upon the subject. Many of these recommendations have since been carried out, notwithstanding the general opposition at first manifested by the railroad companies. Lands have been acquired for the freight terminals of the Boston & Maine system substantially as recommended by the Commission; the tracks of the Providence Division of the New York, New Haven, & Hartford Railroad are to be elevated and increased in number, substantially in accordance with the Commissioners' plan; and this company has shown an entire willingness to coöperate with the city in the improvement of the freight facilities of the Old Colony Division, though not upon the exact lines recommended by the Commission. On the other hand, the recommendation of the Commission of elevated drawless bridges across the Charles River, and of a second-story Union Station, on Causeway street, for the Boston & Maine and Fitchburg Railroad Companies, was defeated in the Legislature of 1893, although it received the endorsement of the State Railroad Commission and of the special committee of the Legislature appointed to consider the subject. The action of the corporations in this matter and the construction of the new Union Station at the level of the street is now understood to be regarded by many of the railroad officials and engineers as a great mistake. The building has cost fully as much as the second-story station would have cost; the expense of abolishing the grade crossings on the north of the river will be very much more than if the tracks had been elevated instead of the streets; and the great advantage to be derived from a two-story station and drawless bridges across the Charles has been indefinitely postponed, if not forever lost.

It is earnestly to be hoped that the Federal authorities will permit the Boston Transit Commission to build a new bridge to Charlestown without a draw, but at an elevation sufficient to permit of the passage of tugs, barges, and small boats at all stages of the tide. This would close the river to masted navigation, and thus cause some inconvenience, and possibly pecuniary loss, to the wharf owners along the upper basin of the Charles; but the gain to the transportation interests of the city would be immeasurably greater than any loss due to the exclusion of masted vessels from the Charles; and the construction of such a bridge would be likely to lead to the reconstruction at some future time of the other bridges across the river at a level sufficient to permit the continuous and uninterrupted passage of mastless craft at all stages of the tide.

CHAPTER 18.

MUNICIPAL INVESTMENTS.

The subject of municipal ownership is attracting great attention, and suggestions for the purchase and management by the community of the various kinds of semi-public business hitherto controlled by private corporations are becoming frequent. The city of Boston has during its seventy-two years of corporate life been engaged on a large scale in five distinct works of this character; namely, the improvement of the "Public Lands," the Quincy market, the Cochituate water-works, the East Boston ferries, and the Mystic water-works; and it is evident that accurate information as to the results of these undertakings may be of great service to the public, not only in the management of these particular enterprises, but in respect to others upon which the city may be urged to embark.

This information, only to be obtained after laborious research in the books and accounts of the city, has been prepared at various times during the past three years by the City Auditor and his clerks in response to inquiries from the Executive Department. I have had the accounts of these different enterprises struck off upon tables and forms specially prepared for the purpose and brought down to date. They will be found in the Appendix, Tables 25 to 45.

SECTION 1. *The Public Lands.* The first undertaking in the nature of an investment or speculation which attracted the attention of the City Government was the improvement and sale of the flats surrounding the city. These were recognized at a very early period, not only as a means of developing and expanding the city, but as a possible source of profit. In fact, for many years it was customary to assume that the proceeds of the public lands thus acquired would be sufficient to pay the city debt.[1] The Mill Pond lands, the Neck Lands acquired by filling on either side of Boston Neck, the South Bay lands on the borders of the tidal basin called by that name, the South Boston lands, and the Back Bay lands, were the principal undertakings of this character, and the financial operations relating to them cover a period of about seventy years; the first expenditures having been in 1824 and the last receipts in 1892. A profit of nearly $3,000,000 was realized on the Neck lands; the South Boston lands netted about $300,000; and the Mill Pond lands about $200,000; while there was a loss on the South Bay scheme of about $700,000, and on the Back Bay lands of about $850,000. The exact net profit of the five undertakings has been $1,847,559.23.[2] This figure takes no account of the subsequent expenditures for streets laid out and constructed on these lands, nor, on the other hand, of the public benefit derived from the increase in the building area of the city. It covers merely the expenditures and receipts charged or credited in the city books to the Public Lands Account.

During the ten or fifteen years succeeding the close of the Civil war three special improvements — the Northampton-street, Suffolk-street, and Church-street improvements — were undertaken and carried out for sanitary reasons. The total cost of these undertakings was $4,174,167.33, and the receipts were $1,258,632.26, making the net cost of the improvements $2,915,535.07.

Other investments or speculations in land have from time to time been entered into, and the result of these operations as a whole, including those already named, is that they have cost the city, net, $1,011,603.96, taking no account, however, of the great collateral advantages derived from the increase of the street and building area of the city. It will be seen that the expectation of the authorities during the earlier period of our municipal history, that there was suffi-

---

[1] See inaugural addresses of the early Mayors.
[2] See Appendix, Table 25.

cient profit in the development of the tidal flats about the city to pay off the city debt, was justified so long as the net debt of the city was under $2,000,000, a financial condition which ceased about the year 1848.

SECTION 2. *The Quincy Market.* The next undertaking or investment of the kind under discussion was the establishment of the Quincy market. This undertaking, begun during the elder Quincy's administration, had paid for itself by 1848, and has since yielded an aggregate profit above all expenses of nearly $3,000,000. Table 26 in the Appendix contains the accounts of the Quincy market from 1825 to January 1, 1894, and may be summarized as follows:

	Principal.	Income.	Totals.
Payments,	$1,240,280 62	$969,316 06	$2,209,596 68
Receipts .	1,178,753 35	3,888,877 65	5,067,631 00
Balance .	— $61,527 27	+$2,919,561 59	+$2,858,034 32

The property now consists of 27,400 square feet of land, assessed at $822,000, and of a building assessed at $300,000, making the total assessed value of the estate $1,122,000. The annual income exceeds the annual expenditure by about $57,000, which is a little over five per cent. on the assessors' valuation. Taking the loss in tax receipts due to its ownership by the city into account, the net profit to the city amounts to about three and three-quarters per cent. per annum. While this is less than the average return from private investments in land, yet it will hardly be denied that an undertaking which paid for itself in twenty years, which has since yielded and is still bringing in a net revenue of nearly $60,000 a year, and which furnishes public accommodations of great value, has been a success, regarded from the standpoint of a municipal investment.

SECTION 3. *The Mystic Water-Works.* After an agitation lasting seven years an act was procured by the city of Charlestown from the Legislature of 1861,[1] and accepted

---
[1] St. 1861, ch. 105.

by the voters September 10, 1861,[1] permitting the city to procure a water supply from Mystic Lake. Work was begun in September, 1862; in 1863 additional legislation[2] was procured; and the works were substantially completed in 1864, the water having been turned on November 29 in that year. The first cost of the works was about $750,000, including $12,000 for interest; and was defrayed by money borrowed principally on short-time notes and afterwards funded in five and six per cent. bonds.

Construction still kept on, and by 1870 the water debt amounted to over $1,000,000. A sinking-fund was established in that year, to consist of surplus earnings above maintenance and interest. The receipts seem to have equalled the payments for maintenance and interest for the first time in 1869, but the accounts were kept in such a manner as to make it very difficult to ascertain the facts; and in 1871 Mayor Kent, "feeling that the time had arrived when the exact state of the accounts should be ascertained,"[3] had the accounts made up from the beginning to February 28, 1871. The results thus obtained are assumed to be correct, and are made the basis of the tables prepared for the appendix to this message.[4] It appears that the works had cost to that date $1,247,633.19 for construction, $150,287.42 for maintenance, and $304,602.12 for interest, a total of $1,702,522.73; and that the receipts from sales of water had been $518,626.34; making the net cost to March 1, 1871, $1,183,896.39.

The water bonds then outstanding amounted to $1,172,-000, — approximately the net cost of the works. In 1872 arrangements were made to supply the town of Everett[5]

---

[1] An act passed in 1860 had been vetoed by Governor Banks, on the ground that the proposed dam might injure the harbor.

[2] St. 1863, ch. 9.   [3] Inaugural address, 1872.

[4] The figures are those given by Mayor Kent, but are differently used. He struck interest on the items on both sides of the account — a process that does not seem to serve any useful purpose.

[5] Chelsea and Somerville are also supplied with water from the Mystic works. The distributing system outside Charlestown was built and is owned by the several municipalities. Boston collects the rates and pays one-half to the several towns by virtue of contracts entered into in 1886 under St. 1871, ch. 400.

with water. The receipts from the sale of water had equalled or exceeded the payments for maintenance and interest since 1868 or 1869, but were still inadequate to meet the expense of the necessary annual extensions, which was continued as a charge against construction and defrayed by the issue of bonds until the fiscal year 1873-4, when for the first time the receipts showed a clear surplus above expenditures of all kinds. Mayor Stone very properly considered that it was time to close the construction account and to use the surplus revenue above maintenance and interest for all necessary extensions or improvements.

At the date of the annexation of Charlestown to Boston (January 5, 1874) the accounts stood as follows:

Payments for construction	. . .	$1,460,000 00
" " maintenance	. . .	344,876 29
" " interest	. . . .	524,962 45
Total	. . . . . .	$2,329,838 74
Receipts	. . . . . .	1,068,199 17
Net cost to January 1, 1874	. . .	$1,261,639 57

Bonds to the aggregate amount of $1,460,000 had been issued, of which $57,000 had been paid, leaving a gross debt of $1,403,000 00
Amount of sinking-funds . . . 97,597 95

Net Mystic debt on annexation . $1,305,402 05

These figures show that about $140,000 had been borrowed in excess of the actual cost of the works. This was in part represented by the money in the sinking-funds.

The undertaking was then, however, earning a profit above annual interest and expenses; that is, was already on a self-supporting basis, and, if rates were properly maintained, would eventually clear itself from debt.

Since annexation, $220,000 of bonds have been issued by the city of Boston for improvements; but these, as well as the water bonds issued by the city of Charlestown, have since been paid out of water rates. The last bond was paid April 1, 1894; and there is now no Mystic water debt, but an apparent surplus in the sinking-funds of $163,210.26,[1] which is used under St. 1892, chap. 213, for extension of mains or other purposes connected with the Cochituate Water-Works. The net cost of the works, meaning the difference between total expenditures to a given date for construction, maintenance, and interest, and total receipts from sales of water, surplus land, etc., was, at the date of annexation, about $1,250,000, and has gradually been reduced, until this year for the first time a net profit is shown on the whole undertaking. On December 31, 1894, the receipts for the entire period, 1865-1895, exceeded the expenditures by $24,603.45;[2] and from this time on the works should yield an annual profit, after paying for all necessary improvements along the Abbajona River and its tributary streams.

One of the principal arguments used to induce the people of Boston to vote for the annexation of Charlestown was the prospective profit to be made on the Mystic Water-Works after the debt was extinguished. It has taken twenty years to realize this expectation; but from this time forth, unless rates are reduced, the Mystic Works should be a source of revenue, to be applied under the Act of 1892 to extension of mains in other parts of the city, or to the reduction of the debt incurred for the Cochituate and Sudbury Works.

SECT. 4. *The Cochituate and Sudbury Water - Works.* After a discussion lasting twenty years, in which innumerable sources of supply were considered, it was determined to take the waters of Long Pond or Lake Cochituate for that purpose. An act of the Legislature was obtained in 1845, but was rejected by the people because the power to

[1] As of January 31, 1894. See Appendix, Table 34.
[2] The net cost January 31, 1894, was $78,868.07 (Appendix, Table 32); and the surplus revenue from February 1 to December 31, 1894, amounted to $103,471.52.

authorize the water loans was vested by the terms of the act in the commission to be appointed to execute its provisions.[1]

The next year a new act was obtained, which left the power to vote appropriations for the water-works with the City Council, and this act was accepted by the people.[2] The commission was appointed in May, 1846, possession taken of the lake on August 10, and ground broken August 20. The mains leading from the lake to the city, the various reservoirs in Brookline, Boston, South Boston, and East Boston, and the distributing system for the entire city, was completed in about three years and a half, at a cost of about $5,000,000,[3] all defrayed by loan. The extensions found necessary from time to time after the close of the construction account in 1851 were provided for partly by loans and partly by taxes; and in 1859 a new main was laid from the Brookline reservoir to the city, for which a special loan was authorized. In 1865 the construction of the large reservoirs at Chestnut Hill was begun under the authority of St. 1865, ch. 131, and completed in five years, at a cost of about $2,500,000.

The annexations of Roxbury,[4] Dorchester,[5] Brighton, and West Roxbury involved an expenditure of over $2,000,000 for extensions of the distributing system to the annexed territory, and also made it necessary to establish a high-ser-

---
[1] St. 1845, ch. 220, rejected by 3,999 nays to 3,670 yeas.
[2] St. 1846, ch. 167, accepted by 4,637 to 348, April 13, 1846.
[3] The original estimate was $2,651,643, and the Act of 1846 authorized a loan of $3,000,000. Water was turned on for the city proper October 25, 1848, and for South Boston on November 28, 1849. In the meantime, however, it had been determined to extend the system to East Boston, at an estimated cost of $500,000; and an act was procured (St. 1849, ch. 187) authorizing a loan of $1,500,000 to cover the East Boston extension and the cost of the works in the city proper in excess of the original loan. The Water Acts also permitted the city to issue loans in addition to the $4,500,000 specifically authorized to cover the payments for interest during construction and for two years after the completion of the works. The construction account of the water-works was declared closed on April 30, 1851, and interest between that date and April 30, 1853, as well as the interest previously paid, was met by the issue of bonds.
[4] The distributing system for Roxbury was completed and water turned on October 26, 1868.
[5] Water turned on July 19, 1870.

vice system,[1] which has cost to date about $1,125,000. The increase of population due to the annexations and other causes, as well as the unexpected *per capita* increase in consumption,[2] rendered an additional source of supply imperative, and authority was procured in 1872[3] to take the waters of the Sudbury River. Under this act and subsequent amendments the greater part of the upper courses of the Sudbury River have been taken for the purposes of "additional supply;"[4] five large impounding basins[5] have been constructed, besides Whitehall Pond, reacquired in 1890; and a sixth basin (called No. 5) is now in process of construction. There had been spent under these acts for additional supply over seven and a quarter millions to the first of February, 1894, and the new basin now in process of construction is estimated to cost $2,500,000 more.[6]

The total cost of the Cochituate and Sudbury system,

---

[1] The high-service works were begun in 1869. The reservoir at Parker Hill was begun in 1873 and completed in 1874, under St. 1873, ch. 287.

[2] At the inception of the works, it was estimated that 28½ gallons per day per capita would be sufficient, but the actual amount used in 1851 was 49 gallons, and it has steadily increased to 107½ gallons in 1893.

[3] St. 1872, ch. 177.

[4] The original taking was made January 21, 1875.

[5] The following tables give area, cost, and other statistics relating to the artificial basins already constructed on the Sudbury water-shed.

	Acres. H. W.	Area not flowed.	Total area Land.	Storage in Million Gals.	Daily Supply Proportional to Capacity. Million Gals.
Basin 1	143	64	207	280	1
" 2	134	50	184	530	1.8
" 3	253	90	343	1,080	3.7
" 4	167	94	261	1,400	4.9
" 6	185	270	465	1,530	5.2

Cost to December 31, 1894.

	Dam.	Basin.	Land Damages.	Total Cost.
Basin 1	$144,929 15	$44,455 20	$67,759 46	$257,143 81
" 2	152,992 51	147,957 82	145,013 78	465,954 11
" 3	194,950 13	183,939 98	40,512 61	419,409 72
" 4	521,998 45	265,517 93	26,330 00	813,846 38
" 6	549,241 57	334,183 02	26,876 59	910,301 18

[6] This basin will cover 1,200 acres of land; its storage capacity will be 7,436,000,000 U.S. gallons.

including, besides the above-named works of large construction, all payments for extension and maintenance of the works to January 31, 1894, was $32,121,785.09, and the payments for interest amounted to $24,154,688.96; making a total of $56,276,474.05. The receipts or income of the water-works (including charges for hydrants and public buildings) have been $34,896,724.18, and from other miscellaneous sources $1,763,939.71; making a total of $36,660,663.89. The difference between the total receipts and the total payments is $19,615,810.16, and represents the net cost[1] of the works on January 31, 1894. Of the total cost of the works ($56,276,474.05), $21,449,420.45 was derived from loans, $33,068,041.69 from water revenue (that is, water rates, premiums on loans, etc.), and $1,759,011.91 from taxes.

Upon the creation of the Board of Commissioners of Sinking-Funds in 1871, the sum of $1,100,000 was set aside from the funds turned over by the Committee on the Reduction of Debt, and apportioned to the sinking-fund created for the payment of the Cochituate water-debt. All the moneys in the hands of the Committee on Reduction of Debt had been raised by taxes, and this sum of $1,100,000 was

---

[1] The expression "net cost" of a municipal water-works is commonly understood to be the difference between the total expenditures on account of the undertaking, including the interest on loans issued, if any, for the purpose, and the total receipts derived from the operation of the works, the sale of surplus land, old material, premium on loans, etc. An attempt was made by the Water Board about twenty years ago to reduce the net cost of the Cochituate Water-Works by the sum of $1,352,000. This was the amount claimed by the Water Board as that portion of the money in the hands of the committee for the reduction of the debt which should have been credited to the Cochituate water loans; and for several years the Water Board deducted this amount from the real net cost for the purpose of making it appear that the total cost of the water-works was so much less than was really the case. In this undertaking they followed a course similar to that pursued by the Directors of the East Boston ferries in their trial balance statement (see p. 157). The City Auditor, however, very properly objected to this method of ascertaining the cost of the water-works, as the sum in question was not derived from the income of the works, but had been contributed from the tax levy; but he was overruled, and for some years, between 1871 and 1878, the Auditor's annual reports contained a statement of the net cost of the Cochituate Water-Works with this credit of $1,352,000 deducted. The views of the Auditor, however, finally triumphed, and in 1879 this ingenious fiction disappeared for good.

therefore a contribution from the general taxpayers for the reduction of the water debt. Since 1871 over three millions and a half have been added to the Cochituate water sinking-fund from the income of the water-works, and nearly a million more from taxes and city income. The present annual additions to the Cochituate water sinking-fund amount to about $300,000 from water rates, $300,000 from interest on investments, and $50,000 from interest on bank deposits, premium on loans, etc., or about $650,000 per annum.

The total amount of water loans issued to January 31, 1894, was $21,563,711.11, of which there was on hand on that date an unexpended cash balance of $114,272.73, and the sum of $17.93 (being the unexpended balance of the loans for the construction of the Chestnut-hill reservoir) had been paid into the sinking-fund; leaving the total amount derived from loan and expended on the water-works to January 31, 1894, at the sum already mentioned, — $21,449,420.45.

As water loans have not in recent years been issued to the full extent of the additions to the sinking-funds from water rates and interest on investments, and as large additions to the sinking-fund were made from the general tax levy prior to 1877, the net debt of the Cochituate Water-Works to-day is much less than the amount borrowed for the construction of the water-works, being only $9,443,032.90 on December 31, 1894.

The Cochituate water debt, which was about $5,000,000 upon the completion of the original water-works in 1851, was gradually reduced to less than $3,000,000 in 1865; after which time it gradually rose, until between 1886 and 1891 it averaged about ten and a quarter millions. During the past four years there has been a reduction, due principally to the abandonment of the practice of borrowing money for annual extensions.

Although the debt is now decreasing, and will continue to decrease unless more than $600,000 or $700,000 is borrowed annually for construction,[1] it does not follow that it is not very much more than it ought to be. In the first place, money has

---

[1] Or rates are reduced.

been borrowed for purposes the cost of which in any properly regulated municipal or private water-works would have been defrayed from income rather than from the proceeds of bonds.

The original cost of the works, with interest during the construction period and for two years thereafter, was rightly met by loan, according to the terms of the Act of 1846; and for these purposes scrip to the amount of $5,430,711.11 was issued. Further loans were properly authorized and issued as follows: for the construction of Chestnut-hill reservoir, $2,449,982.07; for new mains from the Brookline and Chestnut-hill reservoirs into the city, $654,991.83; for additional supply, $7,334,687.56; for the high-service works, $1,103,144.69; for the shops on Albany street, $60,000; and for extensions in the annexed districts, $2,085,000; making a total of $19,118,517.26 procured by loan, and expended for lands, water rights, and construction between 1846 and 1894.

These loans were all for purposes for which stock or bonds would be issued by a private corporation, and for which a municipal water-works would issue loans; but in addition to this sum, which represents the actual amount of money borrowed for real estate and construction, there has been borrowed $215,175.92 for maintenance and "general expenses," $330,000 for meters, and $1,900,000 for ordinary annual extensions of mains: a total of $2,445,175.92, representing items of expenditure which on any correct or customary business theory should have been charged to income and not met by loan.

No one will question that the loans for current expenses should have been avoided, and few will doubt the propriety of charging the cost of meters, stopcocks, and similar articles to income rather than to capital; but the question as to the extension of mains is more difficult, as many corporations issue stock for such purposes. That under ordinary circumstances, however, the cost of annual extensions would not be capitalized, at least in the form of bonds, by a gas or water works is abundantly shown by the annual reports of the Board of Gas and Electric Light Commissioners, the only official publication which attempts to give the exact financial operations of semi-public corporations. It is also to be noted that in the case of the Mystic Water-Works the city of Boston itself has pursued the business-like policy of charging all expenses of this sort to income;[1] and in almost every well-managed municipal water-works the same practice is followed. If the income of a municipal water-works is not sufficient to cover the cost of ordinary extensions, the deficiency had better be met by taxation than by borrowing money.

Prior to 1885 it had been the custom of the Boston Water Board and its predecessors to defray the cost of these extensions from the water rates or from taxes; but between that year and 1892 loans were issued for this purpose aggregating, as already stated, $1,900,000 in amount. The practice was stopped in 1892; extra activity in the office of the Water Registrar resulted in a considerable increase of income without an increase of rates; and it was thus found possible to pay for all necessary extensions out of the income. The result has been a reduction in the Cochituate water debt of nearly a million dollars and the establishment of the works upon a strictly self-supporting basis.[2]

---

[1] The result has been that in the case of the Mystic Water-Works the debt has been paid off and the works are now yielding a clear profit above the cost of maintenance and extensions; but it should be borne in mind that the task of supplying the city of Boston with an adequate supply of water is a relatively very much more difficult and expensive undertaking than the exploitation of Mystic Lake for the towns dependent upon it.

[2] It should be stated that the borrowing of money for the extension of mains was justified by an opinion of the Corporation Counsel (see Doc. 12 of 1885). With this opinion I was never able to agree; but believing that the matter was not free from doubt and that the abandonment of the unbusiness-like practice of borrowing money for current extensions would be criticised in some quarters as long as any one could maintain that the law necessitated such a course, I applied to the Legislature of 1892, and an act was procured which justified the Water Board in returning to the correct practices obtaining prior to 1885. St. 1892, ch. 213, also permitted the Water Board to consolidate the financial operations of the Cochituate and Mystic Water-Works, and between the two the surplus revenues of the year above maintenance and interest have been sufficient to pay for all extensions of mains and to meet the annual requirements for the sinking-funds for the entire water debt. The Cochituate Water-Works have not yet reached this point, as the surplus of the Cochituate revenues above the cost of maintenance, interest, and extension of mains has not yet been quite equal to the amount necessary to meet the sinking-fund requirements; but it should be during the coming year. In any event, the two systems together yield a revenue more than sufficient to cover all expenditures that on any theory should be charged to income; that is, they constitute together a self-supporting system — and before the expiration of another year the Cochituate Water-Works should be self-supporting in themselves, while the Mystic Water-Works should yield a clear profit of between $100,000 and $150,000 a year.

The net Cochituate water debt and the net cost of the works would also be considerably less to-day than they are, if it had not been for continual and injudicious reductions in rates. The original tariff for dwelling-houses established in 1849 was raised in 1850, and again in 1855, while the rates for meters, introduced in 1859, were raised in 1865; and from that time until 1877 there was practically no change in the rates either for dwelling-houses or meters.[1] Up to that year there had been a conscientious effort on the part of the Cochituate Water Board and the City Council to make the water-works self-supporting, and to reduce the debt with a view to its final extinguishment, as was contemplated by the provisions of the Act of 1846, and by those who were responsible for the establishment of the water-works; but about 1877 the theory began to prevail that the chief aim of the administration of the water-works should be to reduce the rates, rather than to pay off the debt. The "sacred duty of providing for the debt"[2] was lost sight of; some encouragement was even given to the idea that the water should be made entirely free — that is to say, that the whole cost of maintaining the works should be transferred from the water takers to the general taxpayers of the city; and a reduction of $16\frac{2}{3}$ per cent. was made that year in the rates for consumption by meter. In 1879 a further reduction of 20 per cent. was made in the meter rates,[3] and in 1886 the meter rates were again reduced by over 10 per

---

[1] Since 1854 charges have been made to the city for water used in the public buildings, and since 1870 a special charge has been made for fire hydrants.

[2] See remarks of Nathan Hale on the introduction of water into the city in 1848.

[3] The ostensible cause of the reduction of 1879 was the assumed illegality of paying any part of the water income for interest on the difference between the cost of the works and the outstanding water debt. Inasmuch as a considerable part of the cost of the water-works had been met by general taxes and not by water loans or rates, it had been the practice of the Treasurer since 1858 to charge the water-works interest on the amount thus contributed, which was described as the unfunded water debt. The City Government of 1879 felt that this practice should be discontinued (see Mayor's message of April 21); and there was much to commend this view of the case if the money thus released was to be covered into the sinking-fund for the funded Cochituate water debt, as such a course would have resulted in a reduction of the debt. As a matter of fact, however, the remission of the obligation to pay interest on the funded water debt was simply used as an excuse for the reduction in meter rates made that year and in 1879, and thus under the pretence of correcting a book-keeping error, the ability of the water-works to pay off the debt was seriously impaired.

cent., and there was a general reduction in dwelling-house rates equivalent to about 10 per cent. In 1888 there was a still further reduction to large consumers of metered water.

Still further uncalled-for reductions were made in the years 1885,[1] 1889, and 1890, in the form of rebates upon the annual water bills for the ensuing year. The reduction for 1886 was 6 per cent., and amounted to $43,588.97; that for 1890 was 7 per cent., and amounted to $61,921.17; and that for 1891 was 10 per cent., and amounted to $93,970.43 — an aggregate loss in receipts and a resulting increase in the debt of $199,450.57.[2]

If no reductions and rebates had been made since 1877, it is easy to compute that the net cost of the water-works would have been less than it is by six or seven millions of dollars, and the net debt of the Cochituate water-works would probably have been extinguished. It will hardly be claimed that the saving to the individual water takers during the past sixteen years is a sufficient compensation for the fact that the net cost of the works has been steadily increasing, instead of diminishing, and that we have to-day a water debt of over nine millions of dollars. For the first thirty years the Cochituate water-works, though never self-supporting, were yet managed with a view to the gradual reduction and ultimate extinction of the debt — that is, in the interest of the city as a corporation; but between 1877 and 1891 they were operated for the benefit of the water-takers as a class.

During the past four years there have been no rebates or reductions of any kind for the benefit of the water takers;[3] the income for the year 1893-4 was $1,692,159.73; and this

[1] The Water Board had increased the rates for 1885, but rescinded this action upon request of the City Council, and after much pressure from prominent water takers. (See Doc. 31 of 1885.) At the close of the year a rebate of six per cent. on the bills for 1886 was ordered, notwithstanding the expressed opinion of the Board that the rates were already too low.

[2] This amount, if saved, could have been used for construction, and so much less money borrowed, or turned into the sinking-fund as surplus revenue. Either course would have resulted in a reduction of the net debt by the amount in question. As large loans were issued every year, these "rebates" were practically loans for distribution among the water takers.

[3] Reductions have, however, been made in the charge of fire hydrants, which have been reduced to an almost nominal amount ($2 per annum); and no charge is made

amount exceeded the total expenditures for maintenance, interest, and extensions of mains, by $186,952.47, an amount nearly equal to the sinking-fund requirements for the year. With the assistance of the profits from the Mystic Water-Works there was paid into the Cochituate sinking-fund not only the requirements for the year, but about $50,000 in addition. Thus the water-works, taken as a whole, Cochituate and Mystic, have been for the first time placed upon a strictly self-supporting basis; and during the ensuing year it ought to be possible to make that statement concerning the Cochituate system considered by itself.

The next step which should be taken is to effect a more rapid reduction in the debt, and a diminution of the figures indicating the net cost of the works. As it has not been thought best during the past four years to increase the water rates for the purpose of making the works self-supporting, so an increase in the rates will not be necessary for the purpose of reducing the debt; for if no further reductions in rates are attempted it ought to be possible, with the increase of consumption and consequent receipts, not only to issue all the loans necessary for the construction of the new basin on the Sudbury River without increasing the net debt, but to reduce it by annually increasing amounts. It will not be possible to make this reduction as rapidly as if the rates had not been tampered with between 1877 and 1888; but a very considerable reduction during the next five years can still be effected if the present schedules are maintained.[1]

I will close this brief review of the financial history of our water-works by calling attention to the series of tables in the Appendix relating to the Cochituate Water-Works, which have been prepared at great labor by the City Auditor and

---

for water used for street-watering purposes or for the public urinals. As the additional protection afforded in case of fire and the improvement of the sanitary condition of the city are among the main justifications for a public supply of water, it seemed proper that none or nominal charges should be made for water used for these purposes. On the other hand, water used in the public buildings is paid for at the usual rates.

[1] These calculations may not hold after it becomes necessary to procure additional sources of supply beyond the Sudbury River. An increase in rates may then be necessary.

his assistants.[1] The difficulty of getting accurate and collated information relating to the cost and management of our water-works is very great. The annual reports of the Water Board contain most complete and elaborate accounts of everything concerning the engineering and sanitary aspects of the problem, but almost nothing relating to finances except the receipts and expenditures for the year. The two histories of our water-works—that of Mr. Bradley, covering the period from 1846 to 1868, and that of Mr. Fitzgerald, covering the period from 1868 to 1876 — are practically silent in respect to the financial operations of the works. It is not pretended that the tables printed in the Appendix, prepared partly for the occasion and partly at various times during the past four years, are in any sense exhaustive ; but they will at least serve to facilitate the work of inquiry into the results obtained by the city of Boston in its largest public undertaking.

SECTION 5. *The East Boston Ferries.* In 1832 the proprietors of Noddle's Island procured a ferry license from the Mayor and Aldermen, and in 1833 were incorporated [2] as The East Boston Company. This company maintained the ferry for the purpose of developing and selling its lands until 1835, when it was transferred to an unincorporated ferry company. In 1836 the Eastern Railroad bought the control of this latter company, and in 1842 the Eastern Railroad and the East Boston Company became the sole stockholders.

The growth of East Boston, as it was then called, stimulated a demand for better ferry accommodations, and in 1852 the East Boston Ferry Company was incorporated.[3] This company bought the existing ferry, paying to the East Boston Company and the Eastern Railroad Company $200,000 in stock, an amount representing rather the losses of the previous twenty years than the actual value of the property.[4]

---

[1] See Appendix, Tables 35 to 45. They do not always agree with the figures given in the reports of the Water Board, but are, I believe, more accurate.
[2] St. 1833, ch. 152.   [3] St. 1852, ch. 244.
[4] It was claimed that the net loss to 1852 had been $203,000.

The charter of the East Boston Ferry Company provided that the Mayor and Aldermen of the city should have the power to fix rates or tolls, but that they should never be made so low as to reduce the dividends below eight per cent. upon the capital invested. There was also a provision for purchase by the city. The capital stock was fixed at $200,000, with the right to increase to $300,000. Two hundred thousand of this was issued at once, as already explained, and in 1853 $25,000 more was issued. The tolls were fixed by the Mayor and Aldermen October 4, 1852.

In 1853 the company made money, and declared a dividend; but during that year an opposition company was started and incorporated as the People's Ferry Company,[1] with a charter similar to that of the East Boston Ferry Company. Late in 1854 the Mayor and Aldermen fixed the tolls for the People's Ferry Company, substantially as for the East Boston Ferry Company. The East Boston Ferry Company operated what is now known as the South Ferry, and the People's Ferry Company what is now known as the North Ferry.

The East Boston Ferry Company prospered in 1854, as during the previous year, and paid a dividend; but these two years, 1853 and 1854, were the only years in which any ferry company to East Boston ever declared a dividend.

The People's Ferry Company began operations late in the year, and a ruinous competition between the two companies ensued. During 1855 and 1856 both companies were operated at a loss, and in the latter year both petitioned for an increase in tolls. The Aldermen rejected the petition, in accordance with objections by citizens, who suggested a public subsidy in the nature of a money payment for laying out highways leading to the ferries over the property of the companies. The companies paid no attention to this refusal, and in June, 1856, increased the rates of their own accord to a figure about 40 per cent. higher than the original schedule. In 1857 numerous citizens petitioned the City

---

[1] St. 1853, ch. 422.

Council either for the establishment of free ferries, or for a subsidy to the companies sufficient to enable them to reduce the tolls. In 1858 the agreement between the two companies entered into in 1856 was broken, competition again broke out, and the tolls were reduced to figures lower even than the original schedule of 1852.

In 1859 the city paid each ferry company $125,000 in cash for certain avenues, wharves, slips, piers, etc., and leased the same at a nominal rental to the companies for ten years; both agreeing to run the ferries for that period at rates to be fixed by the Mayor and Aldermen. Under this agreement the companies renewed operations under the low rates prevailing in 1858 and 1859; but they could make no money on this arrangement, notwithstanding the reduction in fixed charges through the payment of the subsidy, and in June, 1860, the companies raised the tolls to the original schedule. On July 23 the Mayor and Aldermen attempted to establish the tolls on the basis of the rates obtaining in 1858 and 1859; but the companies paid no attention to this order and petitioned for an increase.

In 1862 a subsidy was given to the People's Ferry Company of $5,000, for operating that ferry for four months from June 1, 1862, but in November of that year this company discontinued operations and sold its boats. The city then took possession of the wharves, ships, and other lands of the company which it had bought in 1859, spent $50,000 in repairs, and in 1868 leased them to the East Boston Ferry Company. The People's Company went into liquidation, and the stockholders lost all their capital except a final dividend of $1 a share.

In 1866 the people of East Boston, not satisfied with their experience in the matter, procured a charter[1] for another ferry company, — the Citizens' Ferry Company; but nothing was ever done with this charter.

In 1869 the East Boston Ferry Company started a new line over the slips of the People's Ferry Company, which it had leased from the city. The same year an additional act

---
[1] St. 1866, ch. 213.

authorizing the purchase of the East Boston Ferry Company's franchise and property by the city was obtained.[1] The East Boston Ferry Company petitioned for an increase in tolls, which were then the same as originally established in 1852. The Board of Aldermen refused, and the company brought a petition for a writ of mandamus, which was granted by the Court,[2] and thereupon the Aldermen acquiesced and passed an order raising the tolls.

The city then negotiated a purchase of the property and franchise of the East Boston Ferry Company for $275,000, and on the first of April, 1870, took possession.

Up to this time the city had expended, including this sum of $275,000, nearly $700,000, net, for property, franchise, and subsidies.

Under the Act of 1869 the city, upon purchasing the ferry, could either make it a toll ferry; or a free ferry, and assess betterments on real estate in East Boston; or a free ferry for ten years and then a toll ferry, and assess half the betterments on East Boston property. The City Council elected to adopt the first plan, and on March 24, 1870, established a toll ferry, and fixed the rates, including a two-cent fare for foot passengers.

In 1871 a proposition to abolish tolls was defeated in the City Council, and an order to establish one-cent fares for foot passengers passed the Board of Aldermen, but was defeated in the Council.

The agitation for free ferries, begun in 1871, culminated in 1877 in an order which passed both branches of the City Council and was approved by the Mayor, abolishing the tolls from and after January 1, 1878. This order was declared illegal by the Supreme Judicial Court in the case of Attorney-General v. Boston, 123 Massachusetts, 460, on the ground that the city had exhausted its option by the terms of the order of 1870, establishing a toll ferry.

By 1878 the revenues of the ferries under the schedule

---

[1] St. 1869, ch. 155.
[2] See East Boston Ferry Company v. Mayor and Aldermen of the City of Boston, 101 Mass. 488.

of tolls which had remained unchanged since 1870 were approximately equal to the current expenditures; and although the ferries had cost the city up to that time over a million dollars net, and the average annual receipts were not equal to the average annual expenditures for all purposes, a series of reductions in tolls commenced. On January 1, 1879, a reduced schedule went into effect, by which 16 tickets were sold for 25 cents and 60 tickets for 75 cents, and reductions amounting to from 20 to 25 per cent. were also made in the tolls for teams. Later in the year the schedule was again lowered, so as to permit the purchase of 50 tickets for foot passengers for 50 cents. An application was also made in that year to the Legislature by the Mayor and Aldermen for an act permitting the establishment of free ferries. The petition met with vigorous opposition from the taxpayers, and was defeated.

In 1880 further reductions in tolls were made, principally in respect to the price for team tickets by the package. In 1881 a still further reduction was made in the cost of team tickets by the package. In 1887 the tolls were reduced to the lowest point practically possible for foot passengers, — namely, one cent; and the rest of the schedule was practically cut in half. This was the last reduction, and since 1887 the ferries have been maintained upon the schedule which went into effect July 1 of that year. The fight for free ferries was renewed before the Legislature of that year, with the aid of the City Council, but again proved unsuccessful.

In the meantime, the ferry directors went out of their way to misrepresent the financial results of the ferry undertaking. The annual report for 1881–2 is the first to contain a table purporting to show the "actual standing" of the ferries, which has been repeated in succeeding reports, with figures brought down to date. In the report for 1886 a "trial balance," apparently supporting the table of "actual standing," appears for the first time. If it was proper to characterize the reports prior to 1876, as was done by a committee of that year, as based upon inflated values, it would be equally proper to characterize this table of "actual standing" as a deliberate and intentional misrepresentation. In this table, as it appears in the report for 1881-2 and subsequent years, the ferry department is debited with the amount spent from 1859 to date, except that no account is taken of interest on the moneys borrowed, and the department is credited not only with the amounts received from tolls, with the estimated value of the boats, real estate, "franchises," supplies on hand, etc., but also with $250,000, alleged to be an amount "charged to ferry department for avenues that were laid out as streets in August, 1880, and properly should be credited to this department and charged to streets," and by a further sum of $11,530.30 for "paving avenues." The credit of $250,000 is the sum paid the two ferry companies in 1859 as a subsidy or "measure of relief," and, as distinctly appears from innumerable reports and documents of the period, was in no sense an expenditure for streets.

In this way, by taking no account of interest, by crediting two hundred and sixty-odd thousand dollars improperly, and by putting an inflated value on the real estate and franchise, a net loss on the whole undertaking was figured out of only $46,034.07. A glance at Table 29, in the Appendix, will show that on this date the real cost of the East Boston Ferries amounted to about one and a quarter million dollars, and the tangible assets, real estate, boats, etc., were valued by the Directors themselves at $618,591.86 only.[1]

On April 17, 1891, the Board of Ferry Directors was abolished, and a superintendent was appointed in their place. Since then the ferries have been conducted substantially in the same manner as before, as no increase in the tolls as established in 1887 could be hoped for from the City Council; and the ferries are run at an annual loss of about $60,000, without counting the average expenditure for boats and permanent improvements, which amounts to some $30,000 more.

Since the abolition of the Board of Ferry Directors the

---

[1] Report for 1881-2, p. 10. Undoubtedly a speculative valuation.

annual loss has been relatively less than under the management of that Board, the percentage of deficit in the current expenses to receipts from tolls having been 44.9 per cent. between 1888 and 1891, and only 37.7 per cent. between 1891 and 1894; a result which testifies to the advantage of confiding executive work of this character to a single person, rather than to a board of five.

At the close of the last fiscal year, January 31, 1894, the East Boston Ferries had cost the city $2,359,348.38 more than the receipts from all sources; and this deficit appears to be increasing at the rate of nearly $100,000 per annum.

The financial history of the East Boston Ferries is the record of a succession of failures. Single corporations having a monopoly for the time being were unsuccessful; public regulation failed; competition was disastrous to the private interests involved and unsatisfactory to the public; subsidies proved not even of temporary value; and, finally, municipal ownership has turned out to be the most disastrous experiment of all. The investors lost their money; the city has sunk nearly two and a half millions of dollars; and to-day the people of East Boston are no better satisfied with the accommodations furnished by the ferries than they were in 1852.[1]

It is easy to see, however, that if the tolls had been maintained at the figures originally established by the City Council of 1870, the ferries would before 1880 have been on a self-supporting basis, — that is, the total income would have equalled the total annual expenditures, — and by 1895 the greater part of the original expenditure, if not the whole of it, would have been cancelled. Instead of following, as in the case of the Mystic Water-Works, the prudent, business-like course of maintaining tolls at a point sufficient to pay a net profit above expenditures, which would reduce

---

[1] An instructive contrast in ferry management is presented by the experience of New York city, which secures a large yearly revenue from the lease of ferry franchises and docks.

and gradually extinguish the original cost, the City Council has managed this department as though the only interest concerned was that of the passengers on the ferries; has reduced the tolls to the lowest possible figure, and far below the point of profit; and has only been prevented by the courts and the good sense of the Legislature from abolishing them altogether.

As the sole cause of the disastrous results of this undertaking has been the yielding of the City Council to the desire of a section of the people to be transported between East Boston and the city for nothing, — that is, at the expense of other people, — so it is easy to point out the remedy. Stop all loans for boats, buildings, wharves, and slips; increase the tolls to a point that will pay a considerable profit above all annual expenditures; and provide that a small number of taxpayers may procure from the courts an injunction against reducing the tolls until the extinguishment of the cost. The remedy is easy to suggest, but impossible of accomplishment, as it is wholly improbable that a single vote could be obtained in the City Council for an increase in the tolls.

SECT. 6. *Summary.* The five municipal investments undertaken by the city of Boston have now been described. One of them, the improvement of the public lands, may be considered as having been fairly successful, having regard to both the financial and sanitary results. One of them, the Quincy Market, paid for itself in twenty years, and has been a source of large annual profit ever since. Another, the Mystic Water-Works, has paid for itself in thirty years, and from this time on, freed from debt, should be a source of annually increasing profit. The East Boston Ferry, on the other hand, has proved a most disastrous failure, and continues to be a great and annually increasing burden to the city. The fifth undertaking, the Cochituate Water-Works, was the largest and most difficult of them all, and has been so administered as to stand midway, in point of financial results, between the Mystic Water-Works and the

East Boston Ferries. The Cochituate Water-Works might have been managed very much more advantageously than they have been, they ought to be burdened to-day with a debt certainly not more than half the actual amount, and I believe that they might have been entirely cleared from debt; but, on the other hand, they have not been so utterly mismanaged as the East Boston Ferries, and it is still possible without increasing the rates to gradually reduce the debt and thus pave the way for a reduction in rates without violating business principles.

The lesson of these experiments in municipal ownership seems to be that it is possible for a city to manage these undertakings fairly well from the standpoint of private ownership, and distinctly well considered as municipal investments not necessarily undertaken for profit; and that it is also possible to manage them so badly that they constitute in the end a hopeless burden, the weight of which even fictitious bookkeeping cannot conceal. The history of our water-works and ferries is the record of a never-ending struggle between the taxpayer on the one side, and the rate payer on the other; and in view of the unfortunate results of some of these undertakings, we ought on the whole to congratulate ourselves that the results have been no worse in the others. The city should certainly decline to be drawn into such undertakings in the future, unless the necessity is urgent and the utmost precautions are taken to prevent a reduction in rates, tolls, and fares below the point of profit.

SECTION 7. *The Subway.* I regard this enterprise as a municipal investment, believing, as pointed out to the Legislature of 1894,[1] that the rentals received for the use of tracks and other privileges in the subway should be sufficient to pay the sinking-fund and interest requirements of the debt to be issued to build it. This debt will be presumably $5,000,000, the estimated cost of the work, including land. The money can be borrowed at from three and a quarter to

---

[1] See Doc. 86, of 1894.

three and a half per cent. per annum, and the sinking-fund requirements on a forty years' loan are 1.1427 per cent. per annum. This makes a total of about four and a half per cent. or $225,000 per annum for forty years as the income needed to relieve the city treasury from all payments on account of this enterprise, and to make it a source of large annual profit in the year 1935. As pointed out in the argument referred to, I entertain no reasonable doubt that if, as must be assumed, the present commissioners exercise their great powers in the sole interest of the public treasury, and there is no interference or retrograde action taken by the Legislature, this income can readily be secured.

There is of course the danger that the public, through its representatives in the Legislature or the City Government, will some day voluntarily surrender the profits that ought to be derived from this enterprise, or fritter them away in unprofitable extensions, and, as in the case of the East Boston Ferries and the Cochituate Water-Works, insist that the undertaking shall be managed without profit to the city treasury, or even at a loss to be made good by the general taxpayers. This ought to be a purely theoretic danger; but the experience of our city in the two enterprises mentioned, as well as the growing demand for the public ownership and management of all kinds of semi-public enterprises upon terms which imply increased taxation, justifies the fear. On the other hand, it has been proved to be possible for municipal corporations to manage such enterprises upon business lines, — at least in such a manner as to make them profitable regarded as municipal investments, — and in Boston we have two conspicuous illustrations in the Quincy Market and the Mystic Water-Works.

In leaving, therefore, this great project, which has occupied so much of my time during the past four years, to the care of succeeding City Governments and Legislatures, I desire once again to express the fixed opinion that this enterprise can be so handled as to be no charge upon the taxpayers, to pay for itself in forty years, and thereafter to be a source of large profit to the city and the means of reducing the burden of annual taxation. It can also be mismanaged, the rents and profits thrown away, and its cost charged upon the taxpayers. Which course shall be taken depends upon the action of the future rulers of this city, and the responsibility for the financial success or failure of the subway rests, in my opinion, exclusively on them.

CHAPTER 19.

THE CITY CHARTER.

SECTION 1. *The Charter of 1822.* For forty years after the close of the Revolutionary war the people of Boston debated the desirability of procuring a city charter, and finally voted in favor of the change on January 7, 1822. The State constitution of 1780 had previously been amended[1] so as to remove all doubt concerning the power of the Legislature to establish city governments; and on February 23, 1822, the Legislature passed a city charter, which was accepted by the voters of the town on March 4, 1822.[2] Elections were held on April 8 and April 16, and on May 1, 1822, the new city government was inaugurated.

The charter of 1822 created a government consisting of a mayor, of a board of eight aldermen elected at large, and of a common council of forty-eight members — four elected by the voters of each of the twelve wards into which the city was divided.

The financial, executive, and administrative powers of the government were vested partly in the Mayor and Aldermen, to whom the powers of the selectmen of the town were transferred, and partly in the City Council, to be exercised by concurrent vote of both branches. The executive officers of the city were, generally speaking, elected by the City Council, while the Mayor was to preside over the Board of Aldermen, and to constitute with the Board a single body known as the Mayor and Aldermen. Beyond the power to appoint committees which this position gave him, the Mayor was little more than a figurehead; and although he was enjoined by the charter "to be vigilant and active at all times in causing the laws for the government of said city to be duly

---

[1] In the convention of 1820, ratified by the people April 9, 1821.
[2] By 2,797 to 1,881.

executed and put in force," and "to cause all negligence, carelessness, and positive violation of duty to be duly prosecuted and punished," the Legislature omitted to clothe him with the powers necessary for the performance of these duties.

Other features of the charter of 1822 worth noting are the existence of a separate school committee elected by the people, and a board of fire-wards elected by the voters of the several wards. This latter body was abolished in 1825, and a municipal fire department established in its place.

The charter of the city of Boston was, I believe, the first city charter to be granted in the New England States outside of Connecticut. It was not, like the Constitution of the United States, a carefully studied effort to create a new form of government; it was simply an attempt to substitute representative for direct control. The community, then numbering forty thousand people and seven thousand voters, had outgrown the capacity of the town meeting to conduct its affairs with efficiency and despatch, and a representative substitute was all that was thought necessary. A double legislative body, consisting of a Board of Aldermen and a Common Council, with a Mayor, who was practically nothing more than the presiding officer of the former, had existed in many of the towns of England from the Middle Ages, and had also been adopted in some cities in other parts of the United States. It was accepted by the people of Boston without serious question, their principal object being to secure the conduct of municipal business through representative institutions, rather than as hitherto by direct popular vote. The Common Council has sometimes been regarded as a substitute for the town meeting,[1] and the Board of Aldermen was in terms the successor of the Selectmen; analogies are also discovered to the legislative system adopted by the

---

[1] Section 25 of the charter provided for the calling, on request of fifty voters, of general meetings of the citizens "to consult upon the common good," etc. These meetings, not the Common Council, were at the time regarded as a continuation of the town-meeting system; but few have ever been called — none in recent years.

several States and the federal government; but, in substance, the organization provided by the charter was simply an adaptation of a form of municipal government which had existed for centuries in the commercial towns of England.

As already pointed out, the Mayor was, under the new charter of the city of Boston, as in the older municipalities of England, simply the chief officer of the government. He had no charter power of appointment or removal, no right of veto over municipal legislation, and no control of the executive business of the city, except such as was derived from his vote in the Board of Aldermen and the power to appoint its committees.

The difficulties attendant on this form of government in a democratic community were apparent from the outset. The citizens had surrendered all direct share in the administration of the government; but on the other hand the responsibility for the executive business of the government was divided among a very much larger number of elective officers than under the old system, — that is, among 57 instead of 9, — and there was less rather than more efficiency and cohesion in administration. During the first year of the new City Government disappointment was felt that the change had not produced the practical results expected; and the second Mayor determined to use all the powers that ingenuity could spell out of the city charter to the end of concentrating responsibility and control. The means adopted by him to secure this result was to make himself chairman of all the important committees of the Board of Aldermen, and thus personally to become familiar with all the details of the executive business of the city, and responsible for the management of them. This course enabled Mayor Quincy to become a most competent and careful administrator as well as a far-seeing advocate of public improvements; but the control exercised by him over the affairs of the city was necessarily the result of personal influence and industry. It had no technical justification in the charter, and was unaccompanied by legal powers of any kind. It subjected him to much criticism and abuse, and was one of the causes which contributed to his final defeat in the city election of 1829. I am not aware that any of his successors saw fit to imitate his example; and from 1829 to 1885 the executive business of the city was practically directed by committees of the City Council.

After the abandonment of Mayor Quincy's experiment, the weakness of the executive branch of the City Government was tolerated, though not ignored, until the building of railroads and steamships and the great increase in population due to these and other causes had entirely changed the character of the community and its necessities in the way of government. From a seaport town Boston became the distributing centre for the manufacturing industries of New England; new avenues of commercial communication were opened up in all directions; the city increased in population at an unprecedented rate; and it became common to think and speak of it as a metropolis. The "long winter of New England isolation" was broken, and Boston found herself suddenly transformed from a provincial town into a centre of trade and commerce, in close communication with all the other portions of a great country developing with phenomenal rapidity. The people no longer formed a homogeneous community, in respect to race, religion, or wealth. Their life became more complex, their interests more diversified, their aspirations larger; economy in public affairs ceased to be the chief aim of the city authorities; and a demand arose for a greater measure of municipal activity and a more liberal use of the public funds.

SECTION 2. *The Charter of 1854.* Under these changed conditions the inadequacy of the city charter became a matter of common admission, and in 1854 a revision was obtained.[1] This document contained few changes of importance except that it gave the Mayor a qualified veto

---
[1] St. 1854, ch. 448.

over the action of the City Council or either branch of it. It also gave him a power of removal over appointed officers; but as most of the executive officers continued to be elected by the City Council, this power was of nominal value. The veto power did not include the right to disapprove separate items in an appropriation order or a loan bill.

SECTION 3. *The Charter Amendments of 1885.* The charter of 1854 was in only one respect an improvement on the original—it gave the Mayor a qualified power of veto;[1] and as the city increased in population and the public business became still more diversified and complicated, the inherent difficulty of conducting it through committees of a large elective body became annually more apparent. For the next thirty years almost every Mayor at some period of his administration expressed the opinion that a radical change was necessary, and that the executive business of the city should be separated from the legislative. The annexation of the suburban communities of Roxbury, Dorchester, West Roxbury, Charlestown, and Brighton served to emphasize this necessity; and after various commissions[2] had considered the subject, and it had been repeatedly discussed in the City Council and the Legislature, a new charter was procured in 1885.[3]

This act did not attempt, as did the charter of 1854, to revise or reënact the organic law of the city, but took the form of a few short amendments, and is commonly referred to as the Charter Amendments of 1885. It transferred all the executive powers of the city to the Mayor, to be exercised through the several officers and boards of the city, in their respective departments, under his general supervision and control, and placed in charge of these officers and boards everything relating to contracts, the purchase of material, the employment of labor, the construction, repair, and management of the public works, buildings, institutions, and other city prop-

---

[1] As he had lost the power to vote in the Board of Aldermen, the advantage of the change was not great. Plurality elections for Mayor were inaugurated by this charter, a clear majority having previously been necessary.
[2] See especially the report of the last one, Doc. 120 of 1884.
[3] St. 1885, ch. 266.

erty, and generally the direction and control of all the executive and administrative business of the city. It prohibited the City Council, its members and committees, from interfering in any manner in the employment of labor, the making of contracts, the purchase of materials, and generally in the conduct of the executive and administrative business of the city. It gave the Mayor the power of appointing, subject to confirmation by the Board of Aldermen, all officers and members of boards except the city clerk, clerk of committees, and city messenger, and those officers who were then elected by the people. It gave him the power to remove any of the executive officers and boards for such cause as he might deem sufficient and assign in the order of removal. It provided that all contracts exceeding $2,000 in amount should require the approval of the Mayor, and prohibited the departments from expending money or incurring liability beyond the appropriations duly made therefor. It gave the Mayor the right to veto every order passed by the City Council, or either branch of it, and to disapprove separate items in loan bills and appropriation orders; subject to the right of the City Council by a two-thirds concurrent vote to override the veto. It provided that the Mayor should not be a member, or preside at any of the meetings, or appoint any of the committees, of the Board of Aldermen or the School Committee.

Taken in connection with perfecting amendments[1] subsequently passed, this act amounted to a new charter, under which a single officer was annually chosen by the legal voters of the city, and in his hands was placed the entire charge and responsibility for the proper conduct of all the executive business of the city. Other legislation of the

---

[1] Particularly the following: St. 1890, ch. 418, regulating the status of subordinate employees, and the execution of public works (see p. 80); St. 1891, ch. 206, which practically gives the mayor an absolute veto over loan bills; St. 1891, ch. 323, and 1892, ch. 418, which makes the mayor's signature necessary for all streets laid out by the Board of Survey and Board of Street Commissioners; St. 1892, ch. 213, relating to the waterworks; St. 1893, ch. 192, relating to loans; and St. 1893, ch. 261, relating to transfers of appropriations.

same year limited the rate of taxation for municipal purposes, as well as the amount of indebtedness,[1] while the civil service rules for the selection of the subordinate employees of the city went into effect that year.[2]

Since 1885, therefore, we have been living under a form of government which is entirely different from that which preceded, and is a more consistent application of the theory of executive responsibility than can be found in the organic law of any other large city in this country.[3]

A distrust of municipal legislatures and of the capacity of their committees to conduct the executive business of a city government has been the chief feature of municipal development in this country during the past thirty years. The tendency to substitute the "one-man power" of the Mayor for the unwieldy and irresponsible machinery of the City Council and its committees has been deprecated by some as contrary to European precedents; and it has been denounced by others as un-American and un-democratic. It must be conceded that the common argument that as most of the city's work is executive in character, it should for that reason be vested in an executive officer, is refuted by the experience of foreign cities, most of which are admittedly well-governed under the committee system. The concentration of executive power in the Mayor's hands is to be defended, not so much on business, as on political grounds. The legislative system works well enough in the cities of Europe where the property-owners are in control, but it has worked very badly in the larger cities of this country under universal suffrage. As the voting list expands and the membership of the City Council increases, it has been found more and more difficult to elect a body that in its committee work represents with any approach to fidelity the desires of the

---

[1] St. 1885, ch. 178.
[2] St. 1884, ch. 320.
[3] The reform charter of the city of Brooklyn was probably the nearest approximation to this idea prior to 1885, but it gave the Mayor no absolute power of removal, and was otherwise a much weaker act. In New York the Mayor has no power of removal.

CITY CHARTER.   171

citizens as a whole respecting the conduct of executive work.[1]

[1] The following tables show the change that has gradually taken place in the composition of the legislative branch of the City Government.

Board of Aldermen.

YEAR.	Total Number Members.	Number Assessed on Property.	Percentage Assessed on Property.	Total Valuation of the City.	Amounts Assessed to Aldermen.	Percentage of Total Value Assessed to Aldermen.
1822	8	8	100.00	$42,140,200	$146,100	.00347
1830	8	8	100.00	59,586,000	99,400	.00167
1840	8	8	100.00	94,581,600	168,800	.00178
1850	8	8	100.00	180,000,500	261,800	.00145
1860	12	12	100.00	276,861,000	622,900	.00225
1870	12	12	100.00	584,089,400	476,200	.00081
1875	12	12	100.00	793,961,895	769,600	.00097
1880	13	11	84.61	639,462,495	197,900	.00031
1885	12	7	58.33	685,579,072	457,900	.000087
1890	12	8	66.66	822,041,800	206,200	.000025
1895	12	9	75.00	¹928,109,042	¹105,500	.000025

¹ Figures for 1894.

Common Council.

YEAR.	Total Number Members.	Number Assessed on Property.	Percentage Assessed on Property.	Total Valuation of the City.	Amounts Assessed to Councilmen.	Percentage of Total Value Assessed to Councilmen.
1822	48	45	93.75	$42,140,200	$840,300	.01994
1830	49	38	77.55	59,586,000	228,300	.00383
1840	48	40	83.33	94,581,600	204,400	.00216
1850	48	36	75.00	180,000,500	225,850	.00125
1860	48	41	85.41	276,861,000	1,116,400	.00403
1870	64	56	87.50	584,089,400	1,050,900	.00180
1875	74	61	82.43	793,961,895	1,530,800	.00192
1880	75	42	56.00	639,462,495	607,000	.00143
1885	72	29	40.55	685,579,072	290,300	.00042
1890	73	20	27.39	822,041,800	315,700	.00038
1895	75	16	21.33	¹928,109,042	¹266,500	

¹ Figures for 1894.

These tables show the gradual diminution in the representation secured by the property-owners of the city in the legislative branches of the government, and may be summed up in the statement that whereas during the first fifty years of our municipal history from 85 to 95 per cent. of the representatives elected by the people to the City Council were themselves owners of property, the proportion to-day has fallen to less than 30 per cent.

The voters of the city who pay a property tax secure as large a representation in the City Council as they are numerically entitled to, for they constitute only about twenty per cent. of the total number of registered voters (see Appendix, Table 3); but it cannot be doubted that the people as a whole still prefer that those who have

When the public business becomes voluminous and difficult, our municipal legislatures tend to degenerate into irresponsible debating societies; they represent local and special interests rather than the public interest as a whole; their committees are still further removed from responsibility to the public; and the results are inefficiency, extravagance, and a complete failure to administer the business of the city as the people on the whole desire. Under these circumstances the executive powers of the government have in many of our cities been transferred to the Mayor as that member of the City Government nearest and most responsible to the people. The Mayor, unlike the members of the City Council, cannot shield himself behind a committee report or a majority vote; he is less open to influence by the organized private and special interests of the city, because he is elected by the people as a whole and must account to them; and his control makes the government more truly democratic by bringing it closer to the people, and by making it more responsive to the popular will. Thus we turn to a form of government more democratic both in fact and theory. In a pure democracy there is no room for representative institutions; and although government by direct popular vote has failed whenever tried in populous communities, it should be remembered that government by committees of an elective body is not democracy in the true and original sense. The new system is in theory more democratic than the legislative committee system, and is moreover a distinctly American idea; for a strong and independent Executive is that feature of the political institutions of this country which distinguishes them most completely from the parliamentary form of government common in European States.

In practice the plan has, I think, worked well; immeas-

---

a sufficient direct interest in the tax levy to make them conservative in expenditure should have a larger share in the City Government than at present. By propertyowners is meant those who are assessed a tax on real or personal estate. There are also, of course, many voters who are interested in property assessed to others.

urably better, at least, than the old one.[1] It has brought about better results in the separate departments; it has secured a closer coöperation between them; and it has rendered easier the practice of economy. It imposes great labor on the Mayor, and it makes him literally responsible in the eyes of the people for everything that goes wrong, even in respect to matters over which he has no control; but, on the other hand, the honors and opportunities of the office are co-equal with its difficulties.

The doctrine of executive responsibility and control is therefore democratic in theory, American in origin, and successful in practice. The American people may claim to have practically invented two new and distinct forms of municipal government: the town meeting; and the city charter, in which all executive power is reposed in the Mayor. The former has been a successful feature of our political institutions for two centuries and a half; the latter is but a few years old, it is still on trial, and capable of development and improvement.[2]

---

[1] It was from the outset bitterly antagonized by the City Council, and not until 1891 did the legislative branch thoroughly accept the limitations on its power imposed in 1885. Since 1891 there has been little question, even in the City Council, of the wisdom of the change.

[2] See suggestions in Chapter 1.

CHAPTER 20.

THE PROBLEM OF CITY GOVERNMENT.

While we have changed, and as we think improved, the form and organization of our municipal government, it must not be inferred that the inherent difficulties of the problem have been lessened or removed. It has been made easier to handle them; but the difficulties still remain, and are increasing rather than diminishing.

The corruption about which we hear so much — though fortunately not in Boston — is the least of these difficulties. So far as my observation and information go, the government of this city has always been comparatively free from the suspicion of jobbery and fraud. Instances of corruption may be pointed out; but its detection and prevention ought not to be difficult in a city where the legislative body has nothing to do with executive work; and as a matter of fact the City Government of Boston has always been relatively free from this particular evil.

The difficulty here is not Corruption, but Expenditure.

There can be no doubt that our American cities as a whole spend more money than is required for the government of European cities of equal size;[1] and Boston has

---

[1] It also cannot be denied, that in the two particulars of street service and police work most of the foreign cities — especially those on the continent of Europe — are more efficiently administered than ours; but it should not be forgotten that the continental police system is wholly foreign to our institutions, and that no English-speaking people would ever give to any police force the extensive powers which enable the foreign police to accomplish so much. Street cleaning is largely a question of labor, and as labor can be secured in European cities for from a quarter to a half of what is paid by American cities, it is of course proportionately easier to get good results in this branch of municipal service. In everything that relates to schools, hospitals, pauper institutions, and, of late years, parks, it cannot fairly be claimed, I believe, that our American cities as a whole are behind those of the Old Country. Finally, in some respects the cities of this country are generally much better equipped; namely, in water supply, drainage, and popular libraries. On the other hand, a perfectly clear case can be made out that our cities spend very much more money than European cities of similar size.

apparently led them all in this respect, having probably for the last forty years expended more money on public account in proportion to the population than any other city in the world.[1]

Some of the causes of this excessive expenditure have been already pointed out.[2] We cannot supply this community with pure water, wide streets, and good drainage, except at great cost. The city cannot pay higher salaries and wages than private employers; it cannot operate its water-works and ferries at less than cost; it cannot maintain a school system more elaborate than any to be found elsewhere; it cannot provide every suburban village within the municipal limits with school-houses, fire-engine houses, and police-stations;[3] it cannot build streets and sewers for the benefit of speculative land-owners; — it cannot do all these things, or any of them, without an inordinate annual expenditure and a correspondingly heavy tax rate.

The real difficulty to contend with is the demand of individuals, interests, classes, sections, and sometimes of the whole community, for extravagant expenditure; and this difficulty is constantly increasing as the belief gains ground that the community in its corporate capacity owes a liberal living to its individual members. A gradual change has come over the spirit of the people; and a large part of a population once the most independent and self-reliant in the world is now clamoring for support, as individuals or in classes, from the governments of this country, — federal, state, and city. These symptoms, however, are not local; they may be more prominent here than in other cities, but they exist everywhere. They constitute the chief danger of popular government, and a danger that will be greater before it is less: the demand for a systematic distribution of wealth by taxes.

---

[1] See Chapter 3.   [2] Chapters 3 and 5.
[3] The outlying wards contribute in taxes collected from real and personal estate from one-third to one-half only of the amount annually expended from the city treasury in those wards.

The remedies suggested for the evils of city government as conducted in this country are innumerable.

Confining comment to those most frequently proposed, we have in the first place the proposition to restrict the suffrage for municipal purposes to those who have a direct property interest in the government, through the payment of taxes on real or personal estate.[1] Such a reform is, in my opinion, impracticable; it is wholly unlikely that any Legislature could be induced to disfranchise four-fifths of the voters of this city; and if this was once done, it would not last five years.[2] Our political institutions are founded upon the theory that those who have the physical power shall have the legal right, — that is, on universal manhood suffrage;[3] and on that principle they must stand or fall. As I have not hesitated to point out some of the bad results of universal suffrage in municipal affairs, so I desire to record my opposition to all efforts to abolish or restrict it. If the American people cannot in time solve the problem of city government on the basis of universal suffrage, then democracy itself is a failure.

On the other hand, to extend the suffrage by admitting to it women, would be not only to depart from the true theory of universal suffrage, but would reduce still further the percentage of property-owners to the total number of voters; it would more than double the already large majority of non-property owning voters; and it would introduce considerations into the government, the certain tendency of which would be a further and unnecessary increase in expenditure. The result of the limited experience that this city has had with woman suffrage has not been such as to lead thoughtful people to look upon its extension otherwise than with fear.[4]

---

[1] Recommended twenty years ago by a commission of the State of New York, appointed by Governor Tilden, and since then by many earnest students of municipal affairs.

[2] The burden of taxation, although felt more directly by those who pay it in the first place, is yet in the end distributed in rent and prices throughout the whole community; and it seems no harder a task to convince the people of this fact than to abolish manhood suffrage.

[3] All property qualifications were abolished in 1821, and the payment of a poll tax ceased to be a prerequisite to the right to vote in 1892.

[4] Statute 1884, chap. 298, passed at the instance of a few women who desired to

In opposing the extension of the franchise to women I do not wish to be understood as failing to recognize their capacity as individuals for public work. On the contrary, I have had frequent opportunities for observing the excellent work accomplished by the ladies who have served the city on the School Committee, the Overseers of the Poor, and the Board of Visitors for the Public Institutions; and those appointed by me to positions upon the two last-named Boards were the first to receive an executive appointment from any Mayor of Boston. The dilution of the suffrage by means of the addition of all women to the voting list is a wholly different proposition from the capacity of individual women for public work. Woman suffrage has been a conspicuous failure to the limited extent that it has been already tried in this community, and every consideration tends to show that general or municipal suffrage for women could not fail to be attended with the most disastrous results under conditions such as obtain in all populous communities.

"Non-partisanship" in city politics is a common remedy, and on the face of things most plausible, as no real reason can be assigned why municipal elections should turn on considerations of national party politics; but it has not been found possible in the larger cities of the country to maintain for any length of time "citizens'" movements, although occasionally one proves successful. There is, moreover, one possible result of abolishing the party system which seems to be lost sight of by the advocates of non-partisan reform: the division of the people in municipal elections on class and social lines. As a city is a political institution, the people in the end will divide into parties; and it would seem extremely doubtful whether the present system, however illogical its foundation be, does not in fact produce better results, at

---

take an intelligent part in public affairs, has been used almost exclusively as a weapon in an anti-Catholic agitation, kept up, principally by its means, for the benefit of sensational preachers. The influence of the women who started the school suffrage movement has been lost in the flood of votes cast by other women in ignorance and prejudice, it being estimated that nine-tenths of the women voters at the city election follow the "Committee of One Hundred" and other anti-Catholic societies.

least in large cities, than if the voters were divided into groups separated by property, social, or religious bounds. The evils of such division can be read in the history of the cities of Greece, and if, as many people think, similar dangers confront the municipal democracies of the twentieth century, we should be slow to hasten their advent by a deliberate abandonment of the present system. These remarks apply to partisanship in elections rather than to partisanship in administration. The business of the city can, with relatively insignificant qualifications, be conducted without regard to party politics even under the party system. Ninety-nine per cent. of all the questions that come before the City Council and the executive departments are questions of expenditure; there are practically no divisions of the City Council on party lines; and the contest in almost every case is between extravagance and economy, between expenditure and retrenchment, not between Democrats and Republicans. The present system of party nominations makes the successful party responsible for a bad, inefficient, or extravagant administration; and conversely a successful administration enures to the credit of the party responsible for it; but except in the matter of appointments to office partisanship in administration is no part of the system, and even with respect to appointments the doctrine of partisan proscription has never obtained in this city. Nominations for Mayor of Boston have been made by the principal political parties from the beginning;[1] but, as already pointed out (pp. 13 and 120) partisan changes in the heads of departments have been relatively infrequent, even since the power of appointment was lodged in the Mayor. The much-decried system of party responsibility has some merits regarded from the practical standpoint of results; and it may well be doubted whether the

---

[1] In the seventy-three city elections held since 1822 the Federalist candidates were successful ten times, the National Republicans twice, the Whigs seventeen times, the Native American candidates three times, the Republicans thirteen times, various " citizens' " candidates six times, while the Democrats have carried the city in twenty-two elections.

substitution of social groups for national parties would in the end benefit the people.

The same objection applies to minority representation: that it invites the voters to divide into classes and to carry the differences of social and pecuniary conditions into city politics. Majority or plurality rule may not be fair to all interests involved; but the question is not so much whether the special interests of the community secure that representation in the government to which they are numerically entitled, as whether they ought to have any representation at all. The rule of the majority, like every other political device, is open to criticism; but after all it secures a government that more than half the people have voted for, and not a compromise between the interests of special classes. It is a principle that should not be unthinkingly abandoned.

The "initiative" and "referendum," the latest political importations from foreign parts, are nothing but devices for the abolition of representative government. We may concede that representative institutions are not adapted to the proper conduct of executive work; but the Swiss initiative is a scheme to destroy the legislative power of representative governments.[1]

The theory that the affairs of a city should be managed like those of an ordinary business corporation is attractive and widespread; but it is founded on the fallacy of supposing that a municipality is a business corporation; and its advocates are generally driven to support a limitation of the suffrage. While the modern city is technically a corporation, its constitution, machinery, and objects are wholly different from those of private companies. It is not controlled by a limited number of stockholders casting votes propor-

---

[1] The submission in the discretion of the Legislature of important local measures to popular vote is properly frequent here; but the Swiss law for the compulsory submission upon request of bills passed by the Legislature, and of other bills that the Legislature will not pass, is the complete annihilation of representative government. The best-informed critics agree that this system is, as might be supposed, leading the people of Switzerland straight to socialism.

American. Let us leave it so, and we shall 'tain a form of government that cannot be hurried into tho- popular excesses that ruined the cities of Greece, or into at Chinese stagnation which threatens the socialistic city (the future. Let us aim to remain a body of self-respecting, elf-supporting American citizens, and not permit ourselve to be transformed into a pauperized community of na)nalists and socialists. We must rely on the American genus to solve the problem of democratic city government: nt by sudden or revolutionary reforms; not through metho thrust by socialistic agitation upon communities, like som in Switzerland, which have lost the virility to resist; nt by slow degrees in the Anglo-American way, in wih all our political institutions have been developed. A ctain inefficiency, a certain waste, must be conceded as pai)f the price we must pay for the blessings of free institutio ; and success cannot be attained without the most thountful study and unceasing vigilance and effort; but there ouht to be no doubt of the ultimate capacity of the America people to work this problem out, as they have so many thers.[1]

---

[1] In connection with the foregoing remarks I may be permitted to r'int the closing portion of an address delivered on February 27, 1892, before the studen of the Phillips Academy at Exeter, N.H.:

"The great questions of State and national politics make more inesting subjects for popular discussion than the dry details of municipal administrati: but, after all, the questions that will touch you oftenest and closest in your persnl relations are questions of municipal rather than of State or national governme: Out of $100 contributed by the individual in direct taxation to the various cit ounty, State, and national governments to which he owes allegiance, about 80 per nt. goes to the town or city, while the entire burden of the remaining county, Sta. and national taxes amounts to only 20 per cent.; and in respect to debt, his p onal share of his town or city debt is nearly ten times as great as his proportion of national and State debts.

"In other words, so far as your immediate pecuniary interests are ncerned, based on the amount you pay in taxes, more than three-fourths of the tin and attention you can afford to devote to public business should be bestowed upon town or city where you live. However much you may be attracted while pursuir your studies here or in college in after years to the political and economic prlems growing out of State and national affairs, you will do well to recollect that the nin interest of the citizen is at home, and that it is of as much consequence to him tt his town or city affairs should be honestly and economically administered as tu this or that policy should prevail in State affairs, or this or that party succeed in na)nal politics.

"You will find also that there is far more room for discoveries and inrovements in the field of municipal administration than in the broader, but simpler, domn of national life. The fundamental questions that divide parties in State and natn are, except in times of c... unusual excitement, very much the same from year to year and from generati... eneration; they are few in number and easy to understand, and whether one su... the other for the time being prevails is, after all, of little moment in comparison ... what is or might be done in working out the true theory and practice of m... al government.

"Another is ... n why the youth of the community — particularly that portion of it which is rece'v... e benefit of a liberal education — should be urged to devote their attention, whe... v have finished the preparatory period of life, to the problems of city governmen... the little success that has been achieved, in this country at least, in the solution these problems. The town government is, perhaps, as good a working plan f... managing small communities as has ever been devised, and can probably be ver ittle improved; the federal system of our national government, which has sto... the strain of over a century, is as strong in the hearts of the people and the ... pect of the world as it was at the beginning; but no one would claim that the p... le of this country had, on the whole, or in any particular instance, yet devised an ... nomical and efficient system for the government of great cities. Without assert... or believing that municipal government in this country is, as our enemies ha... claimed, a disgrace to us and a condemnation of democracy, we must, neverthe... admit that the general theory of our institutions, as applied to great cities, has it worked so well as in the larger, but simpler, fields of State and nation. Progr... is undoubtedly being made, and I think it cannot be denied that the large cities of o... untry are on the whole better governed to-day — that is to say, that larger results a... oroduced for the same expenditure of money — than twenty years ago; but it is t ..., I think, that by far the greater part of the work of improvement and refor... s still to come. Thus municipal reform offers a practically limitless field for t... ctivities and intelligence of those of our citizens who have the time, the traini... and the inclination to devote themselves to the solution of public problems.

"In appro/'ng this subject you will be confronted with many plausible and apparently sim, remedies. You will be told, for instance, that that government is best which is b.t administered, and that the whole secret consists in electing honorable and capabie en to office. This proposition, though certainly true to the extent that no system cn be made to work well unless administered by honest and capable officials, fails c·pletely, when the system itself is wrong; and when you find, as you will by com ring almost any American city with a city of corresponding size in foreign coun·ies, that the public services and facilities afforded by European cities are muc· rreater in proportion to the amount expended in this country, h /ever capable and honest the city government for the time being may be, you can.ifely assume that the fault lies with the system rather than with the character o.·ie men who are elected to office. You will be told that the true solution of the ·oblem is to eradicate all politics from city government, and to treat a municipal a· ou would a private corporation, managing the one precisely as the other; and : support of this idea you will be informed of the excellent results accomplished i many of the cities of continental Europe. Persons who advocate this theory will owever, omit to tell you that the basis of every political structure in this country. om the town to the federal government at Washington, is universal local suffrage; hile in the cities of continental Europe, to which your attention and admiratio. ure directed, a large part of the local business is controlled and administered l a centralized national government, and the remainder regulated by a suffrage based n property rather than on polls. In the city of Berlin, for instance, which we can· cely admit to be one of the best-governed municipalities in the world, two-thir of the city council are elected by a very small percentage of the voting populati ; for while every citizen has, I believe, a vote, the electors are divided into clses in such manner that the voting power of each is practically

American. Let us leave it so, and we shall retain a form of government that cannot be hurried into those popular excesses that ruined the cities of Greece, or into that Chinese stagnation which threatens the socialistic city of the future. Let us aim to remain a body of self-respecting, self-supporting American citizens, and not permit ourselves to be transformed into a pauperized community of nationalists and socialists. We must rely on the American genius to solve the problem of democratic city government: not by sudden or revolutionary reforms; not through methods thrust by socialistic agitation upon communities, like some in Switzerland, which have lost the virility to resist; but by slow degrees in the Anglo-American way, in which all our political institutions have been developed. A certain inefficiency, a certain waste, must be conceded as part of the price we must pay for the blessings of free institutions; and success cannot be attained without the most thoughtful study and unceasing vigilance and effort; but there ought to be no doubt of the ultimate capacity of the American people to work this problem out, as they have so many others.[1]

---

[1] In connection with the foregoing remarks I may be permitted to reprint the closing portion of an address delivered on February 27, 1892, before the students of the Phillips Academy at Exeter, N.H.:

"The great questions of State and national politics make more interesting subjects for popular discussion than the dry details of municipal administration; but, after all, the questions that will touch you oftenest and closest in your personal relations are questions of municipal rather than of State or national government. Out of $100 contributed by the individual in direct taxation to the various city, county, State, and national governments to which he owes allegiance, about 80 per cent. goes to the town or city, while the entire burden of the remaining county, State, and national taxes amounts to only 20 per cent.; and in respect to debt, his personal share of his town or city debt is nearly ten times as great as his proportion of the national and State debts.

"In other words, so far as your immediate pecuniary interests are concerned, based on the amount you pay in taxes, more than three-fourths of the time and attention you can afford to devote to public business should be bestowed upon the town or city where you live. However much you may be attracted while pursuing your studies here or in college or in after years to the political and economic problems growing out of State and national affairs, you will do well to recollect that the main interest of the citizen is at home, and that it is of as much consequence to him that his town or city affairs should be honestly and economically administered as that this or that policy should prevail in State affairs, or this or that party succeed in national politics.

"You will find also that there is far more room for discoveries and improvements in the field of municipal administration than in the broader, but simpler, domain of national life. The fundamental questions that divide parties in State and nation are, except in times of crisis or unusual excitement, very much the same from year to year and from generation to generation; they are few in number and easy to understand, and whether one side or the other for the time being prevails is, after all, of little moment in comparison with what is or might be done in working out the true theory and practice of municipal government.

"Another reason why the youth of the community — particularly that portion of it which is receiving the benefit of a liberal education — should be urged to devote their attention, when they have finished the preparatory period of life, to the problems of city government, is the little success that has been achieved, in this country at least, in the solution of these problems. The town government is, perhaps, as good a working plan for managing small communities as has ever been devised, and can probably be very little improved; the federal system of our national government, which has stood the strain of over a century, is as strong in the hearts of the people and the respect of the world as it was at the beginning; but no one would claim that the people of this country had, on the whole, or in any particular instance, yet devised an economical and efficient system for the government of great cities. Without asserting or believing that municipal government in this country is, as our enemies have claimed, a disgrace to us and a condemnation of democracy, we must, nevertheless, admit that the general theory of our institutions, as applied to great cities, has not worked so well as in the larger, but simpler, fields of State and nation. Progress is undoubtedly being made, and I think it cannot be denied that the large cities of our country are on the whole better governed to-day — that is to say, that larger results are produced for the same expenditure of money — than twenty years ago; but it is true, I think, that by far the greater part of the work of improvement and reform is still to come. Thus municipal reform offers a practically limitless field for the activities and intelligence of those of our citizens who have the time, the training, and the inclination to devote themselves to the solution of public problems.

"In approaching this subject you will be confronted with many plausible and apparently simple remedies. You will be told, for instance, that that government is best which is best administered, and that the whole secret consists in electing honorable and capable men to office. This proposition, though certainly true to the extent that no system can be made to work well unless administered by honest and capable officials, fails completely, when the system itself is wrong; and when you find, as you will by comparing almost any American city with a city of corresponding size in foreign countries, that the public services and facilities afforded by European cities are much greater in proportion to the amount expended than anywhere in this country, however capable and honest the city government for the time being may be, you can safely assume that the fault lies with the system rather than with the character of the men who are elected to office. You will be told that the true solution of the problem is to eradicate all politics from city government, and to treat a municipal as you would a private corporation, managing the one precisely as the other; and in support of this idea you will be informed of the excellent results accomplished in many of the cities of continental Europe. Persons who advocate this theory will, however, omit to tell you that the basis of every political structure in this country, from the town to the federal government at Washington, is universal local suffrage; while in the cities of continental Europe, to which your attention and admiration are directed, a large part of the local business is controlled and administered by a centralized national government, and the remainder regulated by a suffrage based on property rather than on polls. In the city of Berlin, for instance, which we can freely admit to be one of the best-governed municipalities in the world, two-thirds of the city council are elected by a very small percentage of the voting population; for while every citizen has, I believe, a vote, the electors are divided into classes in such manner that the voting power of each is practically proportionate to his means. It is easy to see how under such a system the city government can be managed as if it were a private corporation, where, also, the influence of the individual stockholder is proportionate to the amount of his financial interest in the company.

"We are told that a city should be regarded as a business corporation rather than as a political organization; but this advice, again, presupposes a condition of things which does not exist in the United States. Those who tender this advice as a ready and complete remedy for the admitted defects of municipal government in this country forget, I think, the history of democracy in its application to large municipal communities. They look to the modern instances of Berlin and Paris and other foreign cities, where the results are admittedly worthy of consideration; but they overlook the fact that those results are obtained by a sacrifice of the principle of local government and the right of equal manhood suffrage. They do not recall the fact that from the earliest times the government of cities has been a difficult and oftentimes an impossible task, wherever democratic theories have prevailed. The city as we know it had, like almost every other institution that flourishes to-day, its origin in ancient Greece; and the conditions obtaining there, so far as the qualifications for suffrage and the temper of the people are concerned, were more similar to those which exist to-day in this country than anything to be found in the cities of continental Europe. I fancy, however, that no one would seriously point to the history of the Greek cities as furnishing examples of government on business principles. No city in this country can be mentioned that permits anything like as much politics — unwholesome, demagogic, and destructive politics — to enter into the administration of its affairs as was the case in Athens, the greatest of the Greek democracies. By politics I do not mean so much the mere struggle for party supremacy that plays so large a part in the political life of this country, but that tendency to decide questions of municipal policy on social and sentimental rather than on business considerations. Political and social agitation was the life of the Greek city, and finally proved its death; and how many people realize that from the destruction of the Greek republics to the great migration into cities which began in this country less than 100 years ago, history does not furnish us with successful instances of the governing of large municipal communities on truly democratic principles.

"We are working out a problem that has received no attention from the educated intelligence of mankind since the days of classic Greece — the problem of self-government on democratic principles for great bodies of people congregated together in a single neighborhood, and without the controlling power of a superior central government. We should face this problem squarely, with no hesitation, on the one hand, to admit that better and more economical results are being obtained to-day in foreign cities under wholly different systems, but with a determination to do as well ourselves, or even better, without abandoning those fundamental principles of government which are the historic property of the nation. No one should despair of eventual success, or give the problem up as hopeless, because of the difficulties that surround it or the little progress that has hitherto been made. When this republic was founded, it was based upon a new and untried application of democracy. Recalling the fact that all previous attempts at governing nations on democratic principles had failed, through the tendency in such communities to attempt too much in the way of government, the men who created this republic invented a new kind of democracy. They worked out a plan which gave to every citizen a share — and an equal share — in the government of his country, but which rigorously limited the functions and attributes of government to the narrowest limits consistent with national unity and power. This system, with its sharp lines between the powers of the federal government and those of the several States, has been the only permanently successful application of democracy to the government of great nations that the world has witnessed; and it now remains for the descendants of the men who worked out this system to exercise their ingenuity and industry and patriotism in devising plans for the application of democracy to the great, unsolved problem of the government of cities. I am confident that our people are as able to devise a successful democratic plan for governing cities as they were to invent and establish a democratic republic for the country at large. The main reliance of the people in this endeavor will now, as then, be the educated intelligence of the country; and I wish to impress upon you, as scholars and as citizens, that the greatest of all duties that will devolve upon you, when you leave the academy or the college and enter into active life, will be to take an intelligent, personal and perpetual interest in the management of the city where you live. You will derive valuable information for purposes of comparison from visiting other cities and studying their methods; but the details of municipal government are generally so intricate that no adequate comprehension of the difficulties of the case can be formed without keeping a close and personal watch upon the management of your own city government. If the opportunity presents itself to enter city politics and become yourself a member of the city council, do not hesitate to seize it. To accomplish this end, you will generally find it necessary to ally yourself with one party or the other; but you should always bear in mind that the only justification for party politics in municipal business is the opportunity thus afforded to serve your city faithfully, and sometimes to accomplish great results."

CONCLUSION.

Gentlemen of the City Council:

The main objects which I have tried to keep in view during the past four years have been to simplify the organization and machinery of the government; to systematize the books and accounts of the various departments; to secure a more efficient coöperation between the different departments; to reduce the cost and increase the value of our public works by the introduction of business methods in all that relates to the purchase of materials, the letting of contracts, and the building operations of the city; to secure such legislation as seemed from time to time to be necessary; to defend the city treasury against hostile attack; to maintain a conservative management of the city finances; to keep the current expenses of the government within its current income; to use the public credit only for improvements of general and admitted utility; to improve the sanitary condition of the city; to provide better accommodations and treatment for the sick, the poor, and the insane; to procure better streets and pavements; to provide new school-houses and other public buildings; to complete the parks; to readjust upon a fairer basis the relations between the city and the private corporations enjoying privileges in the streets; and to facilitate travel and rapid transit through the city.

In a city where the people are accustomed more than in other cities of this country to rely on the municipal corporation rather than on private enterprise for the development of its material interests; with a system of taxation under which every person with land to develop and improve is invited to secure the means to do so out of the public treasury; in a community burdened with elections so frequent

CONCLUSION. 187

as to create a condition of perpetual politics; with State and municipal legislatures, many of whose members spend their time in attacking the financial interests of the city; — the efficient and economical government of a city, where individuals, sections, classes are continually clamoring, with the assistance of the press (in the news columns, if not on the editorial page), for things that either cannot or ought not to be done, and where the head of the government is theoretically responsible for everything that is done or is not done, is a task of enormous difficulty, and one that is capable of imperfect execution only.

The leading thought which I have endeavored to keep in mind during the administration of the past four years has been that the Mayor should, as contemplated by the charter amendments of 1885, take into his hands a larger share of direction and responsibility than had previously been the case, and thus become more directly accountable to the people for the administration of their affairs. Promising in my first letter of acceptance to literally and in person fulfil the obligations imposed by the city charter, I have endeavored to do my part in the administration of the city government upon this theory, and not to magnify the office beyond the express injunctions of the city charter. I am conscious of innumerable omissions, shortcomings, and mistakes. I know that many things have been left undone for lack of time; and that some things could have been done differently, and some much better. I trust, however, that the administrative and financial methods which have been introduced during these four years may prove a lasting benefit to the city, and tend to make its government easier for those who are to come after me; and that the work of the Board of Survey, the new radial thoroughfares, the Subway, and the Parks, — improvements that will change the face of Boston, — will serve to prepare our city for its metropolitan career.

In laying down the administration of this great trust I desire to express my gratitude and obligation to the citizens of Boston who have so generously supported me at four successive elections, and to thank the members of the City Council, and the heads of departments, for the assistance received on innumerable occasions and in innumerable ways.

APPENDIX.

FINANCIAL TABLES

PREPARED AT VARIOUS TIMES BETWEEN 1891 AND 1894, AND NOW BROUGHT DOWN TO DATE.

[FOR INDEX TO TABLES, SEE PP. 5-7.]

Table No. 1.
POLLS, POPULATION, VALUATION, AND TAX-RATE.

Year	Ratable Male Polls	Population	Valuation Real Estate	Valuation Personal Estate	Valuation Total	Tax-Rate City	Tax-Rate County	Tax-Rate Total City and County	Tax-Rate State	Tax-Rate Total
1822	8,890		$23,364,400	$19,775,900	$42,140,300			$6 30	$1 00	$7 30
1823	9,855		25,367,000	19,529,800	44,896,800			6 00	1 00	7 00
1824	10,897		27,303,800	22,640,000	49,842,800			7 50	1 00	8 50
1825	11,660	58,277	30,992,000	21,450,600	52,442,600			7 00		7 00
1826	12,602		34,203,000	25,246,200	59,449,200			7 00		7 00
1827	12,412		36,061,000	29,797,000	65,858,400			7 00		7 00
1828	12,536		35,908,000	25,615,200	61,523,200			7 10		7 10
1829	13,495		36,963,800	24,104,200	61,068,000			7 14	0 76	8 10
1830	13,098	61,392	36,960,000	22,626,000	59,586,000			7 32	0 78	8 20
1831	13,618		37,675,000	23,023,200	60,648,200			7 14	0 76	8 20
1832	14,184		39,145,200	28,369,200	67,514,400			8 20		8 40
1833	14,899		40,986,400	29,510,800	70,477,200			8 50		8 50
1834	15,137		43,140,600	31,665,200	74,805,800			8 40		9 40
1835	16,188	78,603	47,652,800	31,789,800	79,302,600			9 70		9 70
1836	16,719		53,370,000	34,895,000	88,265,000			9 50		9 50
1837	17,182		56,311,600	33,272,200	89,583,800			10 00		10 00
1838	15,615		57,372,400	32,859,200	90,231,600			9 80		9 80
1839	16,501		58,577,800	33,248,600	91,826,400			11 30		11 30
1840	17,996	93,383	60,424,200	34,167,400	94,581,600			11 00		11 00
1841	18,916		61,963,000	36,048,600	98,046,600			12 00		12 00
1842*	19,636		65,499,900	41,223,800	106,723,700			5 70		5 70
1843	20,063		67,673,400	42,372,600	110,046,000			6 20		6 20
1844	22,329		72,048,000	46,402,300	118,450,300			6 80		6 80
1845	24,257	114,366	71,991,400	63,957,300	135,948,700			5 90		5 90
1846	25,974		90,119,600	58,730,800	148,839,600			6 62		6 62
1847	27,008		97,764,500	64,565,900	162,320,400			6 00		6 00
1848	27,728		100,403,200	67,324,800	167,728,000			6 00		6 00
1849	28,363		102,827,500	71,352,700	174,180,200			6 50	0 20	6 60
1850	28,018	136,881	105,093,400	74,907,100	180,000,500			6 60	0 18	6 60
1851	28,445		109,358,500	78,588,500	187,947,000			7 00		7 00
1852	28,983		110,699,200	76,980,800	187,680,000			6 40	0 50	7 40
1853	29,259		116,080,900	96,423,300	206,614,200			7 10	0 45	7 40
1854	31,130		127,730,200	99,283,000	227,013,200			8 76		8 20

APPENDIX — TABLE No. 1.   191

Year	Polls	Valuation		Tax rate		
1855	31,802		136,351,300	105,580,900	241,932,290		7 06	0 62	7 70
1856	32,074		143,681,700	105,480,500	249,162,500		7 20	0 80	8 00
1857	33,162		149,713,800	108,348,100	258,111,900		8 15	1 15	9 30
1858	32,421		153,505,300	101,208,800	254,714,100		8 16	0 44	8 60
1859	33,456		158,410,900	105,018,100	263,429,000		9 32	0 38	9 70
1860	34,449		163,891,300	112,969,700	276,861,000		8 85	0 15	9 00
1861	35,161		167,682,100	108,078,000	275,760,100		8 99	0 51	9 50
1862	34,169		163,636,000	112,579,000	276,217,000		8 41	3 09	11 50
1863	33,018		169,624,600	132,882,700	302,507,200		8 94	2 56	11 50
1864	32,832		182,072,300	150,377,600	332,449,900		10 95	2 35	13 30
1865	34,704		201,628,900	170,263,875	371,892,775		11 35	4 45	15 80
1866	34,192		225,767,215	189,595,130	415,362,345		11 36	4 24	15 60
1867	35,772		250,387,700	194,558,400	444,946,100		10 65	3 85	14 50
1868	48,416		287,635,800	205,937,900	493,573,700		10 79	2 91	13 70
1869	51,195		332,031,900	217,469,700	549,511,600		10 99	2 51	13 50
1870	56,926		365,593,100	218,496,300	584,089,400		13 65	1 71	15 30
1871	61,148		395,214,050	217,416,600	612,633,550		13 53	1 67	15 20
1872	67,221		443,283,450	239,440,850	682,724,300		10 59	2 11	12 70
1873	70,199	177,840	470,066,300	223,745,300	693,931,400		12 56	1 04	13 60
1874	84,884		554,200,150	239,554,150	798,753,650		14 56	1 04	15 60
1875	85,086	192,318	553,941,600	235,020,845	793,981,185		11 68	1 02	12 70
1876	81,384		528,157,900	222,838,310	748,996,210		12 13	1 17	13 30
1877	86,007		481,375,900	205,433,318	686,340,588		12 30	1 23	13 50
1878	89,452		440,375,900	190,070,966	630,446,866		13 04	2 56	15 60
1879	93,760		428,777,000	184,575,892	613,322,892	$11 84 $0 46	13 00		
1880	99,407	250,526	437,370,100	202,092,395	639,462,495	14 07	0 27	13 98		
1881	102,594		455,388,600	210,165,997	665,554,597	12 84	0 23	13 00		
1882	107,286		467,704,150	204,793,812	672,497,962	13 69	0 28	13 78		
1883	110,481	341,919	478,318,900	204,113,771	682,432,671	13 50	0 29	16 00		
1884	112,104		488,130,600	194,526,058	682,656,658	15 71	0 27	14 50		
1885	112,446		495,973,400	189,605,672	685,579,072	11 82	0 40	17 00		
1886	115,603	362,939	517,503,275	193,118,060	720,421,335	11 65	0 74	12 50		
1887	120,529		547,171,175	200,471,342	747,642,517	11 83	0 80	12 70		
1888	123,335		563,043,275	201,429,273	764,452,548	11 69	0 65	13 40		
1889	125,906	390,393	593,799,975	201,633,769	795,433,744	11 27	0 67	12 90		
1890	132,809		619,990,275	202,051,525	822,041,800	11 76	0 83	13 30		
1891	136,375		630,238,375	204,831,040	835,099,415	11 50	0 53	12 40		
1892	139,767	418,477	680,279,875	213,695,829	843,975,704	11 50	0 92	12 90		
1893	139,789		707,762,275	216,331,478	924,093,751	11 13	0 63	13 30		
1894			723,743,850	204,365,192	928,109,042	11 24	0 73	12 80		

* Previous to 1842 taxes were apportioned on a reduced, or one-half, valuation; but since that time the full valuation has been the basis of apportionment.
1 From 1822 to 1842, inclusive, Poll-tax assessed on all males above 16 years of age.   2 Roxbury annexed.
1843, Poll-tax assessed on all males between 20 and 70 years of age.   3 Dorchester annexed.
1844 and thereafter, Poll-tax assessed on all males above 20 years of age.   4 Brighton, Charlestown, and West Roxbury annexed.

Table No. 2.
POPULATION BY DISTRICTS.

Census.					Annexations.						
Years.	Taken by —	All Boston.	Boston proper, settled, 1630.	Annexed Territory.	East Boston, 1636.	The Islands.	South Boston, March 6, 1804.	Washington Village, May 21, 1855.	Roxbury, Jan. 6, 1868.	Dorchester, Jan. 3, 1870.	West Roxbury, Jan. 5, 1874.	Brighton, Jan. 5, 1874.	Charlestown, Jan. 5, 1874.
1638			¹150										
1675			²4,000										
1698			³7,000										
1704			³6,750										
1720			³11,000										
1722			10,567										
1742			16,382										
1752	Town		15,731										
1765	Town		15,520										2,031
1775	Town		6,573										
1776	Gen. Gage		2,719										
1778	Colony		10,000			282							360
1781	Colony		³15,870			252							¹725
1784	Colony		³17,880			¹619	354						¹1,340
1790	Town	18,320	18,038			284	1,086		1,487	1,360			1,583
1800	United States	24,937	24,055			344	5,595		1,433	1,513		608	2,751
1810	United States	33,787	33,896		18	277	6,176		1,650	1,840		702	4,959
1820	United States	43,298		2,274	24	292	10,020		2,150	2,060			6,591
1825	Town	58,277	56,003			325	13,309		2,226	1,722			
1830	United States	61,392		6,846	607	1,040	16,012		2,765	2,341		972	8,783
1835	City	78,603	72,057	7,908	1,455	1,300	24,921		3,669	2,330		1,425	
1840	City	93,383	85,475	15,330	5,018	1,927	29,383		4,135	3,694			11,484
1845	City	114,366	99,036	23,160	9,526	1,700	39,215		5,247	4,074	4,812	2,356	17,216
1850	United States	136,881	113,721	34,194	15,433	1,927	54,147	²1,319	9,089	4,575	6,310	2,905	21,700
1855	State	160,490	126,296	44,277	18,356	1,545	56,392		18,364	7,969	6,912	3,375	25,066
1860	United States	177,840	133,563	51,225	20,572	2,139	61,534		18,469	8,340	8,696	3,851	26,399
1865	State	192,318	141,063	61,250	23,816		66,701		25,137	9,769	11,783	4,967	28,323
1870	United States	250,526	138,781	111,745	27,420				28,426	10,717	14,032	6,200	33,556
1875	State	341,919	140,669	201,250	30,572				34,753	12,261	17,424	6,603	33,731
1880	State	362,839	147,075	215,764	25,381				60,429	15,788		8,523	37,673
1885	State	390,393	147,138	243,225	29,280				¹57,123	¹17,890			38,348
1890	United States	448,477	161,330	287,147	³36,930				65,968	20,717			
									78,411	29,638	24,997	12,032	

¹ Estimated. ² Included in South Boston after 1865. ³ Including Islands. ¹ Included in South Boston, 1904.

Table No. 3.

AREA, POPULATION, ASSESSED POLLS, REGISTERED VOTERS, AND PROPERTY-OWNING VOTERS BY WARDS.

WARD.	Area in Acres.	Population, Census of 1890.	Assessed Polls, 1893.	Registered Voters, State Election, 1893.	Property Owners registered at the State Election, 1893.
1	1,961	19,633	6,116	4,043	1,028
2	405	17,297	5,090	3,034	456
3	363	13,094	4,017	3,014	457
4	467	12,842	4,007	2,799	505
5	216	12,412	4,183	2,705	383
6	204	18,477	4,329	2,153	292
7	114	13,145	3,471	1,618	265
8	113	13,026	4,548	2,260	323
9	138	12,660	3,868	2.385	330
10	215	8,205	2,985	1,717	299
11	511	21,660	7,683	5,121	1,559
12	244	12,585	3,282	1,947	102
13	598	22,375	6,664	3,296	352
14	1,076	26,367	7,809	4,995	939
15	525	18,049	5,186	3,415	594
16	104	18,048	5,614	2,478	263
17	264	15,638	4,841	3,270	364
18	204	16,035	4,415	2,990	667
19	220	23,016	7,276	3,826	533
20	726	24,335	8,112	5,497	865
21	856	22,930	7,563	5,478	1,442
22	1,361	20,011	6,337	3,781	742
23	8,204	24,997	8,029	5,612	2,069
24	5,652	29,638	9.988	6,999	2,244
25	2,855	12,032	4,290	2,919	733
Total	27,596	448,477	139,703	87,352	17,778
Square miles	43.12				
Number of polls added by supplementary assessment up to the close of registration for State election			4,735		17
			144,438	87,352	[1]17,805

[1] This column gives the number of registered voters assessed a tax on real or personal estate.

Table No. 4.
PERCENTAGE OF TAXES ON PROPERTY AND POLLS COLLECTED
(exclusive of Tax on Bank Stock).[1]

	To Oct. 31.[2]	To Nov. 30.[2]	To Dec. 31.[2]	To Jan. 31[2]
1875–76	29.54	59.00	65.38	83.77
1876–77	31.20	62.57	75.79	84.23
1877–78	32.02	64.00	76.46	85.71
1878–79	45.50	69.35	79.55	85.12
1879–80	45.14	69.05	80.13	85.81
1880–81	42.68	71.64	80.92	86.87
1881–82	47.78	73.03	82.08	87.30
1882–83	44.49	70.79	79.87	86.64
1883–84	47.22	72.17	81.28	87.52
1884–85	47.82	72.05	82.13	87.17
1885–86	56.87	76.45	84.69	88.46
1886–87	49.96	76.66	84.99	88.66
1887–88	46.55	74.47	83.73	87.82
1888–89	47.37	76.98	84.82	89.26
1889–90	51.84	77.11	83.52	88.71
1890–91	49.23	74.08	81.69	88.12
1891–92	51.41	74.96	83.18	88.88
1892–93	50.20	76.16	84.96	90.11
1893–94	46.81	73.78	82.45	88.10
1894–95	52.33	77.85	84.52	

[1] As the tax on bank stock is collected in its entirety, it is omitted from the table.
[2] Including moneys received that day.

TABLE NO. 5.

REVENUES APPLICABLE TO THE GENERAL APPROPRIATIONS, 1860-1 TO 1893-4.

Table No. 5.
REVENUES APPLICABLE TO THE

	1860-61.	1861-62.	1862-63.	1863-64.	1864-65.
City Clerk Dept.	$1,607 62	$1,338 01	$857 53	$874 12	$951 08
City Council: Incidental Expenses,	445 04	1,030 09	189 61	1,002 01	499 68
City Messenger Dept.					
Collecting Bank Tax					
Collecting Dept., or Tax and other Fees,					
Conscience Fund					
Ferry Department					
Fire Department	2,892 21	53 50	1,010 35		152 07
Hay Scales	21 26	23 52	37 32	32 29	19 70
Health Department	105 00	2,749 50	561 26	2,612 37	1,871 00
Hospital Department					3,000 00
Inspection Milk and Vinegar Dept.					
Interest and Premium	70,128 47	55,247 20	56,486 77	141,398 25	109,962 65
Library Department	246 34	350 00	528 49	314 60	385 64
Market "	258 25	173 00	221 75	250 00	526 50
Overseeing of the Poor Department	2,455 31	3,060 26	2,161 55	2,487 58	6,866 74
Park Department					
Pedlers					24 00
Police Department	4,905 41	2,929 17	4,193 58	7,558 97	18,934 03
Public Bldgs. Dept.: Armories	3,600 00	3,600 00	3,600 00		
Miscellaneous	69 88	635 72	1,262 62	2,120 70	424 51
Public Institut'ns Dept.	30,087 93	28,841 10	27,814 16	32,563 14	38,848 25
Registry Department	1,293 00	1,094 00	1,187 50	1,353 50	1,411 00
Rents	87,806 34	87,677 82	87,360 94	86,958 77	93,993 14
School Committee	9,762 08	6,916 81	6,948 00	9,823 28	11,275 06
Sealing of Weights and Measures Dept.				2,524 16	3,274 27
Street Department: Bridge Division				62 00	221 00
Camb'ge Bridges Div.					
Paving Division	11,988 86	5,612 79	11,025 47	4,664 94	10,096 32
Sanitary "	14,803 34	12,818 75	11,932 02	13,253 84	20,147 31
Sewer "	16,660 87	10,247 57	9,992 25	9,880 39	6,735 36
Street-Cleaning Div.					
Watering Division					
Street Laying out Dept.	2,355 92			4,112 59	79,806 63
Dog Fund	1,189 00	895 00	1,036 00	1,005 00	1,053 00
Militia Bounty	8,069 40		14,923 50		
Unclaimed Drafts	2,089 66	1,094 54	1,677 97	2,937 56	1,012 24
Water-Works	372,290 67	380,568 61	400,808 36	434,254 61	463,910 91
Horse Railroads		44 00			
Lamp Department		38 75		33 66	
War Expenses		6 52		446 00	1,061 23
Salaries			22 50		
Advertising				31 25	
Public Grounds Dept.				1,039 58	1,241 15
Harbor Dredging					
City of Roxbury					
Apple Island					
Church-st. District					
Printing Department.					
Carried forward	$645,131 86	$607,046 23	$645,839 50	$763,595 16	$877,704 47

Table No. 5.— Continued.

GENERAL APPROPRIATIONS, 1860-1894.

1865-66.	1866-67.	1867-68.	1868-69.	1869-70.	
$1,432 18	$2,198 88	$2,230 16	$3,097 40	$3,194 30	City Clerk Dept.
					City Council :
333 96	148 72	148 35	....	150 00	Incidental Expenses.
....	....	....	....	....	City Messenger Dept.
....	....	....	....	1,709 20	Collecting Bank Tax.
					Collecting Dept., or
....	....	....	....	....	Tax and other Fees.
....	....	....	....	....	Conscience Fund.
....	....	....	....	....	Ferry Department.
176 02	818 79	844 12	1,114 50	1,729 83	Fire Department.
34 31	102 00	977 19	1,129 16	970 90	Hay Scales.
7,028 92	6,185 50	2,215 35	....	....	Health Department.
6,198 27	7,108 88	4,900 68	3,545 77	4,206 99	Hospital Department.
					Inspection Milk and
....	....	....	....	....	Vinegar Dept.
90,502 70	161,233 81	175,929 81	141,735 07	125,048 91	Interest and Premium.
293 92	504 18	507 72	659 85	996 63	Library Department.
649 10	541 00	514 00	338 00	332 00	Market "
					Overseeing of the Poor
6,759 15	11,549 29	16,425 81	17,177 19	18,580 79	Department.
....	....	....	....	....	Park Department.
32 00	923 00	766 00	952 00	984 00	Pedlers.
9,434 60	11,572 04	14,635 56	14,042 54	15,511 19	Police Department.
					Public Bldgs. Dept. :
12,373 78	11,814 45	11,580 80	11,150 00	10,561 78	Armories.
4,060 79	8,443 37	5,046 64	4,147 08	9,651 48	Miscellaneous.
56,477 88	73,152 22	76,001 64	95,834 24	5117,311 18	Public Institut'ns Dept.
1,488 50	1,501 00	1,679 00	1,808 00	1,947 00	Registry Department.
94,363 47	106,317 26	114,809 66	119,102 00	119,205 70	Rents.
13,575 72	15,457 33	13,024 55	9,096 68	16,941 16	School Committee.
					Sealing of Weights and
3,589 16	3,500 64	3,521 38	2,576 48	2,714 25	Measures Dept.
					Street Department :
....	....	....	....	....	Bridge Division.
....	....	....	....	....	Camb'ge Bridges Div.
3,824 94	2,896 75	4,083 56	9,104 91	13,047 82	Paving Division.
19,637 78	25,661 23	41,102 55	37,536 80	50,233 53	Sanitary "
15,241 83	21,230 06	21,134 30	40,336 01	56,149 90	Sewer "
....	....	....	....	....	Street-Cleaning Div.
....	....	....	....	....	Watering Division.
11,164 47	24,947 06	37,788 23	152,097 81	196,915 32	Street Laying out Dept.
1,725 00	1,527 00	7,536 00	4,516 00	....	Dog Fund.
12,626 50	28,998 00	46,070 30	37,849 00	80,999 18	Militia Bounty.
987 26	266 43	143 75	....	219 84	Unclaimed Drafts.
473,208 75	530,526 80	551,839 36	609,030 49	653,170 86	Water-Works.
....	....	....	....	....	Horse Railroads.
....	54 67	12 00	135 00	82 64	Lamp Department.
8,550 00	....	60 00	1,489 97	....	War Expenses.
....	....	....	....	....	Salaries.
1,025 00	1,425 00	1,212 50	1,487 44	1,320 00	Advertising.
....	580 22	14,311 66	5,400 00	9,500 00	Public Grounds Dept.
....	....	78,531 89	24,162 52	2,938 71	Harbor Dredging.
....	....	....	10 00	....	City of Roxbury.
....	....	....	8,787 87	....	Apple Island.
....	....	....	24 45	....	Church-st. District.
....	....	....	....	....	Printing Department.
$856,775 96	$1,061,185 58	$1,249,584 52	$1,359,474 23	$1,516,325 09	

REVENUE OF THE CITY. — Continued.

	1860-61.	1861-62.	1862-63.	1863-64.	1864-65.
Brought forward ..	$645,131 86	$607,046 .23	$645,839 50	$763,595 16	$877,704 47
Hospital Bld., Springfield St.					
Town of Dorchester..					
City of Charlestown ..					
Atlantic-ave. Market.					
Engineering Dept.....					
Inspection of Buildings					
Town of Brighton....					
Town of West Roxbury					
Mecantile-wharf Market.					
Boston Harbor.......					
Public Lands					
Registration of Voters Dept.					
Cover'd Channel, Stony Brook					
Covered Chan'l, Muddy River.............					
Rebate on Gas					
Board of Aldermen...					
Common Council.....					
Contingent Fund, Joint Com................					
Architect Dept.......					
Surveying Dept.					
Police, Witness Fees..					
Sales of City Property.					
Amounts formerly held under protest.......					
Everett-st. Crossing...					
County of Suffolk	84,007 74	30,418 80	46,791 75	43,158 99	64,984 09
Taxes :					
For prior years.. ..	150,656 95	191,087 70	187,585 95	154,584 48	143,656 80
Current year or general	2,328,862 39	2,191,014 70	2,702,352 82	3,243,813 35	3,952,336 02
City Bank Tax .					
Corporation Tax						391,616 26
Foreign Ships..					
Proportion of State Tax....					
Liquor Licenses (net).					
Balance of Appropriations	108,921 96	145,073 79	33,564 86		
	$3,317,580 90	$3,164,641 22	$3,616,134 88	$4,205,151 98	$5,430,297 64
Cash, beginning of fiscal year					

APPENDIX — TABLE NO. 5.

REVENUE OF THE CITY. — *Continued.*

1865-66.	1866-67.	1867-68.	1868-69.	1869-70.	
$856,775 96	$1,061,185 58	$1,249,584 52	$1,359,474 23	$1,516,325 09	
					Hospital, Bld., Springfield St.
				45,000 00	
				13,374 53	Town of Dorchester.
					City of Charlestown.
					Atlantic-ave. Market.
					Engineering Dept.
					Inspection of Buildings.
					Town of Brighton.
					Town of W. Roxbury.
					Mercantile-wharf Market.
					Boston Harbor.
					Public Lands.
					Registration of Voters Dept.
					Cover'd Channel, Stony Brook.
					Covered Chan'l, Muddy River.
					Rebate on Gas.
					Board of Aldermen.
					Common Council.
					Contingent Fund, Joint Com.
					Architect Dept.
					Surveying Dept.
					Police, Witness Fees.
					Sales of City Property.
					Amounts formerly held under protest.
					Everett-st. Crossing.
75,198 44	122,930 46	179,152 94	81,070 95	113,569 90	County of Suffolk.
					Taxes:
174,620 07	247,809 87	218,275 41	286,740 97	274,569 38	For prior years.
5,520,731 84	5,109,969 15	6,488,300 54	5,767,943 15	6,968,927 02	Current year or general
					City Bank Tax.
402,797 28	383,591 24	439,075 44	418,961 52	453.035 84	Corporati'n Tax.
					Foreign Ships. Proportion of State Tax.
			108,910 89	6,594 13	Liquor Licenses (net).
257,018 68	70,108 36	354,366 45	136 852 73	463,387 82	Balance of Appropriations.
$7,287,143 17	$6,995,594 66	$8,928,755 30	$8,159,954 44	$9,854,783 71	
					Cash, beginning of fiscal year.

REVENUE OF THE CITY. — Continued.

	1870-71.	1871-72.	1872-73.	1873-74.	1874-75.
City Clerk Dept..	$3,517 29	$3,555 75	$3,569 70	$3,727 63	$5,295 66
City Council : Incidental Expenses,	48 65	44 50	4,112 20	957 02	207 34
City Messenger Dept..					
Collecting Bank Tax .	1,257 82			7,701 17	5,158 27
Collecting Dept., or Tax and other Fees,					
Conscience Fund					
Ferry Department....	180,058 54	184,600 00	205,000 00	219,507 50	200,000 00
Fire Department	3,810 73	2,472 10	2,749 36	2,213 52	1,864 16
Hay Scales	1,210 46	1,228 80	1,446 09	1,341 75	1,160 71
Health Department...		600 00	5,585 51	5,329 23	5,947 59
Hospital Department..	5,686 88	4,393 83	3,948 64	3,591 86	3,145 92
Inspection Milk and Vinegar Dept........					
Interest and Premium,	227,213 54	98,281 05	78,883 79	162,467 19	271,158 81
Library Department ..	1,150 00	1,472 44	1,573 21	2,775 00	2,360 24
Market "	475 50				
Overseeing of the Poor Department	15,485 01	23,293 69	24,387 77	20,756 61	29,446 87
Park Department.....					
Pedlers	879 00	930 00	998 50	1,355 60	1,120 00
Police Department....	11,525 78	9,385 61	8,602 95	10,269 73	10,288 65
Public Bldgs. Dept. Armories	10,038 08	9,470 00	9,250 00	12,355 00	19,829 17
Miscellaneous	28,428 20	940 00	1,014 50	861 50	5,704 06
Public Institut'ns Dept.	114,179 21	107,444 40	98,394 03	75,831 11	67,923 67
Registry Department..	2,046 00	2,168 50	2,232 50	2,344 50	2,226 00
Rents	119,725 34	119,139 72	122,014 32	139,074 40	149,253 81
School Committee	28,900 35	26,859 98	28,113 93	30,883 73	26,220 82
Sealing of Weights and Measures Dept.	87 86	110 00	115 00		160 00
Street Department: Bridge Division ...	5 00	400 00	818 75	19 47	2,875 80
C'b'dge Bridges Div.		25 00	125 25	76 00	25 00
Paving Division ...	10,407 64	8,560 78	9,769 20	18,755 80	51,134 22
Sanitary "	48,926 58	47,358 15	40,679 25	26,303 12	36,286 77
Sewer "	51,638 22	52,318 19	54,944 82	87,676 78	81,828 30
Street-Cleaning Div.					
Watering Division..					
Street Laying outDept.	11,787 50				
Dog Fund					
Militia Bounty	46,285 50	38,038 50	72,685 92	5,257 96	
Unclaimed Drafts ...	593 83	717 83	547 20	525 85	1,767 57
Water-Works	789,123 37	841,972 82	902,022 68	989,266 86	1,013,051 02
Horse Railroads.....					
Lamp Department....	92 26	8 00	27 75	304 24	84 35
War Expenses					
Salaries					
Advertising					
Public Grounds Dept..	1,063 00	3,381 51	3,000 00	1,500 00	2,548 75
Harbor Dredging ...	12,850 00				
City of Roxbury	1,046 53	586 40	3,384 51	493 41	
Apple Island					
Church-st. District ...					
Printing Department..			48 80		121 41
Carried forward ...	$1,729,543 67	$1,589,757 55	$1,690,046 13	$1,833,523 04	$1,998,194 94

APPENDIX — TABLE No. 5. 201

REVENUE OF THE CITY. — *Continued.*

1875-76.	1876-77.	1877-78.	1878-79.	1879-80.	
$4,800 64	$5,552 81	$5,198 76	$5,000 20	$5,329 32	City Clerk Dept.
					City Council :
291 26	24 50	277 70	8,418 80	712 50	Incidental Expenses.
					City Messenger Dept.
6,950 51	6,202 55	6,030 01	5,048 98	4,839 00	Collecting Bank Tax.
					Collecting Dept., or
....	36,907 04	32,259 15	3,045 27	5,362 36	Tax and other Fees.
					Conscience Fund.
179,300 00	176,032 00	175,795 48	166,530 31	174,437 00	Ferry Department.
2,804 49	4,024 53	5,774 59	3,255 62	2,224 08	Fire Department.
1,050 93	776 12	816 46	775 37	792 44	Hay Scales.
5,397 68	3,876 09	4,782 24	12,388 04	3,666 28	Health Department.
1,349 40	5,195 78	8,117 15	7,980 42	8,472 96	Hospital Department.
					Inspection Milk and Vinegar Dept.
248,378 81	198,649 59	176,056 79	118,990 27	110,187 82	Interest and Premium.
2,505 35	3,092 12	3,266 31	2,618 32	2,984 12	Library Department.
		347 94	460 71	357 35	Market "
					Overseeing of the Poor
29,229 72	32,928 01	28,679 73	29,895 87	24,618 93	Department.
					Park Department.
1,065 50	952 00	918 00	835 00	400 00	Pedlers.
10,928 40	8,010 27	8,866 85	10,186 52	13,447 08	Police Department.
					Public Bldgs. Dept. :
18,114 00	11,233 55	18,381 44	10,200 00	10,083 34	Armories.
2,740 78	3,924 84	3,747 87	3,723 46	2,786 33	Miscellaneous.
58,453 13	49,175 27	47,239 55	79,681 83	75,270 55	Public Ins'tions Dept.
1,903 50	1,679 00	1,711 00	1,815 00	1,931 50	Registry Department.
140,120 18	130,684 66	125,857 82	122,119 92	105,505 48	Rents.
20,635 72	21,999 03	30,109 31	32,145 54	49,090 28	School Committee.
					Sealing of Weights and
134 10	824 33	9 54	....	....	Measures Dept.
					Street Department :
2,372 80	2,866 70	1,206 20	1,998 79	1,488 76	Bridge Division.
75 00	89 00	87 58	48 40	....	Camb'ge Bridges Div.
58,719 72	38,831 18	29,411 11	17,613 98	16,650 19	Paving Division.
43,581 21	55,136 33	45,035 03	37,690 57	32,583 85	Sanitary "
69,198 56	115,950 12	74,119 81	35,336 52	32,718 34	Sewer "
					Street-Cleaning Div.
					Watering Division.
					Street Laying out Dept.
					Dog Fund.
538 48	1,580 12	1,359 31	871 50	473 20	Militia Bounty.
1,095,713 14	1,002,758 85				Unclaimed Drafts.
					Water-Works.
155 37	134 17	81 29	29 50	20	Horse Railroads.
					Lamp Department.
					War Expenses.
					Salaries.
					Advertising.
					Public Grounds Dept.
					Harbor Dredging.
					City of Roxbury.
					Apple Island.
200 00	....			....	Church-st. District.
39 90	139 91	44 62	102 36	42 61	Printing Department.
$2,006,748 28	$1,019,230 47	$835,088 64	$718,807 07	$686,455 87	

REVENUE OF THE CITY. — *Continued.*

	1870-71.	1871-72.	1872-73.	1873-74.	1874-75.
Brought forward.....	$1,729,548 67	$1,589,757 55	$1,690,046 13	$1,833,523 04	$1,998,194 94
Hospital Bldg., Springfield St............					
Town of Dorchester..	11,671 15		249 00		
City of Charlestown...				143,121 96	6,826 76
Atlantic-ave. Market .				6,744 61	7,162 48
Engineering Dept.....				125 00	
Inspection of Buildings				453 40	226 62
Town of Brighton ...				3,754 89	8,575 96
Town of West Roxbury				59,865 35	3,679 56
Mercantile-wharf Market...............					
Boston Harbor					
Public Lands........					
Registration of Voters Dept...............					
Covered Chan'l, Stony Brook........					
Covered Chan'l, Muddy River					
Rebate on Gas					
Board of Aldermen ...					
Common Council.					
Contingent Fund, Joint Committee.........					
Architect Dept.....					
Surveying Dept.....					
Police, Witness Fees..					
Sales of City Property.					
Amounts formerly held under protest.......					
Everett-st. Crossing ..					
County of Suffolk ...	144,899 25	141,607 34	137,129 23	156,395 21	133,912 35
Taxes:					
For prior years...	458,085 33	583,633 87	599,734 09	780,122 58	629,079 85
Current year or general	8,209,467 12	7,160,241 14	6,884,857 14	7,885,745 25	10,895,539 93
City Bank Tax...		217,193 22	257,765 56	205,156 58	296,906 82
Corporation Tax..	436,826 78	445,025 49	428,876 66	346,995 87	354,909 48
Foreign Ships....					
Proportion of State Tax	2,102 54		2,102 54		
Liquor Licenses (net).					
Balance of Appropriations	470,923 00	257,401 08	109,747 12	238,519 59	854,332 33
	$11,463,518 84	$10,394,859 69	$10,110,507 47	$11,660,523 33	$15,189,347 08
Cash, beginning of fiscal year...........					
Grand Total					

APPENDIX — TABLE NO. 5. 203

REVENUE OF THE CITY. — *Continued.*

1875-76.	1876-77.	1877-78.	1878-79.	1879-80.	
$2,006,748 28	$1,919,230 47	$835,088 64	$718,807 07	$686,455 87	
					Hospital Bld., Springfield st.
					Town of Dorchester.
858 72	4 00			886 38	City of Charlestown.
					Atlantic-ave. Market.
					Engineering Dept.
					Inspection of B'ildings.
1,475 20		1,435 90	230 75	264 69	Town of Brighton.
					Town of West Roxb'ry.
	1,145 00	240 00			Mercantile-wharf Market.
			30 00		Boston Harbor.
					Public Lands.
					Registration of Voters Dept.
					Covered Chan'l, Stony Brook.
					Covered Chan'l, Muddy River.
					Rebate on Gas.
					Board of Aldermen.
					Common Council.
					Contingent Fund, Joint Committee.
					Architect Dept.
					Surveying Dept.
					Police, Witness Fees.
					Sales of City Property.
					Amounts formerly held under protest.
					Everett-st. Crossing.
100,687 85	106,253 09	96,933 38	62,644 02	71,544 00	County of Suffolk.
					Taxes:
1,130,443 37	1,061,989 83	829,464 77	668,629 64	568,291 56	For prior years.
9,449,113 81	8,372,284 86	8,036,536 72	7,263,419 65	6,986,240 75	Current year or general.
241,405 56	211,842 78	213,056 95	179,571 41	173,118 97	City Bank Tax.
352,738 92	301,774 48	284,075 89	294,034 93	293,501 18	Corporation Tax.
					Foreign Ships. Proportion of State Tax.
	125,000 00	182,630 32	141,138 67	159,614 10	Liquor Licenses (net).
814,553 60	577,958 77	404,387 57	658,988 66	114,159 09	Balance of Appropriations.
$14,098,020 31	$12,677,483 28	$10,883,850 14	$9,987,494 80	$9,054,076 59	
		715,164 28	712,646 42	731,509 22	Cash, beginning of fiscal year.
		$11,599,014 42	$10,700,141 22	$9,785,585 81	Grand Total.

REVENUE OF THE CITY. — Continued.

	1880-81.	1881-82.	1882-83.	1883-84.	1884-85.
City Clerk Dept.....	$3,528 50	$4,194 43	$4,334 70	$4,689 25	$6,082 75
City Council: Incidental Expenses,	568 38	664 41	125 30	209 21	523 08
City Messenger Dept..					
Collecting Bank Tax..	6,838 09	6,583 30	6,893 13	6,662 04	7,836 33
Collecting Dept., or Tax and other Fees,	4,664 55	5,334 27	5,690 90	4,733 03	4,337 53
Conscience Fund.....					
Ferry Department....	166,508 48	165,513 06	162,827 91	159,081 03	156,801 60
Fire Department	2,097 89	2,142 33	2,114 37	1,911 43	2,248 03
Hay Scales...........	770 53	795 32	877 28	626 27	600 71
Health Department ...	3,590 25	4,836 60	5,182 48	9,801 00	5,819 02
Hospital Department..	10,812 29	13,379 88	13,651 94	13,805 28	15,658 29
Inspection Milk and Vinegar Dept......					
Interest and Premium,	114,323 55	114,820 62	123,291 06	143,260 24	130,409 92
Library Department ..	3,497 03	2,945 74	3,223 14	3,018 01	2,952 68
Market "	173 46	454 78	531 31	1,007 80	538 96
Overseeing of the Poor Department........	18,541 87	15,863 59	24,222 13	20,741 85	24,022 95
Park Department.....					
Pedlers.............	325 00	500 00	350 00	700 00	500 00
Police Department...	17,951 66	18,465 63	19,834 99	22,152 65	21,582 15
Public Bldgs. Dept.:					
Armories	10,116 66	10,000 00	10,150 00	10,225 00	10,150 00
Miscellaneous	2,436 60	677 29	1,192 51	1,055 96	1,254 83
Public Institut'ns Dept.	83,818 42	99,913 05	123,201 05	110,332 85	112,993 18
Registry Department..	2,120 50	2,296 50	2,406 50	2,437 00	2,367 50
Rents	105,322 44	97,783 86	98,011 36	102,109 29	99,864 46
School Committee	71,992 43	68,500 28	72,430 36	78,304 00	38,560 76
Sealing of Weights and Measures Dept.		3,846 33	3,157 27	3,342 91	3,348 88
Street Department: :					
Bridge Division	1,688 47	1,212 31	1,211 25	703 50	575 59
Camb. Bridges Div..	94 83	163 88	94 00	150 55	224 46
Paving Division	26,536 20	30,516 26	28,807 08	27,963 30	17,821 13
Sanitary "	39,881 77	42,321 64	49,624 68	52,025 09	57,191 77
Sewer "	28,412 03	55,184 69	58,340 89	49,021 86	29,724 36
Street-Cleaning Div.					
Watering Division.					
Street Laying out Dept.					
Dog Fund					
Militia Bounty........					
Unclaimed Drafts.....	869 57	509 32	1,235 04	676 98	2,130 52
Water-Works					
Horse Railroads......					
Lamp Department....	59 65			455 87	352 46
War Expenses.......					
Salaries					
Advertising					
Public Grounds Dept..		15 00	518 00	653 97	
Harbor Dredging.....					
City of Roxbury.....				28 16	33 00
Apple Island........					
Church-st. District....					
Printing Department..	20 27	66 18	51 79	145 79	27 15
Carried forward...	$727,561 37	$769,500 55	$823,582 42	$831,981 17	$765,534 05

APPENDIX — TABLE No. 5.

REVENUE OF THE CITY. — *Continued.*

1885-86.	1886-87.	1887-88.	1888-89.	1889-90.	
$5,896 00	$5,640 55	$5,367 25	$5,892 50	$5,657 17	City Clerk Dept.
					City Council:
1,296 30	264 44	419 22	1,101 71	1,197 47	Incidental Expenses.
....	29 43	31 39	54 25	45 99	City Messenger Dept.
5,881 94	6,060 65	6,430 95	6,253 93	6,466 28	Collecting Bank Tax.
					Collecting Dept., or
4,546 33	4,435 33	4,585 52	3,970 45	1,353 40	Tax and other Fees.
....	....	....	....	500 00	Conscience Fund.
159,558 14	164,497 69	140,001 13	138,760 65	141,633 00	Ferry Department.
2,186 15	2,259 05	1,984 99	1,357 80	2,256 47	Fire Department.
643 08	812 87	702 66	789 60	925 72	Hay Scales.
7,325 68	3,758 29	4,609 96	5,899 35	4,612 50	Health Department.
35,567 36	31,365 54	34,008 54	33,665 68	38,583 62	Hospital Department.
					Inspection Milk and
....	878 00	634 00	552 90	590 00	Vinegar Dept.
111,438 32	116,894 33	148,564 38	116,969 79	137,114 76	Interest and Premium.
2,136 76	3,932 18	1,414 17	....	....	Library Department.
526 87	529 81	579 42	610 51	473 07	Market Department.
					Overseeing of the Poor
22,777 61	16,977 30	12,826 36	13,782 30	15,231 10	Department.
2 25	103 22	....	....	....	Park Department.
600 00	775 00	1,425 00	2,225 00	1,550 00	Pedlers.
20,329 32	23,814 62	25,863 75	25,994 07	12,622 75	Police Department.
					Public Bldgs. Dept.:
9,950 00	9,700 00	9,955 91	10,250 00	10,200 00	Armories.
1,176 42	1,374 87	1,901 15	2,616 39	1,156 38	Miscellaneous.
105,915 11	82,851 20	67,080 91	47,886 59	59,277 18	Public Institut'ns Dept.
2,392 50	2,619 50	2,753 50	2,853 00	2,917 50	Registry Department.
99,907 20	100,051 70	100,326 70	99,376 70	99,364 20	Rents.
30,376 07	32,678 20	36,298 56	88,349 33	38,055 52	School Committee.
					Sealing of Weights and
3,380 58	3,288 60	3,171 91	3,454 74	3,622 26	Measures Dept.
					Street Department:
520 03	571 50	515 60	443 47	425 00	Bridge Divison.
468 41	254 19	437 85	387 81	425 45	Camb. Bridges Div.
36,944 28	23,436 74	19,620 70	16,313 71	13,929 79	Paving Divison.
48,295 71	40,259 51	37,435 59	39,548 17	40,643 49	Sanitary "
127,704 66	51,039 57	26,672 42	28,751 08	43,544 44	Sewer "
....	....	....	....	....	Street-Cleaning Div.
....	....	....	....	....	Watering Division.
....	20 00	....	....	....	Street Laying out Dept.
......*...	....	....	....	....	Dog Fund.
....	....	....	....	....	Militia Bounty.
....	....	....	....	....	Unclaimed Drafts.
....	....	....	....	....	Water-Works.
....	....	....	....	....	Horse Railroads.
72 25	86 16	131 62	829 05	56 35	Lamp Department.
....	....	....	....	....	War Expenses.
....	....	....	....	....	Salaries.
....	....	....	....	....	Advertising.
1 00	1 20	82	....	....	Public Grounds Dept.
....	....	....	....	....	Harbor Dredging.
349 60	84 00	....	....	281 80	City of Roxbury.
....	....	....	....	....	Apple Island.
....	....	....	....	....	Church-st. District.
10 50	69 00	17 00	37 02	46 15	Printing Department.
$848,196 43	$731,394 24	$695,768 93	$648,797 55	$684,758 81	

REVENUE OF THE CITY. — Continued.

	1880-81.	1881-82.	1882-83.	1883-84.	1884-85.
Brought forward...	$727,561 37	$769,500 55	$823,582 42	$831,981 17	$765,534 05
Hospital Bld., Springfield st............					
Town of Dorchester ..					
City of Charlestown ..					
Atlantic-ave. Market..					
Engineering Dept. ...					
Inspection of Buildi'gs,	5 00	30 00	30 00		
Town of Brighton					
Town of W. Roxbury.					
Mercantile-wharf Market					
Boston Harbor					
Public Lands........			30 00		
Registration of Voters Department		7 48			
Cover'd Channel, Stony Brook			276 50		
Cove'd Channel, Muddy River				577 76	
Rebate on Gas.......				3,083 14	
Board of Aldermen ...					138 54
Common Council					6 50
Contingent Fund, Joint Committee					
Architect Dept.					
Surveying Dept.					
Police, Witness Fees .					
Sales of City Property,					
Amounts formerly held under protest.......					
Everett-st. Crossing...					
County of Suffolk	62,847 55	83,289 31	90,551 56	94,296 41	91,461 50
Taxes:					
For prior years. ...	502,428 31	566,915 96	520,881 50	623,879 35	548,949 57
Current year or general	8,896,757 36	8,515,620 97	9,263,483 37	9,096,627 65	10,653,369 23
City Bank Tax ...	238,741 35	229,052 53	240,175 06	225,620 02	258,387 59
Corporation Tax.	465,045 67	603,377 12	596,061 72	592,727 21	605,318 42
Foreign Ships....			7,540 63	11,698 54	16,101 61
Proportion of State Tax					
Liquor Licenses (net),	167,108 13	163,445 71	184,967 33	202,831 39	365,600 51
Balance of Appropriations	- 209,486 94	122,991 98	129,569 41	150,082 99	239,291 46
	$11,269,981 68	$11,054,261 61	$11,857,119 50	$11,833,405 63	$13,544,158 98
Cash, beginning of fiscal year	445,781 81	906,266 49	865,601 10	842,705 60	883,787 23
Grand Total	$11,715,763 49	$11,960,528 10	$12,722,720 60	$12,676,111 23	$14,427,946 21

APPENDIX — TABLE NO. 5. 207

REVENUE OF THE CITY. — Continued.

1885-86.	1886-87.	1887-88.	1888-89.	1889-90.	
8848,196 43	$731,394 24	$695,768 93	$648,977 55	8684,758 81	
					Hospital Bldg., Springfield st.
					Town of Dorchester.
					City of Charlestown.
					Atlantic Ave. Market.
					Engineering Dept.
	93 50	30 00	25 00	144 16	Inspection of Build'gs.
					Town of Brighton.
					Town of W. Roxbury.
					Mercantile Wharf Market.
					Boston Harbor.
					Public Lands.
					Registration of Voters Dept.
					Cover'd Channel, Stony Brook.
					Cover'd Chan'el, Muddy River.
					Rebate on Gas.
9 00					Board of Aldermen.
	4 97				Common Council.
30 00					Contingent Fund, Joint Com.
	62 00				Architect Dept.
			7 00	9 00	Surveying Dept.
					Police, Witness Fees.
					Sales of City Property.
					Amounts formerly held under protest.
					Everett-st. Crossing.
127,526 28	125,116 25	157,270 03	210,256 42	306,548 59	County of Suffolk.
					Taxes:
681,162 72	427,809 54	408,319 41	464,835 02	493,597 53	For prior years.
8,156,904 04	8,450,958 94	9,379,104 68	9,590,413 00	9,512,762 89	Current year or general.
185,277 76	187,069 22	198,337 99	198,167 14	195,863 71	City Bank Tax.
548,097 18	633,900 09	868,857 02	815,701 46	807,021 90	Corporation Tax.
10,777 30	9,422 31	9,025 18	8,499 90	6,567 75	Foreign Ships.
					Proportion of State Tax.
356,781 30	270,084 70	382,083 19	331,069 42	550,344 28	Liquor Licenses (net).
50,112 14	6,791 33	85,540 07	42,166 96	7,256 80	Balance of Appropriations.
$10,964,874 15	$10,842,707 09	$12,184,336 50	$12,310,118 87	$12,564,875 42	
991,111 21	769,830 36	500,977 45	197,414 95	223,421 82	Cash, beginning of fiscal year.
$11,955,985 36	$11,612,537 45	$12,685,313 95	$12,507,533 82	$12,788,297 24	Grand Total.

REVENUE OF THE CITY. — *Continued.*

	1890-91.	1891-92.	1892-93.	1893-94.
City Clerk Department	$5,655 86	$4,843 50	$6,052 25	$6,041 25
City Council:				
Incidental Expenses	725 33	285 93	305 54	30 66
City Messenger Department	40 54	43 96	31 28	29 80
Collecting Bank Tax	6,913 74	6,428 81	6,527 86	6,392 30
Collecting Department, or Tax and other Fees	9,688 78	10,475 21	12,451 86	12,192 15
Conscience Fund		54 00		25 00
Ferry Department	146,276 80	116,353 00	154,660 65	152,069 54
Fire Department	1,764 58	919 35	2,400 12	1,449 34
Hay Scales	581 63	447 42	491 44	465 21
Health Department	5,041 75	4,311 00	12,100 70	8,766 78
Hospital Department	36,445 48	51,442 29	50,375 80	54,455 15
Inspection Milk and Vinegar Department	602 50	540 50	646 00	694 00
Interest and Premium	187,621 58	114,963 24	110,324 86	117,077 25
Library Department				
Market "	622 88	340 92	484 22	581 67
Overseeing of the Poor Dept.	13,373 20	10,152 41	11,208 47	11,825 23
Park Department	2,097 88	13,608 14	2,632 44	4,769 96
Pedlers	1,025 00	1,375 00	2,000 00	1,450 00
Police Department	11,736 13	11,396 48	13,256 18	13,132 74
Public Buildings Department:				
Armories	10,850 00	11,700 00	10,900 00	10,800 00
Miscellaneous	1,800 50	1,138 55	1,437 87	1,440 25
Public Institutions Dept.	67,853 93	57,944 35	60,479 39	76,758 61
Registry Department	3,072 00	2,488 50	2,115 75	800 00
Rents	103,126 70	73,985 65	100,972 55	101,176 70
School Committee	39,128 71	29,608 38	34,799 19	36,756 75
Sealing of Weights and Measures Department	3,612 80	1,986 13	2,649 13	3,569 61
Street Department:				
Bridge Division	1,162 04	357 50	1,481 04	2,099 50
Cambridge Bridges Div.	2,120 67	316 70	581 11	752 68
Paving Division	17,834 61	12,271 60	45,402 68	9,823 83
Sanitary "	44,368 19	31,623 19	35,856 70	28,969 27
Sewer "	18,609 40	19,202 17	55,281 11	38,447 37
Street-Cleaning Division		497 00	1,585 02	2,732 62
Watering Division			100 00	110 00
Street Laying-out Department,		6,025 00		84 00
Dog Fund				
Militia Bounty				
Unclaimed Drafts				
Water-Works				
Horse Railroads				
Lamp Department	211 30		11 00	
War Expenses				
Salaries				
Advertising				
Public Grounds Department			32 50	
Harbor Dredging				
City of Roxbury	136 91			
Apple Island				
Church-st. District				
Printing Department	21 43			
Carried forward	$744,122 85	$597,125 88	$739,634 71	$706,969 22

APPENDIX — TABLE NO. 5.

REVENUE OF THE CITY. — *Concluded.*

	1890-91.	1891-92.	1892-93.	1893-94.
Brought forward............	$744,122 85	$597,125 88	$739,634 71	$706,969 22
Hospital Bldg., Springfield st....				
Town of Dorchester..........				
City of Charlestown				
Atlantic-avenue Market.......				
Engineering Department......		9,034 25		
Inspection of Buildings Dept.,	2,021 38	92 67	38 97	
Town of Brighton		30 80		
Town of West Roxbury........				
Mercantile-wharf Market......				
Boston Harbor				
Public Lands.................				
Registration of Voters Dept....				
Covered Channel, Stony Brook,				
" " Muddy River,				
Rebate on Gas				
Board of Aldermen............				
Common Council				
Contingent Fund, Joint Com...				
Architect Department.........				
Surveying Department........	10 00			
Police, Witness Fees..........	3,889 10			
Sales of City Property........			195,197 28	
Amounts formerly held under protest, Taxes, etc..........		212,526 41		
Everett-st. Crossing				13,108 31
County of Suffolk.............	205,004 89	132,853 22	161,871 88	172,639 02
Taxes:				
For prior years..............	448,623 99	515,311 80	989,493 15	866,981 06
For current year or general,	10,163,910 36	9,647,778 47	10,495,453 77	10,510,141 22
City Bank Tax	199,931 83	184,812 77	188,390 41	181,208 09
Corporation Tax	892,126 89	810,574 81	1,047,406 49	1,025,098 97
Foreign Ships	4,213 70	4,009 51	4,036 82	3,474 23
Proportion of State Tax				
Liquor Licenses (net)	599,618 10	717,218 56	707,213 64	797,128 50
Balance of Appropriations....		230,292 95		
Totals.....	$13,263,473 09	$13,061,662 10	$14,528,737 12	$14,276,748 62
Cash, beginning of fiscal year..	303,537 95	403,373 27	84,034 10	400,537 66
Grand Totals............	$13,567,011 04	$13,465,035 37	$14,612,771 22	$14,677,286 28

Table No. 6.
OPERATION OF THE TAX LIMIT. — 1885-1895.

YEAR.	Average valuation for five years, less abatements to Dec. 31 preceding.	Product of $9 law.	Extra for county purposes under the law of 1887.	Miscellaneous revenue as estimated by the City Auditor.	Total income available for department expenditures.	Interest and sinking-fund requirements as estimated by the City Auditor.	Total possible appropriations for city and county purposes.	Annual appropriation order.
1885-86...	$661,011,076	$5,949,099	.....	$2,804,550	$8,753,649	$2,171,569	$10,925,218	$10,608,100
1886-87...	670,035,172	6,030,316	.....	2,588,490	8,618,806	2,176,357	10,795,163	10,553,690
1887-88...	678,763,000	6,108,867	$425,000	2,694,800	9,228,667	2,425,465	11,654,132	11,654,094
1888-89...	694,078,430	6,246,705	425,000	2,261,080	8,932,785	2,517,522	11,450,307	11,450,307
1889-90...	711,071,286	6,399,641	425,000	2,408,090	9,232,731	2,492,510	11,725,241	11,725,241
1890-91...	733,736,943	6,603,632	425,000	2,470,240	9,498,872	2,990,942	12,489,814	12,489,814
1891-92...	761,236,068	6,851,124	425,000	2,635,390	9,911,514	2,887,916	12,799,430	12,799,430
1892-93...	790,036,144	7,110,325	425,000	2,914,675	10,450,000	3,150,420	13,600,420	13,600,420
1893-94...	819,313,202	7,373,818	425,000	2,756,590	10,555,408	2,910,219	13,465,627	13,465,627
1894-95...	850,076,262	7,650,686	425,000	2,490,000	10,565,686	2,826,068	13,391,754	13,391,754
1895-96...	876,794,390	7,891,149	425,000	2,598,665	10,914,814	3,098,229	14,013,043	.....

Table No. 7.

TAX CALCULATIONS FOR THE YEAR 1894.

CITY OF BOSTON, MAYOR'S OFFICE,
August 10, 1894.

Warrants of the City Council:		
Appropriation orders		$13,891,754 00
Deduct estimated income		2,490,000 00
Net appropriations for City and County purposes to be raised by taxation under P. S., ch. 103, sect. 34, as per Auditor's certificate of June 28, 1894:		
City	$10,034,358 00	
County	867,396 00	
		$10,901,754 00
Calculation to see if this amount is within the tax limitation laws:		
Average valuation December 31, 1893, for five preceding years, less abatements		$850,076,262 00
Percentage allowed by St. 1885, ch. 178		·009
		= $7,650,686 36
Add amount allowed for County expenses, under St. 1887, ch. 281		425,000 00
Add amount allowed for debt and interest requirements:		
City debt (St. 1885, ch. 178)	$2,628,672 00	
County debt (St. 1887, ch. 101)	197,396 00	
		2,826,068 00
Total amount allowed by law to be raised by taxation for City and County purposes		$10,901,754 36
Warrants from the Commonwealth:		
State tax, under St. 1894, ch. 510		$731,500 00
Armory assessments under St. 1888, ch. 384		28,056 27
Metropolitan sewer assessments, under St. 1889, ch. 439, and St. 1894, ch. 307		46,517 66
Grade crossing assessments, under St. 1890, ch. 428, and St. 1893, ch. 283,		5,263 04
Total State tax		$811,336 97
Total Warrants:		
City		$10,034,358 00
County		867,396 00
Total by order of the City Council		$10,901,754 00
State		811,336 97
Total amount to be raised by taxes		$11,713,090 97

Calculation of Taxes to be Assessed on Property:

	City.	County.	State.	Total.
Amount of warrants.. Deduct one-half tax on polls (P. S., ch. 11, § 48)	$10,034,358	$867,396 139,743	$811,336 97 139,743 00	$11,713,090 97 279,486 00
Total proportion of warrants to be assessed on property.. Add 4% for overlay authorized by P. S., ch. 11, § 49, and St. 1887, ch. 226	$10,034,358 401,374	$727,653 29,106	$671,593 97 26,864 00	$11,433,604 97 457,344 00
Tax to be assessed on property	$10,435,732	$756,759	$698,457 97	$11,890,948 97

Calculation of the Rate of Tax on Property:
Total valuation of real and personal property as assessed by the Board of Assessors and announced August 10, 1884 = $928,092,456.

    The city tax . . . $10,435,732 00 is . . 1.12442%
    The county tax . . . 756,759 00 is . . .08154%
    The State tax . . . 698,457 97 is . . .07526%

    The total tax . . $11,890,948 97 is   1.28122%

Rate declared August 10, 1894, as follows.
    City . . . . $11 24 in the $1,000
    County . . . . 81 " " "
    State . . . . 75 " " "

    Total . . . . $12 80 " " "

TABLE NO. 8.

ORDINARY DEPARTMENT EXPENDITURES.

1884–5 TO 1893–4.

214   VALEDICTORY ADDRESS.

Table No. 8.
ORDINARY DEPARTMENT EXPENDITURES.

	1884-85.	1885-86.	1886-87.	1887-88.
Ancient Records Department	$4,324 08	$4,002 26	$4,107 24	$3,667 95
Architect Department	14,638 09	17,792 49	18,955 06	24,344 47
Assessing Department	104,955 69	107,220 63	108,284 86	110,533 59
Auditing Department	18,319 59	20,571 62	22,998 87	23,717 59
Board of Aldermen	5,870 30	6,030 02	10,513 75	10,782 29
Soldier's Relief [1]			60,000 00	
Board of Police:	942,010 01	953,155 99	1,072,452 14	1,080,993 26
Department Expenses	942,010 01	953,155 99	1,072,452 14	1,080,993 26
Liquor Licenses, Expenses				
Police Signal Expenses				
City Clerk Department:	19,809 50	19,026 00	19,728 24	20,228 72
General Expenses	19,809 50	19,026 00	19,328 24	20,228 72
Election Expenses				
City Council:				
Contingent Fund, Joint Committees	9,074 53	10,120 51	5,078 82	11,411 97
Incidental Expenses	58,184 62	54,911 39	79,400 13	55,242 99
City Messenger Department	5,105 55	5,150 00	17,997 60	19,073 49
Clerk of Committees Department	5,820 00	5,419 16	6,702 40	7,518 84
Collecting Department	51,835 45	52,835 96	53,939 40	58,656 91
Common Council	10,991 28	11,354 88	13,339 71	13,026 36
Engineering Department	30,047 95	29,999 28	29,999 29	32,999 94
Ferry Department	234,877 56	230,209 04	189,737 51	207,652 69
Fire Department, including Inspection of Wires	696,017 15	695,104 49	713,763 74	772,989 21
Harvard Bridge Commissioners				
Health Department	109,173 37	126,269 74	114,609 20	107,667 16
Hospital Department	155,499 45	166,616 58	174,324 43	182,541 83
Inspection of Buildings Department	43,771 22	41,982 59	48,766 41	50,908 82
Inspection of Milk and Vinegar Department	3,781 94	10,467 03	8,761 55	8,994 01
Inspection of Provisions Department			363 92	2,221 15
Lamp Department:	481,001 98	499,937 50	524,923 45	573,661 15
Electric Lights	91,813 48	101,978 65	111,572 51	131,097 97
Gas	251,503 19	257,906 90	262,483 69	262,236 19
Care and Cleaning Lamps	102,115 77	103,813 86	109,812 86	121,740 91
Oil and Naphtha Lighting	5,100 34	5,253 78	5,193 29	5,468 84
Miscellaneous	30,469 20	30,984 31	35,861 10	53,117 24
Law Department	22,743 21	22,942 30	23,199 85	23,484 28
Library Department	128,396 18	117,558 03	129,081 07	126,949 85
Market Department	9,724 91	9,576 28	9,698 63	9,787 71
Mayor	7,296 85	18,105 11	21,551 74	22,853 56
Mount Hope Cemetery Department [1]	15,000 00	10,000 00	14,000 00	10,000 00
Park Department	16,049 68	20,372 03	24,220 55	21,465 44

[1] Amount paid from taxes.

APPENDIX — TABLE No. 8. 215

Table No. 8. — *Continued.*
ORDINARY DEPARTMENT EXPENDITURES.

1888-89.	1889-90.	1890-91.	9 months, 1891-92.	1892-93.	1893-94.
$4,480 61	$4,414 71	$4,515 17	$2,917 55	$2,037 50	
22,396 67	19,365 01	22,563 50	16,876 24	22,216 16	$22,338 41
109,764 50	109,293 94	114,864 22	110,639 64	140,523 90	136,934 31
23,816 11	24,044 65	25,518 25	20,163 91	27,200 00	28,700 00
14,307 48	22,333 15	22,354 31	18,879 45	25,044 13	29,336 00
15,000 00	30,000 00	42,000 00	65,000 00	82,000 00	75,000 00
1,140,346 25	1,134,867 48	1,136,102 76	876,489 35	1,143,396 62	1,280,530 02
1,140,346 25	1,134,867 48	1,136,102 76	876,489 35	1,143,396 62	1,196,498 28
					32,527 87
					51,503 87
21,082 87	21,469 44	59,005 27	60,099 63	71,998 57	78,568 87
21,082 87	21,469 44	37,069 58	21,979 70	32,915 18	33,894 40
		32,835 69	38,119 93	39,083 39	44,674 47
13,058 51	6,044 38	10,520 26	14,768 65	6,343 46	8,948 06
49,282 43	38,708 04	31,496 33	28,882 26	67,485 83	51,542 48
20,576 72	21,939 97	23,751 11	17,719 06	24,749 13	25,638 04
7,546 90	7,638 28	9,489 99	7,970 24	11,551 64	12,016 92
60,798 69	61,564 58	71,504 63	63,661 66	39,399 40	85,998 08
10,757 79	13,376 94	11,560 07	6,656 19	10,785 88	10,607 12
33,890 21	34,965 54	35,465 78	26,989 69	39,999 22	41,909 91
214,846 22	194,967 77	204,520 72	158,905 56	211,567 19	213,746 76
853,824 19	854,928 54	910,659 27	777,859 72	989,225 26	1,018,712 64
		3,159 58	1,920 44	3,141 64	
113,512 39	115,719 23	117,802 45	105,170 31	142,709 89	147,588 32
219,239 58	229,040 45	225,624 92	189,714 62	255,610 49	261,025 36
58,997 47	67,990 70	59,992 36	50,307 11	68,511 75	70,417 35
9,158 13	9,133 32	11,436 80	8,109 67	11,195 39	12,498 68
2,600 62	2,236 70	2,362 26	1,797 88	3,232 13	3,167 03
566,961 91	592,317 70	541,757 64	420,179 21	582,113 83	572,293 70
158,503 26	184,210 07	149,248 91	146,908 73	216,451 00	225,776 82
234,411 02	229,026 53	213,054 94	134,883 09	193,702 52	169,919 17
124,974 40	127,607 86	127,633 11	98,020 04	109,892 23	92,562 00
6,902 24	8,695 82	9,876 62	5,806 26	27,748 43	59,299 54
42,170 99	42,777 42	41,944 06	34,561 09	34,319 65	24,736 17
23,719 66	28,743 15	28,606 77	21,829 66	29,424 05	30,901 01
146,518 11	161,827 42	152,576 11	119,826 45	170,251 30	165,309 63
9,615 63	9,584 84	11,691 88	7,508 10	11,588 36	12,133 49
22,730 63	19,065 65	[1] 25,079 61	[1] 21,573 42	[1] 32,017 31	[2] 42,540 76
10,000 00		2,500 00	6,000 00	10,000 00	10,391 67
34,692 80	50,556 24	58,682 11	62,229 32	77,779 88	106,431 80

[1] Includes entertainment of distinguished guests.
[2] Includes entertainment of distinguished guests and expenses of Bay State gas investigation.

216 VALEDICTORY ADDRESS.

Table No. 8. — *Continued.*
ORDINARY DEPARTMENT EXPENDITURES.

	1884-85.	1885-86.	1886-87.	1887-88.
Printing Department [1]	$41,000 00	$38,500 00	$40,000 00	$47,000 00
Public Buildings Department:	162,228 28	162,550 11	131,648 21	160,229 27
General Expenses, care, repairs, etc.	118,087 80	115,224 94	77,939 58	102,091 88
Armories	26,295 66	29,123 83	29,762 25	33,229 65
Rents	17,844 82	18,201 34	23,946 38	24,907 74
Election Expenses				
Public Celebrations	19,350 24	20,424 90	19,556 46	20,343 14
Public Grounds Department	66,710 11	66,565 02	63,524 34	65,982 19
Public Institutions	505,316 31	508,468 14	525,689 41	557,697 48
Registration of Voters	26,203 75	27,858 12	28,390 02	29,503 00
Registry Department	12,233 68	12,158 07	13,087 22	13,566 29
Relief of the Poor Department	115,328 78	109,126 90	108,825 00	104,399 14
School Committee:	1,701,967 80	1,672,762 12	1,647,051 96	1,755,786 78
General Expenses	1,503,908 69	1,484,326 49	1,483,940 58	1,535,548 98
School-Houses	198,059 11	188,435 63	163,111 38	220,187 80
Sealing of Weights and Measures	9,588 26	10,088 40	11,077 35	10,364 07
Sinking-Funds Department	1,572 15	1,730 22	2,330 95	2,401 91
Street Department:	2,131,896 71	1,552,298 26	1,422,624 65	1,655,771 73
Central Office				
Bridge Division	70,328 31	76,406 72	91,941 88	98,456 74
Cambridge Bridges Division	8,397 22	6,816 50	11,172 97	6,668 98
Paving Division	1,248,415 30	791,145 32	667,199 83	821,430 61
Sanitary Division	433,424 36	431,842 73	452,125 40	503,713 86
Sewer Division	328,894 50	202,232 31	155,244 18	174,135 81
Street-Cleaning Division				
Street Police Division				
Watering	42,437 00	43,854 68	44,940 35	51,365 73
Street Laying Out Department, office expenses	12,146 02	13,879 06	13,879 06	13,685 11
Surveying Department	29,999 59	31,144 93	31,144 93	32,000 00
Treasury Department	28,953 07	28,570 10	28,570 10	32,566 23
Advertising	2,085 53	1,828 81	1,828 81	2,034 21
Election Expenses	13,899 01	12,957 02	12,957 02	12,002 91
Boston Harbor	5,481 41	3,124 82	3,124 82	6,839 31
Cedar Grove Cemetery [1]	8,825 00	4,000 00	4,000 00	
Chestnut Hill Driveway	2,997 48	3,165 38	3,166 38	
Free Concerts	2,973 05	2,980 10	2,980 10	
County of Suffolk	380,923 70	416,970 03	416,970 02	472,019 24
House of Correction	109,227 37	98,050 55	98,050 55	102,247 72
Totals	$8,595,227 44	$8,065,922 97	$8,162,063 91	$8,692,764 96

[1] Amount paid from taxes.

APPENDIX — TABLE NO. 8.   217

Table No. 8. — *Concluded.*
ORDINARY DEPARTMENT EXPENDITURES.

1888-89.	1889-90.	1890-91.	9 months. 1891-92.	1892-93.	1893-94.
$46,000 00	$46,500 00	$47,500 00	$39,000 00	$45,000 00	$45,000 00
178,871 34	175,430 69	185,747 98	162,485 78	185,369 78	157,481 27
117,357 17	117,768 48	118,134 00	108,837 33	113,303 42	82,414 08
42,770 24	38,877 09	26,604 56	14,843 46	17,770 55	17,676 43
18,743 93	18,785 12	21,092 61	20,195 90	29,432 52	30,275 00
....	....		19,916 81	18,609 09	24,863 29	27,115 76
22,201 15	25,470 51	50,486 52	26,705 11	27,479 63	35,078 13
74,282 50	83,852 62	94,248 93	82,180 54	95,200 00	82,582 09
590,655 28	577,555 71	567,442 13	419,561 34	569,603 66	606,894 92
38,994 16	50,940 30	43,033 13	34,618 60	46,089 77	45,007 04
13,883 85	14,132 60	14,494 84	8,503 28	20,068 66	32,604 52
114,984 00	110,006 69	110,269 98	75,912 01	109,615 76	112,544 78
1,847,601 26	1,898,593 88	1,946,684 03	1,500,208 29	1,988,606 15	2,011,610 24
1,595,865 09	1,653,351 76	1,684,162 03	1,295,329 02	1,766,800 62	1,821,145 18
251,736 17	245,242 12	262,522 00	204,879 27	221,805 53	190,465 06
10,423 50	10,537 61	11,690 19	9,292 90	18,316 71	19,349 73
2,448 82	2,457 51	2,416 52	1,822 30	2,324 92	2,380 87
1,901,243 01	1,659,331 15	1,950,891 26	1,794,795 67	2,177,095 87	2,174,095 35
			16,050 00	18,793 60	20,805 96
94,778 87	99,891 82	108,201 10	98,236 54	128,954 37	133,159 94
5,935 12	8,966 15	8,770 70	10,322 94	11,079 76	11,493 16
776,099 89	669,955 59	867,507 93	648,600 32	707,960 99	745,681 52
493,347 31	490,044 90	527,212 16	330,567 64	469,370 74	481,300 63
490,495 24	342,635 23	381,232 03	370,825 28	458,108 19	373,517 38
			215,464 92	288,320 42	308,707 80
			464 41		
40,586 58	47,837 46	57,967 34	104,263 62	94,507 80	99,430 16
13,754 34	13,434 44	13,580 67	10,980 76	18,916 92	17,377 67
33,495 91	35,000 00	38,271 56	29,205 98	35,193 87	48,163 39
36,049 55	37,048 70	36,775 77	28,915 67	38,583 59	39,391 50
2,168 08	2,496 24				
14,283 07	119,135 35				
3,625 14					
522,921 63	530,168 77	507,755 66	378,215 52	520,009 12	549,018 91
110,756 84	100,035 96	87,984 24	67,875 14	91,191 10	97,592 36
$9,412,166 51	$9,378,266 55	$9,687,337 54	$7,960,923 68	$10,346,765 42	$10,631,489 19

VALEDICTORY ADDRESS.

Table No. 9.
PAYMENTS FOR SALARIES AND WAGES, 1893-94.

	Heads of Departments.	Assistants.	Clerk-hire.	Wages.	Totals.
Architect Dept.	$3,500 00	$15,271 05			$18,771 05
Assessing Dept.	27,633 33	39,349 00	$57,319 00		124,301 33
Auditing Dept.	5,000 00		22,325 00		27,325 00
Board of Aldermen	18,000 00		1,260 50		19,260 50
Soldiers' Relief	3,500 00		6,018 66		9,518 66
City Clerk Dept.	5,000 00	3,800 00	19,819 36		28,619 36
City Messenger Dept.	2,991 56	12,758 74			15,750 30
Clerk of Committees Dept.	3,500 00	2,500 00	4,263 15		10,263 15
Collecting Dept.	5,000 00	42,090 22	31,975 56		79,065 78
Common Council	3,000 00		1,596 98		4,596 98
Engineering Dept.	6,000 00	28,620 89			34,620 89
Ferry Dept.	3,500 00	133,677 99	3,500 00		140,677 99
No. Ferry, Boston side, Wid'g berth		573 00			573 00
Fire Dept.	10,470 72	736,375 36	8,077 31	$20,993 55	775,916 94
Fire Alarm	3,190 72	43,989 00			47,179 72
Health Dept.	9,000 00	49,347 97	9,059 08	24,065 89	91,472 94
Hospital Dept.	4,000 00			68,425 13	72,425 13
New Bldgs., City Hospital		760 00			760 00
Improved Sewerage		8,556 24		42,862 55	51,418 79
Inspection of Bldgs. Dept.	5,000 00	44,000 00	14,690 33		63,690 33
Board of Appeal	1,035 00	299 40			1,334 40
Inspection of Milk and Vinegar Dept.	3,000 00	7,620 50			10,620 50
Inspec. of Provisions Dept.	1,700 00	733 34			2,433 34
Lamp Dept.	3,500 00		2,700 00	92,562 00	98,762 00
Law Dept.	6,000 00	22,083 32	947 56		29,030 88
Laying Out and Construction of Highways	12,500 00	44,157 50	2,500 00	125,311 60	184,469 10
Library Dept.	4,986 80	92,745 07			97,731 87
Market Dept.	3,000 00	7,581 95			10,581 95
Mayor	10,000 00		8,926 66		18,926 66
Carried forward	$164,008 13	$1,336,890 54	$194,979 15	$374,220 72	$2,070,098 54

APPENDIX — TABLE NO. 9. 219

PAYMENTS FOR SALARIES AND WAGES, 1893-94. — *Cont'd.*

	Heads of Departments.	Assistants.	Clerk-hire.	Wages.	Totals.
Brought forward ...	$164,008 13	$1,336,890 54	$194,979 15	$374,220 72	$2,070,098 54
Mt. Hope Cemetery Dept.	4,300 00	......	929 65	26,989 02	32,218 67
Overseeing of the Poor Dept.	......	24,355 00	7,900 00	......	32,255 00
Park Dept.	......	......	5,071 91	72,945 19	78,017 10
Public Parks	......	13,338 20	2,839 32	223,249 39	239,426 91
Police Dept.	12,500 00	1,126,401 91	9,379 85	17,649 71	1,165,931 47
Printing Dept.	2,991 56	......	2,299 68	......	5,291 24
Public Buildings Dept. ...	3,600 00	17,784 91	6,908 80	......	28,293 71
Public Grounds Dept. ...	3,000 00	1,800 00	1,500 00	44,111 67	50,411 67
City Nursery and Greenhouses	......	......	......	6,495 94	6,495 94
Public Institutions:					
Office Expenses ...	11,000 00	......	8,800 00	......	19,800 00
House of Industry ..	2,500 00	35,003 17	......	2,520 00	40,023 17
Lunatic Hospital ...	2,500 00	27,307 62	......	......	29,807 62
Marcella-street Home .	2,000 00	10,864 92	......	......	12,864 92
Almshouse, Charlestown	1,300 00	1,617 99	......	......	2,917 99
Home for Paupers:					
Rainsford and Long Islands	562 50	2,419 95	......	......	2,982 45
Rainsford Island ...	1,687 50	2,860 00	......	......	4,547 50
Long Island	1,330 00	6,323 69	......	......	7,653 69
Pauper Expenses ..	......	9,321 56	......	......	9,321 56
Steamer "J. Putnam Bradlee"	......	8,460 00	......	......	8,460 00
New Bldgs., Long Island .	......	......	......	180 00	180 00
New Lunatic Hospital ..	......	......	......	6,805 97	6,805 97
Registration of Voters Dept.	9,000 00	5,408 00	15,060 78	......	29,468 78
Registry Dept.	4,000 00	......	14,043 60	......	18,043 60
School Committee ...	......	1,579,688 38	11,398 50	......	1,591,086 88
Carried forward	$226,279 69	$4,209,845 84	$281,111 24	$775,167 61	$5,492,404 38

PAYMENTS FOR SALARIES AND WAGES, 1893-94. — *Cont'd.*

	Heads of Departments	Assistants.	Clerk-hire.	Wages.	Totals.
Brought forward ...	$226,279 69	$4,209,845 84	$281,111 24	$775,167 61	$5,492,404 38
Public Building, Schools .	1,400 00	6,400 00	......	......	7,800 00
Sealing of Weights and Measures	2,991 04	11,452 40	1,235 18	......	15,678 62
Sinking-Funds Dept....	......	1,400 00	700 00	......	2,100 00
Street Dept.:					
Central Office	7,500 00	6,962 78	2,599 20	......	17,061 98
Bridge Division ...	3,000 00	54,715 62	4,412 60	32,065 63	94,193 85
Camb'dge Bridges Div.......	......	3,861 00	250 00	......	4,111 00
Paving Division ...	3,500 00	16,644 51	12,412 33	306,266 53	338,823 37
Sundry Appropriations	......	5,422 71	......	190,496 23	195,918 94
Sanitary Division ..	3,000 00	......	5,511 60	299,059 05	307,570 65
Sewer Division	3,500 00	33,541 25	8,409 13	177,519 77	222,970 15
Sundry Sewers	......	566 00	......	1,831 28	2,397 28
Street-Cleaning Div. .	3,000 00	137 22	4,530 80	218,412 40	226,080 42
Watering Division ..	......	......	......	9,693 73	9,693 73
Abolishment of Grade Crossings	......	2,069 50	......	......	2,069 50
Allston Bridge......	......	119 50	......	......	119 50
Sundry Bridges	......	360 25	......	810 40	1,170 65
Street Laying Out Dept. .	9,000 00	......	2,500 00	......	11,500 00
Surveying Dept......	3,840 76	38,663 54	......	......	42,504 30
Treasury Dept.	6,000 00	......	28,300 00	......	34,300 00
Cochituate Water-Works (Supply)	7,011 11	32,121 06	14,417 69	205,447 72	258,997 58
Cochituate Water-Works (Income)	3,600 00	43,166 99	......	......	46,766 99
Add'l Supply of Water ..	......	2,965 22	......	63,414 39	66,379 61
Extension of Mains, etc. .	......	1,099 98	......	73,102 26	74,202 24
High Service	......	......	......	540 95	540 95
Mystic Water-Works (Supply)...........	4,006 40	8,072 85	2,594 44	83,652 70	98,326 39
Carried forward	$287,629 00	$4,479,588 22	$368,984 21	$2,437,480 65	$7,573,682 08

APPENDIX — TABLE No. 9. 221

PAYMENTS FOR SALARIES AND WAGES, 1893-94. —*Concluded.*

	Heads of Departments.	Assistants.	Clerk-hire.	Wages.	Totals.
Brought forward	$287,629 00	$4,479,588 22	$368,984 21	$2,437,480 65	$7,573,682 08
Mystic Water-Works (Income)				9,870 72	9,870 72
Library Building, Dartmouth street				4,714 50	4,714 50
Buildings, Gallop's Island and Swett street		60 00			60 00
	$287,629 00	$4,479,648 22	$368,984 21	$2,452,065 87	$7,588,327 30

Table No. 10.

PAYMENTS FOR PENSIONS, ETC.

	Fire Department.	Police Department.	Police Charitable Fund.
1872-73			$21 50
1873-74			20 00
1874-75			300 00
1875-76			839 00
1876-77			1,531 00
1877-78			1,910 00
1878-79			¹8,109 00
1879-80		$3,040 00	²14,232 75
1880-81		14,259 00	4,705 00
1881-82		15,544 00	5,300 00
1882-83		20,945 94	5,660 00
1883-84		22,936 24	6,690 00
1884-85	$595 50	25,577 98	7,265 00
1885-86	1,775 00	27,872 67	7,940 00
1886-87	1,905 00	28,696 46	8,485 00
1887-88	1,992 86	29,235 16	8,845 00
1888-89	3,641 28	29,770 36	9,035 00
1889-90	8,175 02	31,407 92	9,060 00
1890-91	12,348 05	31,459 96	7,445 00
1891-92	10,360 42	23,883 17	8,411 34
1892-93	13,524 89	31,632 68	8,830 00
1893-94	23,415 48	64,303 55	9,175 00
	$77,733 50	$400,565 09	³$133,809 59

1 Five pension rolls, $5,609, paid from this amount.
2 Nine pension rolls, $7,980, paid from this amount.
3 Paid from fees of police officers, earned in municipal courts.

APPENDIX — TABLE NO. 11.

Table No. 11.

WAR PAYMENTS.

	Expenditures.	Receipts.		Expenditures.	Receipts.
Recruiting:			*Brought forward*	$4,675,071 45	$2,258,981 34
1862-63	$937,012 26	$42,350 00	1875-76	84,219 50	86,100 00
1863-64, State			1876-77	82,225 36	81,900 00
Bounty Tax,	255,365 52	64,296 00	1877-78	81,629 51	84,254 57
1863-64	513,026 41		1878-79	119,981 12	79,730 88
1864-65	549,050 43	150,086 84	1879-80	91,445 66	109,498 00
1867-68		60 00	1880-81	99,020 21	81,819 50
1868-69		1,489 97	1881-82	100,310 55	78,610 00
			1882-83	97,276 61	80,567 50
Other Expenses:			1883-84	92,475 79	83,538 68
1861-62	90,151 63	6 52	1884-85	94,134 31	80,505 07
1862-63	15,856 53		1885-86	97,052 74	75,625 50
1863-64	33,010 34		1886-87	96,911 46	78,619 00
1864-65	19,457 60	1,061 23	1887-88	99,516 82	79,671 00
1865-66	23,371 13	8,580 00	1888-89	105,254 35	82,030 50
1866-67	19,795 05		1889-90	115,726 75	85,966 00
1867-68	7,750 98		1890-91	137,095 56	90,910 75
1868-69	1,959 00		1891-92	120,007 54	102,273 00
1869-70	900 50		1892-93	177,520 01	109,778 62
1870-71	52 00		1893-94	182,516 59	142,974 48
1886-87	40,000 00				
			Burial Expenses,		
Soldiers' Relief:			chap. 395,		
1861-62	129,309 00	479 12	Acts 1889:		
1862-63	309,553 09	61,071 02	1889-90	1,772 00	
1863-64	297,328 33	257,066 51	1890-91	2,247 50	
1864-65	293,987 67	310,759 87	1891-92	2,647 50	932 25
1865-66	117,469 30	290,007 28	1892-93	3,968 00	1,177 50
1866-67	257,407 60	164,000 00	1893-94	4,818 02	1,845 00
1867-68	109,179 79	205,000 00			
1868-69	108,709 95	145,387 63		$6,764,844 91	$3,957,309 14
1869-70	102,845 29	102,500 00			
1870-71	96,564 20	99,043 00	Gross Expendi-		
1871-72	89,942 41	95,500 00	tures	$6,764,844 91	
1872-73	83,940 45	87,700 00	Gross Receipts..		3,957,309 14
1873-74	83,435 12	81,600 00			
1874-75	88,639 87	90,936 35	Net Expenses,	$2,807,535 77	
Carried forward	$4,675,071 45	$2,258,981 34			

Table No. 12.

SURPLUS REVENUE,

and its Disposition at Close of each Fiscal Year.

	Amount.	Disposition of.	Authority.
1822–3	$16,589 67	Carried forward	
1823–4	16,468 24	"	
1824–5	51,655 40	"	
1825–6	14,516 32	"	
1826–7	35,640 02	Sinking-Fund	Order City Council, April 23, 1827.
1827–8	1,617 50	"	"
1828–9	Deficit	$3,688 12	
1829–30	"	9,762 59	
1830–1	"	5,134 61	
1831–2	218 82	Sinking-Fund	"
1832–3	669 74	"	"
1833–4	3,591 57	"	R. O. of 1834, chap. 51, sects. 3 and 4.
1834–5	333 92	"	"
1835–6	14,381 41	"	"
1836–7	12,268 57	"	"
1837–8	59,730 98	"	"
1838–9	73,178 89	"	"
1839–40	196 27	"	"
1840–1	5,741 95	"	"
1841–2	19,531 68	"	"
1842–3	46,205 63	"	"
1843–4	74,870 67	"	"
1844–5	130,872 56	"	"
1845–6	131,723 60	"	"
1846–7	35,400 08	"	"
1847–8	213 30	"	"
1848–9	Deficit	$27,758 85	
1849–50	9,553 91	Sinking-Fund	
1850–1	60,391 51	"	R. O. of 1850 on Finance, sects. 9 and 10.
1851–2	5,605 59	"	"
1852–3	122,912 66	"	"
1853–4	157,343 79	"	"
1854–5	161,667 53	"	"
1855–6	47,937 23	"	"
1856–7	81,645 44	"	R. O. of 1856 on Finance, sects. 9 and 10.
1857–8	85,064 71	"	"
1858–9	289,175 64	"	"
1859–60	297,515 63	"	"
1860–1	263,150 90	"	"
1861–2	202,721 22	"	"
1862–3	227,337 38	"	"
1863–4	149,481 89	"	R. O. of 1863 on Finance, sects. 9 and 10.
1864–5	151,889 08	"	"
1865–6	1,064,348 17	"	"
1866–7	1,101,760 66	"	"
1867–8	1,096,546 14	"	"
1868–9	1,067,878 44	"	"
1869–70	1,272,139 14	"	R. O. of 1869 on Finance, sects. 9 and 10.

APPENDIX — TABLE No. 12. 225

Table No. 12. — *Concluded*.

SURPLUS REVENUE,
and its Disposition at Close of each Fiscal Year.

	Amount.	Disposition of.	Authority.
1870–1	$1,156,660 84	Sinking-Fund	R. O. of 1869 on Finance, sect. 9, and Ord. of Dec. 24, 1870.
1871–2	894,116 69	"	R. O. of 1869, and Ord. of Dec. 24, 1870.
1872–3	249,475 47	"	"
1873–4	612,002 95	"	"
1874–5	742,084 08	"	"
1875–6	993,595 31	"	"
1876–7	715,164 28	Remained in Treasury for the benefit of the appropriations of the next year.	Ord. on Finance, Mar. 27, 1877, sect. 2.
1877–8	712,646 42	"	"
1878–9	713,509 22	"	"
1879–80	445,781 81	"	"
1880–1	906,266 49	"	"
1881–2	865,601 10	"	"
1882–3	842,705 60	"	R. O. of 1883, chap. 15, sect. 10.
1883–4	883,787 23	"	"
1884–5	991,111 21	"	"
1885–6	769,830 36	"	R. O. of 1885, chap. 15, sect. 9.
1886–7	500,977 45	"	"
1887–8	197,414 95	"	"
1888–9	223,421 82	"	"
1889–90	303,537 95	"	R. O. of 1890, chap. 10, sect. 5.
1890–1	403,373 27	"	"
1891–2	84,034 10	"	"
1892–3	400,537 66	"	R. O. of 1892, chap. 39, sect. 5.
1893–4	89,291 28	"	"

Table No. 13.

TOTAL EXPENDITURES

Of the City of Boston and County of Suffolk, Exclusive of Debt and Temporary Loans Redeemed, from 1855 to 1894.

Year.	Interest on Debt and Temporary Loan.	State Tax.	Other City Expenditures.	Total actual Expenditure on account of City.	County.	Total.
1855-56	$365,934 86	$148,036 50	$2,094,975 18	$2,608,946 54	$187,437 09	$2,796,383 63
1856-57	378,220 57	155,509 95	2,309,926 82	2,843,657 34	191,422 26	3,035,079 60
1857-58	399,481 68	337,945 05	2,795,548 27	3,532,975 00	207,252 91	3,740,227 91
1858-59	440,615 40	107,608 44	2,661,178 83	3,209,402 67	190,112 60	3,399,515 27
1859-60	448,714 99	98,694 00	2,823,484 35	3,370,893 34	207,478 40	3,578,371 74
1860-61	446,026 31	82,245 00	2,879,970 44	3,408,241 75	174,850 24	3,583,091 99
1861-62	463,119 04	94,575 00	2,710,732 66	3,268,426 70	170,225 21	3,438,651 91
1862-63	688,861 67	¹578,270 56	3,782,979 34	5,050,111 57	153,594 98	5,203,706 55
1863-64	824,068 34	²1,269,626 41	3,000,767 61	5,094,462 36	152,867 32	5,247,329 68
1864-65	1,505,144 71	756,600 00	3,752,200 35	6,013,945 06	146,619 60	6,160,564 66
1865-66	1,889,397 69	1,592,501 00	3,866,973 09	6,348,871 78	173,050 06	6,521,921 84
1866-67	1,035,145 74	1,016,490 00	4,276,046 93	6,327,682 67	205,937 10	6,533,619 77
1867-68	1,277,278 13	1,694,150 00	5,128,986 84	8,100,414 97	233,245 65	8,333,660 62
1868-69	1,152,377 79	723,140 00	7,614,331 26	9,489,849 05	226,488 17	9,716,337 26
1869-70	1,179,688 64	903,925 00	10,467,741 61	12,551,335 25	314,840 81	12,866,176 01
1870-71	1,500,433 36	933,775 00	9,789,982 87	12,224,191 23	272,342 38	12,496,533 62
1871-72	1,560,489 26	933,775 00	9,650,712 08	12,144,976 34	271,941 38	12,416,917 70
1872-73	1,859,283 56	736,480 00	11,991,630 39	14,587,393 95	337,526 95	14,924,920 98
1873-74	2,279,394 06	828,540 00	15,133,971 71	18,241,909 77	310,702 71	18,552,612 48
1874-75	2,671,496 12	802,120 00	11,542,694 17	15,016,310 29	372,321 99	15,388,632 21
1875-76	2,607,933 20	802,120 00	11,704,336 52	15,114,389 72	361,510 29	15,475,900 09
1876-77	2,572,057 28	742,932 00	10,805,276 07	14,120,265 35	345,976 34	14,466,241 68
1877-78	2,461,600 59	619,110 00	10,434,694 47	13,515,405 06	328,646 92	13,844,051 91
1878-79	2,352,160 26	412,740 00	9,413,015 15	12,177,915 41	327,833 50	12,505,748 90
1879-80	2,377,050 59	206,370 00	9,320,836 79	11,904,257 38	296,140 82	12,200,308 20
1880-81	2,220,171 43	619,110 00	10.252,967 39	13,092,248 82	305,871 68	13,398,120 58
1881-82	2,188,564 72	619,110 00	10,422,476 44	13,230,151 16	338,261 12	13,568,412 28
1882-83	2,184,580 49	825,480 00	11,879,562 33	14,889,622 82	362,908 06	14,252,530 81
1883-84	2,227,045 73	578,055 00	12,852,436 08	15,657,536 81	368,352 40	16,025,889 21
1884-85	2,238,518 17	770,740 00	12,456,798 17	15,466,056 34	393,785 77	15,859,842 21
1885-86	2,242,102 19	578,055 00	11,480,449 18	14,300,606 37	852,613 93	15,153,220 30
1886-87	2,237,479 04	555,870 00	11.542,638 27	14,335,987 31	990,056 20	15,335,043 51
1887-88	2,315,833 49	833,805 00	12,920,866 74	16,070,505 23	1,086,026 43	17,156,531 66
1888-89	2,324,476 50	833,805 00	12,974,131 56	16,132,413 06	1,334,640 21	17,467,053 27
1889-90	2,353,785 54	738,420 00	13,508,467 28	16,600,272 82	1,265,160 36	17,865,433 18
1890-91	2,447,882 87	645,767 50	14,585,464 60	17,679,114 97	1,133,121 18	17,812,236 15
Nine mos. ending Jan. 31, 1892	1,764,671 04	553,515 00	13,856,842 03	16,195,028 07	777,496 32	16,972,524 39
1892-93	2,522,587 58	640,062 50	16,954,626 31	20,117,276 39	1,183,388 65	21,300,665 04
1893-94	2,476,430 94	914,375 00	17,287,020 68	20,677,826 62	1,019,172 73	21,696,999 35

¹ Including $221,262.00, National direct tax assumed and paid by the State.
² Including $513,026.41, State Bounty Tax.

Table No. 14.

TOTAL DEBT ISSUED

In each Financial Year between 1822 and 1865-66, and in each Calendar Year since 1865-66.

1822 (town debt),	$100,000 00	1858-9	. . .	$1;232,950 00
1822-3	. . . 3,550 00	1859-60	. . .	735,800 00
1823-4	. . . 103,500 00	1860-1	. . .	992,700 00
1824-5	. . . 283,257 75	1862-3	. . .	1,604,850 00
1825-6	. . . 318,685 32	1863-4	. . .	850,000 00
1826-7	. . . 873,475 00	1864-5	. . .	639,709 80
1827-8	. . . 181,000 00	1865-6	. . .	712,150 00
1828-9	. . . 147,250 00	1866	. . . .	1,499,000 00
1829-30	. . . 295,480 75	1867	. . . .	1,037,175 00
1830-1	. . . 281,000 00	1868	. . . .	2,937,000 00
1831-2	. . . 199,743 18	1869	. . . .	531,500 00
1832-3	. . . 466,592 53	1870	. . . .	3,561,500 00
1833-4	. . . 593,044 00	1871	. . . .	5,238,000 00
1834-5	. . . 744,626 69	1872	. . . .	2,981,000 00
1835-6	. . . 707,186 03	1873	. . . .	7,255,176 65
1836-7	. . . 359,304 65	1874	. . . .	4,478,500 00
1837-8	. . . 217,300 00	1875	. . . .	2,206,200 00
1838-9	. . . 283,200 00	1876	. . . .	3,533,300 00
1839-40	. . . 478,332 56	1877	. . . .	667,000 00
1840-1	. . . 345,000 00	1878	. . . .	1,349,000 00
1841-2	. . . . . .	1879	. . . .	1,890,000 00
1842-3	. . . . . .	1880	. . . .	2,701,000 00
1843-4	. . . . . .	1881	. . . .	123,000 00
1844-5	. . . 11,566 62	1882	. . . .	2,078,500 00
1845-6	. . . 109,653 16	1883	. . . .	3,278,500 00
1846-7	. . . 297,860 32	1884	. . . .	1,837,500 00
1847-8	. . . 1,419,683 39	1885	. . . .	1,742,700 00
1848-9	. . . 1,085,367 51	1886	. . . .	3,838,800 00
1849-50	. . . 528,371 23	1887	. . . .	3,324,700 00
1850-1	. . . 1,195,285 00	1888	. . . .	1,529,800 00
1851-2	. . . 1,180,513 05	1889	. . . .	3,784,000 00
1852-3	. . . 2,044,711 11	1890	. . . .	5,462,000 00
1853-4	. . . 944,118 00	1891	. . . .	2,716,500 00
1854-5	. . . 306,400 00	1892	. . . .	2,642,800 00
1855-6	. . . 158,100 00	1893	. . . .	6,115,525 00
1856-7	. . . 431,900 00	1894	. . . .	5,808,800 00
1857-8	. . . 1,168,400 00			

Table No. 15.

THE SINKING-FUNDS TO 1871.

Receipts of Committee on Reduction of Debt from 1827 to April 30, 1871.

Fiscal Year.	Sales of Land, Rents, etc.	Interest.	Unexpended Balances, etc.	Taxes.	Miscellaneous.	Total.
1827-28	$45,407 43	$486 59	$35,640 02	$15,000 00	....	$96,534 04
1828-29	30,785 00	....	1,617 50	15,000 00	....	47,402 50
1829-30	44,260 81	....	4,530 61	20,000 00	....	68,791 42
1830-31	24,678 55	....	5,438 80	15,000 00	....	45,117 35
1831-32	42,414 56	....	865 39	20,000 00	....	63,279 95
1832-33	18,159 71	....	218 82	20,000 00	....	38,378 53
1833-34	37,872 24	....	669 74	15,000 00	....	53,541 98
1834-35	74,253 30	....	3,591 57	15,000 00	....	92,844 87
1835-36	58,631 49	....	333 92	15,000 00	....	73,965 41
1836-37	29,012 24	....	14,381 41	15,000 00	....	58,393 65
1837-38	18,393 67	....	12,268 57	15,000 00	....	45,662 24
1838-39	20,152 44	....	59,730 98	15,000 00	....	94,883 42
1839-40	14,182 77	....	73,178 89	45,000 00	....	132,361 66
1840-41	15,578 92	....	5,938 22	45,000 00	....	66,517 14
1841-42	20,968 48	....	19,531 68	50,000 00	....	90,500 16
1842-43	15,414 20	....	46,205 63	50,000 00	....	111,619 83
1843-44	86,406 79	....	74,870 67	50,000 00	....	211,277 46
1844-45	112,643 93	....	61,706 60	50,000 00	....	224,350 53
1845-46	192,138 18	....	11,306 41	50,000 00	....	253,444 59
1846-47	171,386 19	....	35,400 08	50,000 00	....	256,786 27
1847-48	93,749 42	....	213 30	50,000 00	*$250 00	144,212 72
1848-49	89,863 99	....	....	50,000 00	....	139,863 99
1849-50	64,476 58	....	9,553 91	50,000 00	....	124,030 49
1850-51	89,719 12	....	78,329 50	50,000 00	....	218,048 62
1851-52	67,076 43	....	5,605 59	55,000 00	....	127,682 02
1852-53	190,141 68	....	122,912 66	54,000 00	....	367,054 34
1853-54	263,036 37	....	157,343 79	59,000 00	....	479,380 16
1854-55	163,388 32	....	161,667 53	60,000 00	†3,666 34	388,722 19
1855-56	191,917 18	....	47,937 23	60,000 00	....	299,854 41
1856-57	172,684 98	....	81,645 44	60,000 00	....	314,330 42
1857-58	224,210 25	....	85,064 71	80,000 00	....	389,274 96
1858-59	303,970 61	....	289,175 64	105,000 00	....	698,146 25
1859-60	234,866 99	....	297,515 63	220,000 00	....	752,382 62
1860-61	205,524 35	....	263,150 90	220,000 00	....	688,675 25
1861-62	82,959 75	....	202,721 22	300,000 00	....	585,680 97
1862-63	255,959 73	....	227,337 38	200,000 00	....	683,297 11
1863-64	48,864 27	....	149,481 89	300,000 00	....	498,346 16
1864-65	85,244 17	....	151,889 08	300,000 00	....	537,133 25
1865-66	67,468 10	....	1,064,348 17	350,000 00	....	1,481,816 27
1866-67	101,762 10	26,856 85	1,101,760 66	360,000 00	....	1,590,379 61
1867-68	136,732 09	77,626 74	1,096,546 14	400,000 00	....	1,710,904 97
1868-69	174,346 23	232,389 52	1,067,878 44	417,000 00	....	1,891,614 19
1869-70	170,782 79	267,520 50	1,272,139 14	577,000 00	....	2,287,392 43
1870-71	814,149 36	280,499 42	1,156,660 84	719,000 00	....	2,970,309 62
	$5,366,585 76	$885,379 62	$9,558,304 30	$5,681,000 00	$3,916 34	$21,494,186 02

* Discount on debt purchased.   † C. W. Works.

TABLE NO. 16.

ADDITIONS TO THE SINKING-FUNDS FOR THE CITY AND COUNTY DEBT, SINCE 1871.

Table No. 16.
ADDITIONS TO THE SINKING-FUNDS
[SINCE THE ESTABLISHMENT OF THE BOARD

Fiscal Year.	Premium on Loans.	Sales of Land, Betterments, Assessments, etc.	Interest on Investments.	Interest on Bank Deposits.	Unexpended Balances of Appropriations and Excess of Income.
Apl. 30, 1871..		Received from the Committee on Reduction of Debt.........			
1871-72	....	$832,790 59	$424,154 62	$84,321 61	$885,116 69
1872-73	....	873,165 14	576,492 00	48,760 31	219,385 47
1873-74	....	724,262 21	652,113 92	25,058 16	536,029 67
1874-75	....	1,243,183 43	736,360 70	31,202 75	676,530 08
1875-76	....	915,138 89	732,203 71	35,878 64	758,781 31
1876-77	....	887,916 63	747,513 23	45,945 44	....
1877-78	....	563,067 25	691,691 84	53,551 93	....
1878-79	....	417,329 23	675,666 37	36,885 58	....
1879-80	....	201,757 74	676,828 29	32,036 13	....
1880-81	....	263,247 75	644,182 56	8,476 60	....
1881-82	....	403,187 87	630,730 52	39,222 14	....
1882-83	....	176,471 17	647,446 16	35,682 52	....
1883-84	$224,777 00	369,166 46	661,485 78	24,094 00	....
1884-85	....	271,003 71	639,227 29	44,188 53	....
1885-86	....	123,579 89	642,012 33	39,853 46	....
1886-87	70,860 00	99,426 62	659,528 45	22,501 92	....
1887-88	....	115,416 28	681,743 16	41,869 50	....
1888-89	129,106 80	159,720 11	627,915 10	60,210 94	....
1889-90	102,140 04	70,039 62	588,597 71	71,500 56	....
1890-91	43,521 20	34,581 01	645,699 93	74,599 65	....
1891-92	14,120 00	59,020 59	486,986 93	49,929 98	....
1892-93	115,696 10	64,087 28	618,601 36	112,332 26	....
1893-94	74,060 43	167,037 74	532,920 21	52,107 13	....

Table No. 16. — *Concluded.*
FOR THE CITY AND COUNTY DEBT.
OF SINKING-FUND COMMISSIONERS IN 1871.]

Unexpended Balances from Loans.	Interest on Redeemed Sterling Debt.	Appropriation Orders. Taxes.	Miscellaneous.	Total.	Fiscal Year.
....	....	....	....	$9,553,734 83	Apl. 30, 1871
....	....	$68,250 00	....	2,294,633 51	1871-72
....	....	....	....	1,717,802 92	1872-73
....	....	....	[1] $55,958 29	1,993,422 25	1873-74
....	$23,788 75	....	....	2,711,065 71	1874-75
....	7,263 06	....	[2] 130,000 00	2,579,265 61	1875-76
....	5,700 00	....	....	1,687,075 30	1876-77
....	32,172 78	458,200 00	....	1,798,683 80	1877-78
$312,801 85	19,582 75	457,447 00	....	1,919,712 78	1878-79
....	22,087 46	495,704 00	....	1,428,413 62	1879-80
....	23,581 59	593,655 00	....	1,533,143 50	1880-81
....	26,285 98	702,928 00	....	1,802,354 51	1881-82
....	27,719 76	668,371 00	....	1,555,690 61	1882-83
116,608 90	33,454 89	756,991 00	....	2,186,578 03	1883-84
11,688 37	33,454 89	758,856 00	....	1,758,418 79	1884-85
....	40,623 80	643,938 00	....	1,490,007 48	1885-86
180 84	44,925 14	548,134 00	....	1,445,556 97	1886-87
....	44,925 13	749,107 00	....	1,633,061 07	1887-88
....	52,094 04	808,930 00	....	1,837,976 99	1888-89
....	40,145 87	882,272 00	....	1,754,695 80	1889-90
....	45,881 00	1,230,634 00	....	2,074,916 79	1890-91
....	48,748 55	1,459,161 00	....	2,117,967 05	1891-92
....	84,115 15	1,277,392 00	[3] 50,166 21	2,322,390 36	1892-93
....	106,099 79	1,222,219 00	....	2,154,444 30	1893-94
				$53,351,012 58	

[1] From City of Charlestown.

Table No. 17.
FUNDED DEBT, GROSS AND NET, AT THE CLOSE OF EACH FISCAL YEAR.

	Gross Funded Debt.	Means of Redemption.	Net Funded Debt.
April 30, 1822	$100,000 00		$100,000 00
May 31, 1823	103,550 00	$3,267 27	100,282 73
" 1824	207,050 00	3,254 61	203,795 39
" 1825	305,873 85		305,873 85
April 30, 1826	364,800 32	145,980 93	218,819 39
" 1827	1,011,775 00	299,096 38	712,678 62
" 1828	949,350 00	279,124 85	670,225 15
" 1829	911,850 00	267,505 76	644,344 24
" 1830	891,930 75	228,028 30	663,902 45
" 1831	880,330 75	264,095 69	616,235 06
" 1832	817,123 93	175,734 75	641,389 18
" 1833	940,358 28	168,094 70	772,263 58
" 1834	1,078,088 28	153,636 46	924,451 92
" 1835	1,147,398 97	102,075 55	1,045,323 42
" 1836	1,264.400 00	182,245 56	1,082,154 44
" 1837	1,497,200 00	217,955 45	1,279,244 55
" 1838	1,491,400 00	97,436 60	1,393,963 40
" 1839	1,596,600 00	93,931 59	1,502,668 41
" 1840	1,698,232 56	171,439 31	1,526,793 25
" 1841	1,663,800 00	90,349 56	1,573,450 44
" 1842	1,594,700 00	88,930 79	1,505,769 21
" 1843	1,518,700 00	134,389 31	1,384,310 69
" 1844	1,423,800 00	302,149 09	1,121,650 91
" 1845	1,613,266 62	378,400 45	784,866 17
" 1846	1,153,713 16	717,610 79	436,102 37
" 1847	1,296,626 98	800,977 82	495,649 16
" 1848	3,452,606 37	478,213 28	2,974,393 09
" 1849	5,334,846 54	388,396 02	4,946,450 52
" 1850	6,195,144 35	310,259 40	5,884,884 95
" 1851	6,801,541 35	473,634 98	6,327,906 87
" 1852	7,110,679 70	489,065 22	6,621,614 48
" 1853	7,859,435 66	872,674 15	6,986,761 51
" 1854	7,799,855 32	1,411,858 00	6,387,997 32
" 1855	7,151,149 77	1,042,977 90	6,108,171 87
" 1856	7,107,149 77	1,088,483 92	6,018,665 85
" 1857	7,259,299 77	1,054,976 27	6,204,323 50
" 1858	8,101,199 77	1,108,147 09	6,993,052 68
" 1859	8,954,649 77	1,331,565 05	7,623,084 72
" 1860	8,491,599 77	967,175 69	7,524,424 08
" 1861	8,894,499 77	988,922 61	7,905,577 16
" 1862 — War debt included this year and after	9,031,207 77	851,659 08	8,179,548 69
" 1863	10,335,857 77	1,190,901 13	9,144,956 64
" 1864	11,015,732 77	1,463.187 67	9,552,545 10
" 1865	11,371,942 57	1,621,255 41	9,750,687 16
" 1866	11,892,375 91	3,039,590 32	8,852,785 59
" 1867	12,998,559 91	4,440,278 32	8,558,281 59
" 1868 — Roxbury debt included	14,011,656 91	5,199,369 72	8,812,287 19
" 1869	16,959,500 91	6,869,989 11	10,089,511 80

APPENDIX — TABLE NO. 17. 233

Table No. 17. — *Concluded.*

FUNDED DEBT, GROSS AND NET, AT THE CLOSE OF EACH FISCAL YEAR.

		Gross Funded Debt.	Means of Redemption.	Net Funded Debt.
April 30,	1870 — Dorchester debt included	$18,687,350 91	$9,215,831 25	$9,471,519 66
"	1871	26,472,916 80	11,632,959 91	14,839,956 89
"	1872	28,628,535 82	12,849,159 31	15,779,376 51
"	1873	30,553,116 80	13,926,777 92	16,626,338 88
"	1874 — Charlestown, Brighton, and W. Roxbury debts included	42,890,785 77	15,417,572 75	27,473,213 02
"	1875	43,414,829 99	16,218,402 92	27,196,427 07
"	1876	43,848,835 73	16,880,387 41	26,967,448 32
"	1877	43,590,497 30	16,109,973 55	27,480,523 75
"	1878	42,457,022 47	16,297,245 80	26,159,776 67
"	1879	42,359,816 23	16,130,150 42	26,229,665 81
"	1880	42,030,125 36	14,188,021 08	27,842,104 28
"	1881	40,949,332 18	14,943,711 59	26,005,620 59
"	1882	40,079,312 04	15,901,650 44	24,177,661 60
"	1883	41,184,358 12	16,422,541 43	24,761,816 69
"	1884	43,185,669 07	16,933,174 61	26,252,494 46
"	1885	42,962,180 02	18,365,600 11	24,596,579 91
"	1886 — County debt included	43,628,322 04	18,915,502 44	24,712,819 60
"	1887	46,799,962 72	20,312,079 64	26,487,883 08
"	1888	48,993,803 45	21,632,559 02	27,361,244 43
"	1889	49,920,475 25	22,266,285 21	27,654,190 04
"	1890	53,930,095 22	22,854,262 88	31,075,832 24
"	1891	55,861,980 06	24,519,341 59	31,342,638 47
Jan. 31,	1892	56,003,997 35	25,569,706 32	30,924,699 70
"	1893	56,908,148 04	25,983,448 34	30,908,879 24
"	1894	54,418,535 36	20,908,860 58	33,509,674 78

Table No. 18.
FUNDED DEBT, GROSS AND NET,
At Close of Each Calendar Year.

	Gross Debt.	Means of Redemption.	Net Debt.
Dec. 31, 1855	$7,195,649 77	$1,172,846 26	$6,022,803 51
" 31, 1856	7,110,249 77	1,151,477 85	5,958,771 92
" 31, 1857	7,967,499 77	1,233,862 82	6,733,636 95
" 31, 1858	9,163,049 77	1,264,415 14	7,898,634 63
" 31, 1859	9,219,599 77	1,774,272 97	7,445,326 80
" 31, 1860	9,236,299 77	1,192,435 48	8,043,864 29
" 31, 1861	9,149,499 77	1,222,053 94	7,927,445 83
" 31, 1862	10,392,207 77	1,028,027 18	9,364,180 59
" 31, 1863	10,193,732 77	1,307,078 27	8,886,654 50
" 31, 1864	11,380,232 77	1,597,034 69	9,783,198 08
" 31, 1865	11,686,375 91	2,065,776 51	9,620,599 40
" 31, 1866	12,845,375 91	3,368,526 00	9,476,849 91
" 31, 1867	13,533,850 91	4,699,280 73	8,834,570 18
" 31, 1868	16,516,849 91	5,618,309 75	10,898,540 16
" 31, 1869	16,607,500 91	7,521,814 55	9,085,686 36
" 31, 1870	23,908,350 91	9,779,442 67	14,128,908 24
" 31, 1871	27,865,916 80	11,770,162 35	16,095,754 45
" 31, 1872	29,718,677 91	13,552,249 33	16,166,428 58
" 31, 1873	35,527,293 45	14,350,895 32	21,176,398 13
" 31, 1874	43,474,841 96	15,661,906 73	27,812,935 23
" 31, 1875	43,886,632 24	16,381,626 50	27,505,005 74
" 31, 1876	44,958,822 30	16,681,789 34	28,277,032 96
" 31, 1877	43,354,444 06	16,498,979 12	26,855,464 94
" 31, 1878	41,809,583 31	15,625,411 89	26,184,171 42
" 31, 1879	43,022,816 20	16,925,033 15	26,097,783 05
" 31, 1880	41,103,750 60	14,445,294 19	26,658,456 41
" 31, 1881	40,018,598 02	15,770,551 42	24,248,046 60
" 31, 1882	41,105,577 88	16,724,552 86	24,381,025 02
" 31, 1883	42,544,123 96	17,232,488 44	25,311,635 52
" 31, 1884	42,981,934 91	18,215,870 64	24,766,064 27
" 31, 1885	43,416,945 84	18,716,931 55	24,700,014 29
" 31, 1886	46,337,887 86	19,983,492 39	26,354,395 47
" 31, 1887	48,682,428 58	21,054,840 11	27,627,588 47
" 31, 1888	48,576,569 29	21,725,667 30	26,850,901 99
" 31, 1889	51,185,741 09	22,863,953 03	28,321,788 06
" 31, 1890	55,440,361 06	24,386,864 08	31,053,496 98
" 31, 1891	56,242,745 90	25,539,387 56	30,703,358 34
" 31, 1892	57,083,563 19	26,544,273 22	30,539,289 97
" 31, 1893	55,831,635 15	22,111,523 22	33,720,111 93
" 31, 1894	58,654,211 56	22,160,347 14	36,493,864 42

APPENDIX — TABLE NO. 19.   235

Table No. 19.

DEBT STATEMENT

December 31, 1894.

Gross funded debt, December 31, 1893 . .		$55,831,635 15
Add funded debt issued in 1894		5,808,800 00
		$61,640,435 15
Deduct funded debt paid in 1894 . .		2,986,223 59
Gross debt, December 31, 1894 . . .		$58,654,211 56
City debt		$37,211,937 58
County debt		3,682,000 00
Cochituate water debt		17,760,273 98
		$58,654,211 56
Sinking-Funds, December 31, 1893 .	$21,700,894 82	
Receipts during 1894	2,770,741 16	
	$24,471,635 98	
Payments during 1894 . .	2,970,099 43	
	$21,501,536 55	
Bonds, betterments, etc., the payments of which are pledged to the payment of debt:		
Bonds $2,000 00		
Betterments, etc. . . . 297,456 45		
Street construction assessments, chap. 323, Acts of 1891 . . . . . 24,613 68		
Sidewalk assessments, chap. 401, Acts of 1892 . . 114,640 58		
Sewer assessments, chap. 402, Acts of 1892 . . 219,419 06		
Sidewalk assessments, chap. 437, Acts of 1893 . . 680 82		
	658,810 59	
Total redemption means, December 31, 1894 . . .		22,160,347 14
Net debt, December 31, 1894 . . .		$36,493,864 42

Table No. 20.

BORROWING CAPACITY

December 31, 1894.

Total Debt City and County . . .			$58,654,211 56
Less Special Loans (Outside of limit) . .	$11,300,000 00		
Cochituate Water Debt,	17,760,273 98		
County Debt (Outside of limit) . . .	2,921,000 00		
		31,981,273 98	
			$26,672,937 58
Sinking-Funds . . .		. $21,501,536 55	
Less Cochituate Water Sinking-Fund . .	$8,318,241 08		
Special Loans Sinking-Funds . . .	1,418,026 96		
County Court-House Sinking-Fund . .	256,892 34		
		9,993,160 38	
			11,508,376 17
Debt, excluding Debts outside of limit and deducting Sinking-Funds for said debt			$15,164,561 41
Two per cent. on §850,076,262 average valuation for five years, less abatements			$17,001,525 24
Debt as above			15,164,561 41
Right to borrow, under chap. 178, Acts of 1885, December 31, 1894			$1,836,963 83
Less loans authorized but not issued, inside of limit . .			1,490,000 00
			$346,963 83

APPENDIX — TABLE No. 21.   237

Table No. 21.
BORROWING CAPACITY
January 1, 1895.

Total Debt City and County			$58,654,211 56
Less Special Loans (Outside of limit)	$11,300,000 00		
Cochituate Water Debt,	17,761,273 98		
County Debt (Outside of limit)	2,921,000 00		
		31,982,273 98	
			$26,671,937 58
Sinking-Funds		$21,501,536 55	
Less Cochituate Water Sinking-Fund	$8,318,241 08		
Special Loans Sinking-Funds	1,418,026 96		
County Court-House Sinking-Fund	256,892 34		
		9,993,160 38	
			11,508,376 17
Debt, excluding Debts outside of limit and deducting Sinking-Funds for said debt			$15,163,561 41

Two per cent. on $850,076,262 average valuation for five years, less abatements		$17,001,525 24
Debt as above		15,163,561 41
Right to borrow, under chap. 178, Acts of 1885, December 31, 1894		$1,837,963 83
Average valuation for five years, less abatements, to December 31, 1894	$876,794,390 00	
Average valuation for five years, less abatements, to December 31, 1893	850,076,262 00	
Two per cent. on increase	$26,718,128 00	
		534,362 56
Interest on Investments, January 1, 1895		60,410 96
Right to borrow, January 1, 1895, under St. 1885, ch. 187		$2,432,737 35
Less loans authorized but not issued		1,490,000 00
		$942,737 35
Carried forward		$942,737 35

Brought forward					$942,737 35

Estimated additions to the Sinking-Funds in 1895:

April	1,	1895.	Interest on Investments . . .	$138,701 00	
July	1,	1895.	Interest on Investments . . .	58,100 00	
Oct.	1,	1895.	Interest on Investments . . .	148,723 00	
"	1,	1895.	Debt paid from Appropriation . .	17,000 00	
Nov.	1,	1895.	Appropriation for Debt . . .	1,033,213 00	
Dec.	31,	1895.	Sterling Debt Redeemed . .	90,000 00	
"	31,	1895.	Interest on Bank Deposits . . .	22,500 00	
Jan.	1,	1896.	Interest on Investments . . .	58,100 00	
					1,566,337 00

Right to borrow, January 1, 1895, under St. 1891, ch. 93 . $2,509,074 35

Table No. 22.

LOANS AUTHORIZED BY SPECIAL STATUTES.

Outside of the Debt Limit from 1885 to 1895.

Year.	Chapter.	Date of Approval.	Object.	Amount Authorized.	Amount Issued to Dec. 31, 1894.
1886	304	June 21, 1886	Public Park Construction	$2,500,000 00	$2,500,000 00
1887	101	March 21, 1887	Suffolk County Court-House [1]		2,781,000 00
1887	282	May 18, 1887	Harvard Bridge	250,000 00	250,000 00
1887	312	May 26, 1887	Public Park Lands	400,000 00	400,000 00
1887	394	June 11, 1887	Sewer, Tremont Street	[2] 75,000 00	
1887	428	June 16, 1887	Stony-Brook Improvement	500,000 00	500,000 00
1888	392	May 23, 1888	Public Park Lands	600,000 00	600,000 00
1889	68	March 1, 1889	New Library Building	1,000,000 00	1,000,000 00
1889	254	April 12, 1889	West Chester Park Extension	[2] 75,000 00	
1889	283	April 26, 1889	Congress-street and Oliver-street Extension	[2] 500,000 00	
1889	322	May 9, 1889	Improved Sewerage	500,000 00	500,000 00
1890	271 and 444	May 5 and June 28, 1890	Public Parks, Charlestown	200,000 00	200,000 00
1891	301	May 7, 1891	Public Parks	3,500,000 00	3,500,000 00
1891	324	May 11, 1891	New Library Building	1,000,000 00	800,000 00
1891	323	May 11, 1891	Laying Out and Construction of Highways [3]		1,500,000 00
1892	288	May 9, 1892	Suffolk County Court-House, Furnishing	100,000 00	100,000 00
1893	478	June 10, 1893	Subway [4]	2,000,000 00	
1894	396	May 17, 1894	Public Parks	1,000,000 00	
1894	548	July 2, 1894	Rapid Transit [5]	7,000,000 00	50,000 00

[1] $2,500,000 in addition to the cost of land. Cost of land, $1,056,469.69; $2,781,000 authorized by City Council. [2] Never approved by City Council.
[3] Not exceeding $1,800,000 each year, and not exceeding $3,000,000 in all in excess of the sinking-funds. The debt authorized in 1891 ($500,000) inside of debt limit; debt authorized thereafter is outside of debt limit. [4] Act accepted by city, but superseded by Rapid Transit Act of 1894.

Table No. 23.
LOANS AUTHORIZED, BUT NOT ISSUED,
December 31, 1894.

Date of Order.	Object.	Inside of Debt Limit.	Outside of Debt Limit.
Oct. 24, 1891...	Library Building, Dartmouth Street,	....	$200,000 00
April 26, 1893...	Additional Supply of Water	....	1,800,000 00
May 17, 1893...	Public Park, Wards 6 and 7	[1] $150,000 00	
Feb. 1, 1894...	New Buildings, City Hospital ...	300,000 00	
Feb. 12, 1894...	Charlestown Bridge	740,000 00	
June 8, 1894....	Public Parks......	....	1,000,000 00
June 25, 1894...	Laying Out and Construction of Highways	....	1,000,000 00
July 12, 1894...	Columbus-Ave. Extension	300,000 00	
Stat. 1894, ch. 548 .	Rapid Transit [2] ...·........	.. ..	$6,950,000 00
		$1,490,000 00	$10,950,000 00

Inside Debt Limit $1,490,000 00
Outside Debt Limit 10,950,000 00

$12,440,000 00

[1] Chap. 282, Acts of 1893, authorizes the city of Boston to take land for a public park or playground in Wards 6 and 7, the assessed valuation of said land not to exceed $300,000; also authorizes the expenditure of $50,000 for preparing said land for public use.
[2] Chap. 548, Acts of 1894, authorizes the city of Boston to borrow not exceeding seven millions of dollars to promote Rapid Transit, and such further amount for Charlestown bridge and its approaches, in addition to the seven hundred and fifty thousand dollars heretofore appropriated by the city council, as may be necessary for the completion of said bridge and approaches.

APPENDIX — TABLE NO. 24. 241

Table No. 24.
STATEMENT OF THE LOANS FOR "LAYING OUT AND CONSTRUCTION OF HIGHWAYS,"
December 31, 1894.

Loans issued to December 31, 1894 . . . . . $1,500,000 00

Payments.

Board of Survey	$229,359 32	
Land damages	73,703 03	
Street and sidewalk construction	316,832 20	
Sewer construction	757,748 04	
Interest	1,000 00	
		1,378,642 59
Balance December 31, 1894		$121,357 41

Receipts.

		Interest.	Total.
Sidewalk Assessments	$119,486 89	$10,215 22	$129,702 11
Sewer Assessments	118,661 44	7,212 94	125,874 38
Street Const'n Assessments	25,318 54	1,409 67	26,728 21
	$263,466 87	$18,837 83	$282,304 70
Sale of property, Washington and Water streets			65,550 00
Premium on loans negotiated			10,754 00
Accrued interest on loans negotiated			2,593 49
			$361,202 19

Paid interest	$73,068 55	
Paid to Sinking-Fund	241,545 07	
To be paid to Sinking-Fund	15,153 04	
Held under protest	31,435 53	
		$361,202 19

Total Assessments to December 31, 1894.

	Net Assessments.	Receipts.	Balance Outstanding.
Sidewalks	$234,127 47	$119,486 89	$114,640 58
Sewers	338,080 50	118,661 44	219,419 06
Street Construction	49,932 22	25,318 54	24,613 68
	$622,140 19	$263,466 87	$358,673 32

Sinking-Fund.

Receipts, Assessments, and Interest on same	$165,241 07
Sale of property, Washington and Water streets	65,550 00
Premium on loans negotiated	10,754 00
Interest on Investments	2,765 01
Interest on Bank Deposits	2,852 83
Total Fund, December 31, 1894	$247,162 91

Net Debt Statement.

Outstanding loans		$1,500,000 00
Means of redemption:		
Sinking-Funds	$247,162 91	
Outstanding Assessments	358,673 32	
		605,836 23
Net Debt, December 31, 1894		$894,163 77

Still to be Issued:

Authorized but not yet issued	$1,000,000 00

Additional Amount that can be Authorized:

Sinking-Funds	$147,162 91
Amount authorized by Statute 1891, chap. 323, in excess of Sinking-Funds	3,000,000 00
	$3,247,162 91
Amount already authorized by City Council	2,500,000 00
Amount that can be authorized by City Council, January 1, 1895,	$747,162 91

Table No. 25.

THE "PUBLIC LANDS" ACCOUNT,

From 1822 to January 31, 1894.

	Expenditures.	Receipts.	Net Profits.	Net Loss.
Neck Lands	$418,885 59	$3,298,524 60	$2,879,639 01	
South Bay Lands	1,202,729 67	506,925 22		$695,804 45
Back Bay Lands	1,029,022 41	179,205 87		849,816 54
South Boston Lands	22,751 42	323,519 74	300,768 32	
Church-st. District	1,183,363 12	222,921 89		960,441 23
Northampton-st. Dist.	561,817 63	172,289 81		389,527 82
Suffolk-st. District	2,428,986 58	863,420 56		1,565,566 02
Roxbury and Roxbury Canal	372,930 51	98,082 50		274,848 01
Miscellaneous Lands	363,887 70	672,652 64	308,764 94	
Mill Pond Lands		135,572 73	135,572 73	
Neck and Mill Pond Lands		77,190 16	77,190 16	
East Boston		6,916 56	6,916 56	
Charlestown Lands		15,548 39	15,548 39	
	$7,584,374 63	$6,572,770 67	$3,724,436 11	$4,736,040 07

Table No. 26.
THE QUINCY MARKET.

Payments.

Fiscal Year.	Plant, Land, Buildings, etc.	Repairs and Alterations, etc.	Salaries, etc.	Miscellaneous.	Interest.	Totals.
1825-26	$532,797 33	......	$916 66	....	......	$533,713 99
1826-27	....	......	1,469 50	......	$31,622 95	33,092 45
1827-28	85,933 94	......	2,380 50	$774 65	31,622 95	120,712 04
1828-29	26,089 13	$117 64	2,373 00	334 25	29,703 21	58,617 23
1829-30	100,241 52	140 23	2,421 60	461 73	28,428 21	131,693 29
1830-31	121,866 87	613 62	1,712 89	276 55	23,973 21	148,443 14
1831-32	38,917 39	863 97	1,416 28	432 65	18,073 21	59,703 50
1832-33	432 47	1,174 00	1,369 45	389 40	16,270 51	19,635 83
1833-34	14,325 78	1,780 14	1,377 62	476 93	15,770 51	33,730 98
1834-35	7,000 00	1,786 52	1,675 58	149 50	15,010 51	25,622 11
1835-36	10,000 00	262 68	1,546 34	184 65	14,292 50	26,286 17
1836-37	69,300 00	703 56	1,836 79	182 70	13,792 50	85,815 55
1837-38	15,621 47	653 45	1,988 10	151 80	10,327 50	28,742 32
1838-39	5,163 51	1,936 22	1,960 98	30 30	10,327 50	19,418 51
1839-40	....	391 29	1,929 20	......	10,327 50	12,647 99
1840-41	2,320 81	977 05	2,425 54	......	10,327 50	16,050 90
1841-42	7,000 00	928 79	2,092 42	......	10,327 50	20,348 71
1842-43	....	355 82	2,192 17	......	10,000 00	12,547 99
1843-44	....	497 35	2,683 56	775 00	10,000 00	13,955 91
1844-45	82,595 13	1,184 56	2,105 68	1,298 61	10,000 00	97,183 98
1845-46	....	2,737 99	2,322 86	1,045 53	6,000 00	12,106 38
1846-47	10,000 00	610 89	3,276 41	710 42	6,000 00	20,597 72
1847-48	....	471 34	3,098 84	1,583 24	5,037 50	10,190 92
1848-49	....	2,027 76	3,539 86	879 67	5,400 00	11,847 29
1849-50	....	633 23	3,360 75	1,411 47	5,400 00	10,805 45
1850-51	....	1,777 29	3,612 20	1,113 73	5,400 00	11,903 22
1851-52	....	11,220 30	4,687 84	1,614 63	5,400 00	22,922 77
Carried forward	$1,129,605 35	$33,845 69	$61,772 62	$14,277 41	$358,835 27	$1,598,336 34

APPPNDIX — TABLE NO. 26. 245

Table No. 26. — *Continued.*

THE QUINCY MARKET.

Receipts.					Net Results.		Fiscal Year.
Sales of Land.	Rents.	Miscellaneous.	Interest.	Totals.	Cost at close of Year.	Profit at close of Year.	
$514,753 58	. . . . . .	$22,604 67	. . . . .	$537,358 25	. . . . .	$3,644 26	1825–26
35,714 18	$14,895 64	4,461 12	$11,109 23	66,180 17	. . . . .	36,731 98	1826–27
21,400 00	26,219 89	2,324 44	9,199 78	59,144 11	$24,835 95	. . . . . .	1827–28
26,500 00	26,169 41	2,776 07	8,129 78	63,575 26	19,877 92	. . . . . .	1828–29
42,402 77	24,681 79	274 92	7,665 48	75,024 96	76,546 25	. . . . . .	1829–30
9,500 00	23,530 31	2'2 11	5,486 64	38,719 06	186,270 33	. . . . . .	1830–31
51,533 79	25,252 65	124 67	5,579 91	82,491 02	163,482 81	. . . . . .	1831–32
601 83	22,940 71	125 00	3,968 09	27,635 63	155,483 01	. . . . . .	1832–33
15,500 00	24,350 46	324 83	3,860 47	44,035 76	145,178 23	. . . . . .	1833–34
31,481 10	32,889 91	402 17	2,893 81	67,666 99	103,133 35	. . . .	1834–35
1,483 10	34,557 64	481 63	918 30	37,440 67	91,978 85	. . . . . .	1835–36
1,583 10	35,341 70	607 64	844 15	38,376 59	139,417 81	. . . . . .	1836–37
3,264 00	35,047 06	572 07	765 00	39,648,13	128,512 00	. . . .	1837–38
1,345 30	33,957 93	737 02	601 80	36,642 05	111,288 46	. . . . . .	1838–39
345 30	32,406 90	1,033 09	534 53	34,319 82	89,016 63	. . . . . .	1839–40
345 30	32,914 32	1,094 04	517 26	34,870 92	70,796 61	. . . . . .	1840–41
. . . . . .	33,979 26	1,099 37	500 00	35,578 63	55,566 69	. . . . . .	1841–42
. . . . . .	34,125 14	997 61	500 00	35,622 75	32,491 93	. . . . . .	1842–43
. . . . . .	34,062 77	1,073 15	500 00	35,635 92	10,811 92	. . . . . .	1843–44
5,000 00	33,821 50	1,274 70	500 00	40,596 20	67,399 70	. . . . . .	1844–45
. . . . . .	33,664 32	1,193 64	250 00	35,107 96	44,398 12	. . . . . .	1845–46
. . . . . .	38,337 24	1,384 46	250 00	39,971 70	25,024 14	. . . . . .	1846–47
. . . . . .	38,240 80	1,426 81	250 00	39,917 61	. . . . .	4,702 55	1847–48
. . . . . .	39,559 97	1,702 39	250 00	41,512 36	. . . . .	34,367 62	1848–49
. . . . . .	39,434 12	1,714 43	250 00	41,398 55	. . . . .	64,960 72	1849–50
. . . . . .	50,462 81	1,323 88	250 00	52,036 69	. . . . .	105,094 19	1850–51
. . . . . .	49,169 34	1,244 28	250 00	50,663 62	. . . . .	132,835 04	1851–52
$762,753 35	$850,013 59	$52,580 21	$65,824 23	$1,731,171 38	. . . . .	. . . . . .	Carr'd forw'd.

Table No. 26. — Continued.

THE QUINCY MARKET.

Payments.

Fiscal Year.	Plant, Land, Buildings, etc.	Repairs and Alterations, etc.	Salaries, etc.	Miscellaneous.	Interest.	Totals.
Brought forward .	$1,129,605 35	$33,845 69	$61,772 62	$14,277 41	$358,835 27	$1,598,336 34
1852–53 .	5,000 00	2,868 43	3,351 84	1,110 91	5,400 00	17,731 18
1853–54 .	45,000 00	600 16	3,019 75	1,380 65	5,100 00	55,100 76
1854–55	40,000 00	899 56	3,135 50	1,505 01	2,400 00	47,940 07
1855–56 .	. . . .	628 00	3,122 20	1,485 12	. . . . . .	5,235 32
1856–57 .	20,675 27	774 80	3,012 50	1,398 54	1,205 00	27,066 11
1857–58 .	. . . .	1,006 49	3,231 02	1,289 50	1,205 00	6,732 01
1858–59 .	. . . .	1,307 24	3,247 50	1,130 27	1,205 00	6,890 01
1859–60 .	. . . .	1,356 24	3,563 50	2,365 27	1,205 00	8,490 01
1860–61 .	. . . .	1,563 88	3,554 25	1,465 22	1,205 00	7,788 35
1861–62 .	. . . .	12,406 06	3,641 75	1,431 96	1,205 00	18,684 77
1862–63 .	. . . .	1,460 89	4,104 60	1,703 41	1,080 00	8,348 90
1863–64 .	. . . .	829 43	4,212 96	2,375 47	1,080 00	8,497 86
1864–65 .	. . . .	613 35	4,769 94	3,035 37	1,080 00	9,498 66
1865–66 .	. . . .	3,005 12	4,966 00	2,397 38	1,080 00	11,448 50
1866–67 .	. . . .	3,106 45	5,609 50	2,093 85	1,080 00	11,889 80
1867–68 .	. . . .	1,393 06	5,722 75	2,032 41	. . . . .	9,148 22
1868–69 .	. . . .	3,700 48	5,717 41	3,026 40	. . . . .	12,444 29
1869–70 .	. . . .	3,500 38	6,575 50	2,668 75	. . . . .	12,744 63
1870–71 .	. . . .	1,500 55	7,669 50	1,810 27	. . . . .	10,980 32
1871–72 .	. . . .	3,802 21	8,249 50	1,354 37	. . . . .	13,406 08
1872–73 .	. . . .	3,700 14	8,395 00	1,221 10	. . . . .	13,316 24
1873–74 .	. . . .	4,951 84	8,931 00	1,288 66	. . . . .	15,171 50
1874–75 .	. . . .	3,065 47	8,663 00	993 64	. . . . .	12,722 11
1875–76 .	. . . .	5,324 19	8,227 00	1,225 39	. . . . .	14,776 58
1876–77 .	. . . .	3,364 56	8,114 00	2,269 37	. . . . .	13,747 93
1877–78 .	. . . .	6,311 23	7,405 00	1,870 54	. . . . .	15,586 77
1878–79 .	. . . .	5,890 04	7,505 00	2,827 32	. . . . .	16,222 36
1879–80 .	. . . .	1,303 21	7,514 00	1,739 86	. . . . .	10,557 07
Carried forward .	$1,240,280 62	$114,079 15	$217,004 09	$64,773 42	$384,365 27	$2,020,502 55

APPENDIX — TABLE No. 26.

Table No. 26. — Continued.

THE QUINCY MARKET.

Receipts.					Net Results.		
Sales of Land.	Rents.	Miscellaneous.	Interest.	Totals.	Cost at close of Year.	Profit at close of Year.	Fiscal Year.
$762,753 35	$850,013 59	$52,580 21	$65,824 23	$1,731,171 38	. . . . .	. . . . .	Bro't forw'd.
49,216 00	52,066 21	1,356 92	18,339 20	120,978 33	. . . . .	$236,082 19	1852–53
215,810 13	48,882 31	1,187 03	18,339 20	284,218 67	. . . . .	465,200 30	1853–54
31,942 92	48,869 81	1,212 61	7,548 69	89,574 03	. . . . .	506,834 26	1854–55
27,325 00	48,951 06	1,170 59	5,951 55	83,398 20	. . . . .	584,997 14	1855–56
14,119 11	52,563 56	1,225 39	4,585 29	72,493 35	. . . . .	630,424 38	1856–57
19,119 11	53,287 15	1,159 92	3,879 34	77,445 52	. . . . .	701,137 89	1857–58
11,363 42	54,883 79	817 86	2,923 39	69,988 46	. . . . .	764,236 34	1858–59
5,883 81	53,840 04	943 83	2,355 22	63,022 90	. . . . .	818,769 23	1859–60
3,236 76	53,878 26	773 83	2,061 03	59,949 88	. . . . .	870,930 76	1860–61
3,236 76	51,810 97	779 04	1,899 19	57,725 96	. . . . .	909,971 95	1861–62
27,452 01	54,768 94	797 41	1,737 35	84,756 61	. . . . .	986,379 66	1862–63
911 75	54,018 20	790 66	364 70	56,085 31	. . . . .	1,033,967 11	1863–64
911 76	58,183 30	1,002 84	319 12	60,417 02	. . . . .	1,084,885 47	1864–65
911 76	56,793 90	1,115 60	273 53	59,094 79	. . . .	1,132,531 76	1865–66
911 76	62,574 10	903 88	227 94	64,617 68	. . . . .	1,185,259 64	1866–67
911 76	66,768 50	872 37	182 35	68,734 98	. . . . .	1,244,846 40	1867–68
. . . . . .	70,410 00	660 00	136 76	71,206 76	. . . . .	1,303,608 87	1868–69
2,735 28	71,747 00	670 70	. . . . .	75,152 98	. . . . .	1,366,017 22	1869–70
. . . . . .	72,210 00	844 47	. . . . .	73,054 47	. . . . .	1,428,091 37	1870–71
. . . . . .	72,721 00	415 37	. . . . .	73,136 37	. . . . .	1,487,822 66	1871–72
. . . . . .	74,017 00	477 32	. . . . .	74,494 32	. . . . .	1,548,999 74	1872–73
. . . . . .	84,966 87	491 03	. . . . .	85,457 90	. . . . .	1,619,286 14	1873–74
. . . . . .	92,817 00	372 91	. . . . .	93,189 91	. . . . .	1,699,753 94	1874–75
. . . . . .	92,067 00	352 31	. . . . .	92,419 31	. . . . .	1,777,396 67	1875–76
. . . . . .	89,817 00	317 00	. . . . .	90,134 00	. . . . .	1,853,782 74	1876–77
. . . . . .	86,286 43	423 66	. . . . .	86,710 09	. . . . .	1,924,906 06	1877–78
. . . . . .	83,799 12	460 71	. . . . .	84,259 83	. . . . .	1,992,943 53	1878–79
. . . . . .	70,511 24	698 72	. . . . .	71,209 96	. . . . .	2,053,596 42	1879–80
$1,178,753 35	$2,683,523 35	$74,874 19	$136,948 08	$4,074,098 97	. . . . .	. . . . .	Carr'd forw'd.

Table No. 26. — *Continued.*

THE QUINCY MARKET.

Payments.

FISCAL YEAR.	Plant, Land, Buildings, etc.	Repairs and Alterations, etc.	Salaries, etc.	Miscellaneous.	Interest.	TOTALS.
Brought forward .	$1,240,280 62	$114,079 15	$217,004 09	$64,773 42	$384,365 27	$2,020,502 55
1880–81	. . . .	2,162 87	7,759 50	1,240 66	. . . . . .	11,163 03
1881–82	. . . .	3,413 58	7,855 75	1,442 79	. . . . . .	12,712 12
1882–83	. . . .	3,488 60	8,255 25	1,242 96	. . . . . .	12,986 81
1883–84	. . . .	7,080 91	8,279 25	2,939 24	. . . . . .	18,299 40
1884–85	. . . .	4,710 32	8,268 00	1,456 91	. . . . . .	14,435 23
1885–86	. . . .	2,223 47	8,276 00	1,301 28	. . . . . .	11,800 75
1886–87	. . . .	2,743 95	8,370 00	1,350 38	. . . . . .	12,464 33
1887–88	. . . .	1,534 31	8,359 00	1,602 26	. . . . . .	11,495 57
1888–89	. . . .	3,003 81	8,287 00	1,350 53	. . . . . .	12,641 34
1889–90	. . . .	4,044 63	8,428 29	1,293 02	. . . . . .	13,765 94
1890–91	. . . .	5,114 57	8,855 84	2,845 04	. . . . . .	16,815 45
1891–92	. . . .	2,221 47	6,747 00	761 10	. . . . . .	9,729 57
1892–93	. . . .	4,709 37	10,106 99	1,482 37	. . . . . .	16,298 73
1893–94	. . . .	2,435 71	10,581 95	1,468 20	. . . . . .	14,485 86
Total .	$1,240,280 62	$162,966 72	$335,433 91	$86,550 16	$384,365 27	$2,209,596 68

APPENDIX — TABLE No. 26.

Table No. 26. — *Concluded.*

THE QUINCY MARKET.

Receipts.					Net Results.		
Sales of Land.	Rents.	Miscellaneous.	Interest.	Totals.	Cost at Close of Year.	Profit at Close of Year.	Fiscal Year.
$1,178,753 35	$2,683,523 35	$74,874 19	$136,948 08	$4,074,098 97	. . . . .	. . . . .	Bro'ht forw'd.
. . . . .	70,686 24	173 46	. . . . .	70,859 70	. . . . .	$2,113,293 09	1880-81
. . . . .	71,122 66	454 78	. . . . .	71,577 44	. . . . .	2,172,158 41	1881-82
. .	70,946 00	531 31	. . . . .	71,477 31	. . . . .	2,230,648 91	1882-83
. . . . .	73,267 25	1,007 80	. .	74,275 05	. . . . .	2,286,624 56	1883-84
. . . . .	71,564 10	538 96	. . . . .	72,103 06	. . . . .	2,344,292 39	1884-85
. . . . .	71,336 00	526 87	. . . . .	71,862 87	. . . . .	2,404,354 51	1885-86
. . . . .	71,293 00	529 81	. . . . .	71,822 81	. . . .	2,463,712 99	1886-87
. . . . .	71,793 00	579 42	. . . . .	72,372 42	. . .	2,524,589 84	1887-88
. . . . .	71,043 00	610 51	. . . . .	71,653 51	. . . . .	2,583,602 01	1888-89
. . . . .	70,543 00	473 07	. . . . .	71,016 07	. . . . .	2,640,852 14	1889-90
. . . . .	74,793 00	622 88	. . . . .	75,415 88	. . . . .	2,699,452 57	1890-91
. . . . .	53,782 25	340 92	. . . . .	54,123 17	. . . . .	2,743,846 17	1891-92
. . . . .	71,713 85	484 22	. . . . .	72,198 07	. . . . .	2,799,745 51	1892-93
. . . . .	72,193 00	581 67	. . . . .	72,774 67	. . . . .	2,858,034 32	1893-94
$1,178,753 35	$3,669,599 70	$82,329 87	$136,948 08	$5,067,631 00			

Table No. 27.

EAST BOSTON FERRIES.

Expenditures.

YEARS.	Current Expenses of Ferry Department.	Other Expenditures charged to Department.	Other Expenditures charged to other Departments.	Interest on Loans.	Total Expenditures.
1858–59...			$125,000 00		$125,000 00
1859–60...			125,000 00		125,000 00
1860–61...			551 22	$12,500 00	13,051 22
1861–62...				12,500 00	12,500 00
1862–63...			9,770 02	12,500 00	22,270 02
1863–64...				9,700 00	9,700 00
1864–65...			236 32	9,700 00	9,936 32
1865–66...			9,665 32	9,400 00	19,065 32
1866–67...			19,626 35	11,600 00	31,226 35
1867–68..			26,976 81	11,600 00	38,576 81
1868–69...			6,474 12	11,600 00	18,074 12
1869–70...		$276,375 00	8,101 14	11,600 00	296,076 14
1870–71...	$196,297 45	16,348 45	267 62	19,260 00	232,173 52
1871–72...	204,449 72	.51,066 47	73 48	19,260 00	274,849 67
1872–73...	191,088 12	51,467 32	481 46	19,260 00	262,296 90
1873–74...	210,395 68	86,987 85		19,260 00	316,643 53
1874–75...	235,191 67	30,217 05	812 84	19,260 00	285,481 56
1875–76...	207,729 80	33,564 54	5,611 54	19,260 00	266,165 88
1876–77...	169,976 96	29,216 67	1,158 08	18,840 00	219,191 71
1877–78...	162,201 60			16,500 00	178,701 60
1878–79...	163,437 69	800 00		16,500 00	180,737 69
1879–80...	154,419 14	44,473 48	2,171 77	16,500 00	217,564 39
1880–81...	168,788 50				168,788 50
1881–82...	179,407 86				179,407 86
1882–83...	199,722 32	39,890 59			239,612 91
1883–84...	242,538 36	39,644 58			282,182 94
1884–85...	234,877 56	65,740 27		1,280 00	301,897 83
1885–86...	230,200 04	15,263 11			245,463 15
1886–87...	189,737 51	11,492 50		625 00	201,855 01
1887–88...	202,090 17	56,924 07		1,920 00	260,934 24
1888–89...	214,846 22			1,920 00	216,766 22
1889–90...	199,030 23			3,000 00	202,030 23
1890–91...	204,520 72	20,985 00		3,000 00	228,505 72
1891–92...	157,240 56	69,215 87		4,920 00	231,376 43
1892–93...	211,567 19	21,498 82		4,920 00	237,986 01
1893–94...	213,746 76	35,623 89		4,920 00	254,290 65
	$4,743,501 83	$996,795 53	$341,978 09	$323,105 00	$6,405,380 45

Table No. 28.

EAST BOSTON FERRIES.

Receipts.

YEARS.	Credited to Ferry Department.	Credited to other Departments.	Total Receipts.
1858-59................	....	....	....
1859-60................	....	$625 00	$625 00
1860-61................	....	1,250 00	1,250 00
1861-62................	....	3,013 56	3,013 56
1862-63................	....	900 00	900 00
1863-64................	....	2,700 00	2,700 00
1864-65................	....	2,700 00	2,700 00
1865-66................	....	3,000 00	3,000 00
1866-67................	....	4,050 00	4,050 00
1867-68................	....	3,850 00	3,850 00
1868-69................	....	3,600 00	3,600 00
1869-70................	....	3,900 00	3,900 00
1870-71................	$180,058 54	3,600 00	183,658 54
1871-72................	184,600 00	3,000 00	187,600 00
1872-73................	205,000 00	3,000 00	208,000 00
1873-74................	219,507 50	3,000 00	222,507 50
1874-75................	200,000 00	3,000 00	203,000 00
1875-76................	179,300 00	2,590 00	181,890 00
1876-77................	176,032 00	3,000 00	179,032 00
1877-78................	175,795 48	3,000 00	178,795 48
1878-79................	166,530 31	3,000 00	169,530 31
1879-80................	174,437 00	2,000 00	176,437 00
1880-81................	166,508 48	1,500 00	168,008 48
1881-82................	165,513 06	....	165,513 06
1882-83................	162,827 91	....	162,827 91
1883-84................	159,031 03	....	159,031 03
1884-85................	156,801 60	....	156,801 60
1885-86................	159,558 14	....	159,558 14
1886-87................	164,497 69	....	164,497 69
1887-88................	140,001 13	....	140,001 13
1888-89................	138,760 65	....	138,760 65
1889-90................	141,633 00	....	141,633 00
1890-91................	146,276 80	....	146,276 80
1891-92................	116,353 00	....	116,353 00
1892-93................	154,660 65	....	154,660 65
1893-94................	152,069 54	....	152,069 54
	$3,985,753 51	$60,278 56	$4,046,032 07

Table No. 29.

EAST BOSTON FERRIES.

Net Results.

YEARS.	Total Expenditures.	Total Receipts.	Deficit for the Year.	Net Cost at close of Year.
1858-59.	$125,000 00		$125,000 00	$125,000 00
1859-60.	125,000 00	$625 00.	124,375 00	249,375 00
1860-61.	13,051 22	1,250 00	11,801 22	261,176 22
1861-62.	12,500 00	3,013 56	9,486 44	270,662 66
1862-63.	22,270 02	900 00	21,370 02	292,032 68
1863-64.	9,700 00	2,700 00	7,000 00	299,032 68
1864-65.	9,936 32	2,700 00	7,236 32	306,269 00
1865-66.	19,065 32	3,000 00	16,065 32	322,334 32
1866-67.	31,226 35	4,050 00	27,176 35	349,510 67
1867-68.	38,576 81	3,850 00	34,726 81	384,237 48
1868-69.	18,074 12	3,600 00	14,474 12	398,711 60
1869-70.	296,076 14	3,900 00	292,176 14	690,887 74
1870-71.	232,173 52	183,658 54	48,514 98	739,402 72
1871-72.	274,849 67	187,600 00	87,249 67	826,652 39
1872-73.	262,296 90	208,000 00	54,296 90	880,949 29
1873-74.	316,643 53	222,507 50	94,136 03	975,085 32
1874-75.	285,481 56	203,000 00	82,481 56	1,057,566 88
1875-76.	266,165 88	181,890 00	84,275 88	1,141,842 76
1876-77.	219,191 71	179,032 00	40,159 71	1,182,002 47
1877-78.	178,701 60	178,795 48	Surplus 93 88	1,181,908 59
1878-79.	180,737 69	169,530 31	11,207 38	1,193,115 97
1879-80.	217,564 39	176,437 00	41,127 39	1,234,243 36
1880-81.	168,788 50	168,008 48	780 02	1,235,023 38
1881-82.	179,407 86	165,513 06	13,894 80	1,248,918 18
1882-83.	239,612 91	162,827 91	76,785 00	1,325,703 18
1883-84.	282,182 94	159,031 03	123,151 91	1,448,855 09
1884-85.	301,897 83	156,801 60	145,096 23	1,593,951 32
1885-86.	245,463 15	159,558 14	85,905 01	1,679,856 33
1886-87.	201,855 01	164,497 69	37,357 32	1,717,213 65
1887-88.	260,934 24	140,001 13	120,933 11	1,838,146 76
1888-89.	216,766 22	138,760 65	78,005 57	1,916,152 33
1889-90.	202,030 23	141,633 00	60,397 23	1,976,549 56
1890-91.	228,505 72	146,276 80	82,228 92	2,058,778 48
1891-92.	231,376 43	116,353 00	115,023 43	2,173,801 91
1892-93.	237,986 01	154,660 65	83,325 36	2,257,127 27
1893-94.	254,290 65	152,069 54	102,221 11	2,359,348 38
	$6,405,380 45	$4,046,032 07 Less	$2,359,442 26 93 88	
			$2,359,348 38	

APPENDIX — TABLE NO. 30. 253

Table No. 30.
MYSTIC WATER-WORKS.
Payments.

Year.	Maintenance, Repairs, etc.	Interest.	Refunded	Paid other Cities and Towns.	Mystic Sewer.	Introduction of Meters and Inspection.	Totals.
To March 1, 1871	Construction as per statement of Mayor Kent, of Charlestown						$1,247,633 19
Year ending Mar. 1, 1872,							116,554 71
Mar. 1, 1873							97,071 51
							$1,461,259 41
Less amount charged to Maintenance to balance amount for which the city had been authorized to issue bonds							1,259 41
							$1,460,000 00
To Mar. 1, 1871,	$150,287 42	$304,602 12					454,889 54
" 1, 1872,	46,819 27	66,373 84					113,193 11
" 1, 1873,	63,335 54	77,376 91					140,712 45
Jan. 1, 1874,	84,434 06	76,609 58					161,043 64
From Jan. 1 to Apr. 30, 1874,	14,148 44	25,692 26					39,840 70
1874-75	114,869 17	101,586 33					216,455 50
1875-76	122,677 49	70,280 00		$14,882 69	$24 00		207,864 18
1876-77	89,700 26	66,290 00		21,688 17	1,220 32		178,898 75
1877-78	104,938 49	68,875 00		22,674 92	79,465 11		275,953 52
1878-79	105,746 57	68,027 50		23,794 62	25,508 93		223,077 62
1879-80	104,413 70	63,865 00		43,582 53	2,027 28		213,888 51
1880-81	108,746 19	65,145 00		26,695 28	4,871 63		205,458 10
1881-82	80,753 92	62,445 00		31,106 23	5,743 89		190,049 04
1882-83	98,405 54	62,185 00		34,694 33	3,882 82		199,167 69
1883-84	109,215 59	53,860 00		37,508 51	6,133 60	$3,458 73	210,176 43
1884-85	120,679 53	48,960 00	$1,330 00	37,622 32	7,368 12	6,873 80	222,833 77
1885-86	131,755 66	48,930 00	10 00	41,641 11		3,545 78	225,882 55
1886-87	134,038 19	43,817 50	542 42	111,310 99		128 25	289,837 35
1887-88	149,846 95	42,617 50	174 33	89,513 43		2 53	282,154 74
1888-89	160,143 33	41,877 50	37 67	95,530 15		104 35	297,693 00
1889-90	143,203 73	41,842 50	138 16	100,902 50		143 75	286,230 64
1890-91	132,469 92	38,547 50	168 81	107,970 25		742 81	279,899 29
1891-92	116,438 21	21,633 75	35 23	23,501 38			161,608 57
1892-93	129,354 49	19,257 50	128 19	137,621 36			286,361 54
1893-94	160,643 97	18,707 59	151 42	144,101 35			323,604 33
	$2,777,065 63	$1,599,404 88	$2,716 23	$1,146,342 12	$136,245 70	$15,000 00	$7,136,774 56

Table No. 31.
MYSTIC WATER-WORKS.
Receipts.

Year.	Water Rates.	Other Sources.	Mystic Sewer.	Total.
From 1865 to Mar. 1, 1871..	$518,626 34			$518,626 34
" " 1872..	185,814 79			185,814 79
" " 1873	200,141 07			200,141 07
to Jan. 1, 1874..	163,616 97			163,616 97
1873-74..	128,080 30	$37 51		128,117 81
1874-75..	272,300 40	12,597 21		284,897 61
1875-76.	261,452 19	11,430 33		272,882 52
1876-77..	289,823 11	3,292 38		293,115 49
1877-78..	267,917 34	5,716 06		273,633 40
1878-79..	264,445 42	4,255 68	$422 81	269,123 91
1879-80..	260,988 62	3,870 67	1,457 37	266,316 66
1880-81..	228,392 47	3,965 30		232,357 77
1881-82..	245,336 77	9,022 06		254,358 83
1882-83..	252,335 27	8,599 13		260,934 40
1883-84.	266,401 20	5,185 40		271,586 60
1884-85..	267,670 59	6,114 25		273,784 84
1885-86..	279,220 87	5,270 63		284,491 50
1886-87..	323,851 03	4,376 91		328,227 94
1887-88..	303,873 18	1,764 47		305,637 65
1888-89..	320,466 35	2,579 49		323,045 84
1889-90..	323,478 65	1,220 02		324,698 67
1890-91..	337,378 13	1,173 74		338,551 87
1891-92..	130,325 75	1,426 19		131,751 94
1892-93..	394,008 75	1,783 72		395,792 47
1893-94..	421,572 93	2,189 67	52,637 00	476,399 60
	$6,907,518 49	$95,870 82	$54,517 18	$7,057,906 49

Table No. 32.
MYSTIC WATER-WORKS.
Net Result of Expenditures and Receipts.

YEAR.	Total Payments.	Total Receipts.	Net Payments.	Net Receipts.	Cost at close of Year.
From commencement to March 1, 1871,	$1,702,522 73	$518,626 34	$1,183,896 39		$1,183,896 39
1871-72	229,747 82	185,814 79	43,933 03		1,227,829 42
1872-73	237,783 96	200,141 07	37,642 89		1,265,472 31
1873-74	199,624 93	291,734 78		$92,109 85	1,173,362 46
1874-75	216,455 50	284,897 61		68,442 11	1,104,920 35
1875-76	207,864 18	272,882 52		65,018 34	1,039,902 01
1876-77	178,898 75	293,115 49		114,216 74	925,685 27
1877-78	275,953 52	273,633 40	2,320 12		928,005 39
1878-79	223,077 62	269,123 91		46,046 29	881,959 10
1879-80	213,888 51	266,316 66		52,428 15	829,530 95
1880-81	205,458 10	232,357 77		26,899 67	802,631 28
1881-82	180,049 04	254,358 83		74,309 79	728,321 49
1882-83	199,167 69	260,934 40		61,766 71	666,554 78
1883-84	210,176 43	271,586 60		61,410 17	605,144 61
1884-85	222,833 77	273,784 84		50,951 07	554,193 54
1885-86	225,882 55	284,491 50		58,608 95	495,584 59
1886-87	289,837 35	328,227 94		38,390 59	457,194 00
1887-88	282,154 74	305,637 65		23,482 91	433,711 09
1888-89	297,693 00	323,045 84		25,352 84	408,358 25
1889-90	286,230 64	324,698 67		38,468 03	369,890 22
1890-91	279,899 29	338,551 87		58,652 58	311,237 64
1891-92	161,608 57	131,751 94	29,856 63		341,094 27
1892-93	286,361 54	395,792 47		109,430 93	231,663 34
1893-94	323,604 33	476,399 60		152,795 27	78,868 07
	$7,136,774 56	$7,057,906 49	$1,297,649 06	$1,218,780 99	

Table No. 33.

MYSTIC WATER SINKING-FUND RECEIPTS,

From the Annexation of Charlestown to the Extinction of the Fund upon the Final Payment of the Mystic Water Debt.

Year.	From Tax Levy and City Income.	Interest on Investments.	Interest on Bank Deposits.	Water Rates.	Premium on Loans and Accrued Interest.	From the City of Charlestown.	Total Receipts.
1873-74	....	$780 15	....	$88,277 11	....	$97,597 95	$186,655 21
1874-75	....	5,124 99	$1,006 45	68,442 11	....	....	74,573 55
1875-76	....	4,814 92	1,605 60	65,042 34	....	....	74,387 86
1876-77	$25,152 96	....	494 54	115,437 06	....	....	141,084 56
1877-78	....	125 00	2,752 99	77,144 99	....	....	80,022 98
1878-79	422 81	1,500 00	3,493 47	71,132 41	....	....	76,548 69
1879-80	1,457 37	8,450 00	2,851 15	52,998 06	....	....	65,756 58
1880-81	....	16,917 34	72 69	31,771 30	....	....	48,761 33
1881-82	28,573 00	17,153 00	1,585 44	80,053 68	....	....	127,365 12
1882-83	52,799 00	16,881 05	4,112 03	65,649 53	....	....	139,441 61
1883-84	....	6,453 71	9,067 32	....	....	....	25,835 03
1884-85	10,314 00	5,849 11	7,419 93	71,002 50	....	....	114,913 54
1885-86	30,642 00	2,400 00	9,465 25	65,192 99	....	....	77,126 63
1886-87	68 39	16,348 35	4,635 61	62,154 73	....	....	84,513 69
1887-88	1,375 00	20,417 64	4,572 90	38,418 84	....	....	63,400 38
1888-89	....	20,611 00	4,787 42	23,485 44	....	....	48,883 86
1889-90	....	20,232 50	6,171 59	25,457 19	....	....	51,861 28
1890-91	....	19,962 50	7,443 39	38,611 78	....	....	66,017 67
1891-92	....	12,515 42	3,368 45	59,395 39	....	....	75,279 26
1892-93	....	17,405 00	3,640 31	50,000 00	....	....	71,045 31
1893-94	....	22,129 53	1,826 72	....	....	....	23,956 25
1894-95	....	3,105 00	578 86	....	....	....	3,683 86
Totals	$150,804 53	$239,176 21	$80,952 11	$1,149,667 45	$2,925 00	$97,597 95	$1,721,123 25

Table No. 34.
MYSTIC WATER DEBT, GROSS AND NET,
At the Close of Each Fiscal Year.

Fiscal Year.	Gross Debt.	Sinking-Funds.	Net Debt.	Surplus.
1862-63 [1]....	$100,000 00	....	$100,000 00	
1863-64.....	308,000 00	....	308,000 00	
1864-65.....	583,000 00	....	583,000 00	
1865-66.....	641,000 00	....	641,000 00	
1866-67.....	958,000 00	....	958,000 00	
1867-68.....	1,020,000 00	....	1,020,000 00	
1868-69.....	1,022,000 00	....	1,022,000 00	
1869-70.....	1,022,000 00	....	1,022,000 00	
1870-71.....	1,172,000 00	....	1,172,000 00	
1871-72.....	1,357,000 00	$18,151 55	1,338,848 45	
1872-73.....	1,364,000 00	77,768 46	1,286,231 54	
1873-74 [2]....	1,403,000 00	186,655 21	1,216,344 79	
1874-75.....	1,280,000 00	138,228 76	1,141,771 24	
1875-76.....	1,318,000 00	45,616 62	1,272,383 38	
1876-77.....	1,228,000 00	96,701 18	1,131,298 82	
1877-78.....	1,228,000 00	175,831 79	1,052,168 21	
1878-79....	1,153,000 00	252,380 48	900,619 52	
1879-80.....	1,153,000 00	318,137 06	834,862 94	
1880-81.....	1,153,000 00	366,898 39	786,101 61	
1881-82	1,127,000 00	468,225 12	658,774 88	
1882-83.....	1,027,000 00	506,705 12	520,294 88	
1883-84 .. .	840,000 00	330,540 15	509,459 85	
1884-85.....	839,000 00	444,453 69	394,546 31	
1885-86.....	839,000 00	521,541 93	317,458 07	
1886-87.....	839,000 00	603,555 62	235,444 30	
1887-88.....	839,000 00	666,965 00	172,035 00	
1888-89....;	839,000 00	715,811 53	123,188 48	
1889-90....·	839,000 00	767,306 65	71,693 36	
1890-91.....	690,000 00	680,929 44	9,070 57	
1891-92.....	482,000 00	550,208 70	....	$68,208 70
1892-93.....	441,000 00	579,254 01	....	138,254 01
1893-94.....	102,000 00	265,210 26	....	163,210 26

[1] The fiscal year of the city of Charlestown began March 1 and ended February 28.
[2] To April 30, Charlestown annexed to Boston January 5, 1874.

Table No. 35.
COCHITUATE AND MYSTIC WATER-WORKS.
Certain Payments from Revenue.

	1884-85.	1885-86.	1886-87.	1887-88.	1888-89.	1889-90.	1890-91.	1891-92. 9 months.	1892-93.	1893-94.
Cochituate Water-Works	$418,368 97	$283,920 78	$327,011 10	$351,238 38	$345,938 81	$367,582 45	$325,068 74	$279,456 33	$348,224 45	$382,929 32
Supply Department							43,394 15	33,025 53	44,537 76	50,478 86
Income Department									87,425 93	285,721 20
Extension of Mains	120,679 53	131,755 66	134,138 19	149,846 95	160,143 33	143,203 73				
Mystic Water-Works										
Supply Department							122,880 80	108,896 64	118,949 83	149,678 79
Income Department							9,589 12	7,541 57	10,404 66	10,965 18
Totals	$539,048 50	$415,676 44	$461,149 29	$501,085 33	$506,082 14	$510,786 18	$500,932 81	$428,920 07	$609,542 63	$879,773 35

TABLE NO. 36.

COCHITUATE WATER-WORKS.

EXPENDITURES 1844-1894, ACCORDING TO APPROPRIATIONS.

Table No. 36.

COCHITUATE WATER-WORKS.

YEARS.	EXPENDITURES.				Totals.
	Special Appropriations.	Payments to Mystic Water, and Refunds.	General Appropriations for Construction and Maintenance.	Interest, Premiums, and Discount.	
1844–45	Sundry expenses, surveys, etc.				$3,106 67
1845–46	Sundry expenses, surveys, etc.				11,635 89
1846–47	Sundry expenses, surveys, etc.				1,193 52
					$15,936 08
1846–47			$415,163 28	$6,011 50	$421,174 78
1847–48			1,540,974 42	127,412 01	1,668,386 43
1848–49			1,572,835 67	182,095 10	1,754,930 77
1849–50			580,610 60	234,173 52	814,784 12
1850–51			362,326 76	282,192 79	644,519 55
1851–52			125,625 90	310,421 05	436,046 95
1852–53			109,138 52	303,984 30	413,122 82
1853–54			76,003 69	268,714 62	344,718 21
1854–55			81,956 28	262,519 38	344,475 66
1855–56			64,578 95	264,740 22	329,319 17
1856–57			90,852 62	261,448 36	355,300 98
1857–58			95,465 67	280,748 31	376,213 98
1858–59	New Main from Brookline Reservoir.	$29,770 47	90,550 65	274,019 74	394,340 86
1859–60	New Main from Brookline Reservoir.	272,223 95	108,270 87	294,873 78	675,368 60
1860–61	New Main from Brookline Reservoir.	2,997 41	117,900 74	284,072 63	404,970 78
1861–62			88,916 22	289,520 04	378,436 26

APPENDIX — TABLE No. 36.

1862–63					413,483 11
1863–64					530,607 47
1864–65	Chestnut-hill Reservoir	107,282 02			765,556 81
1865–66	Chestnut-hill Reservoir	267,601 60			688,665 03
1866–67	Chestnut-hill Reservoir	451,124 65			873,260 79
1867–68	Chestnut-hill Reservoir	737,770 00			1,114,832 77
1868–69	Water-works, Wards 13, 14, 15	280,808 84			
	Chestnut-hill Reservoir	530,035 88		322,644 64	
	Water-works, Wards 13, 14, 15	300,369 56		434,254 21	
1869–70	Water to Deer Island	159 20		659,347 81	
	Chestnut-hill Reservoir	329,957 80		453,925 00	
	New Main, E. Boston	630 33		122,207 37	
	Water to Deer Island	30,895 15	Mystic, 25,765 81	483,451 82	
	Water-works, Wards 13, 14, 15	105,088 38		515,245 33	
	Water-works, Ward 16	237,298 71		605,045 92	1,788,015 65
1870–71				193,858 27	
	Additional Supply of Water	2,302 81	Mystic, 38,932 18	588,179 31	1,588,368 03
	Chestnut-hill Reservoir	26,210 12			
	New Water-pipes, E. Boston	24,247 75			
	Water to Deer Island	12,267 22		238,431 80	
1871–72	Water-works, Wards 13, 14, 15	40,656 34	Mystic, 47,697 84	685,266 48	
	Water-works, Ward 16	14,716 25			
	Water-works, Wards 13, 14, 15, 16	137,701 29			
	Additional Supply of Water	192,955 04		277,120 11	
	High Service, So. Boston	61,278 83		536,876 00	1,666,500 83
	Water to Deer Island	26,832 25			
1872–73	New Water-pipes, E. Boston	3,289 31	Mystic, 52,338 36	253,963 58	
	Water-works, Wards 13, 14, 15, 16	8,732 21		702,177 21	1,312,750 77
		107,044 10			1,215,655 85
Carried forward		$4,342,247 47	$164,734 19	$7,340,464 29	$9,866,361 08	$21,713,807 03

COCHITUATE WATER-WORKS. — Continued.

Years.	Special Appropriations.		Payments to Mystic Water, and Refunds.	Construction, Maintenance, etc.	Interest, Premiums, and Discount.	Totals.
	Brought forward...........	$4,342,247 47		$7,340,464 29	$9,865,361 08	$21,713,807 08
1873-74	Additional Supply of Water	114,102 77	Mystic, $164,734 19	506,888 20	497,016 79	
	Parker-hill Reservoir	32,690 78	Mystic, 43,920 60			
	Water-works, Wards 13, 14, 15, 16....	119,886 01				1,314,505 15
1874-75	Parker-hill Reservoir	106,106 23	Mystic, 71,497 51	680,600 97	540,858 77	
	Water-pipes, Wards 17 and 19	2,388 59				
	Water-works, Wards 13, 14, 15, 16, and extension to Wards 17 and 19 ...	104,250 89				
	Additional Supply of Water.......	224,956 68				1,730,659 64
1875-76	Parker-hill Reservoir	89,449 16	Mystic, 31,246 75	408,173 52	833,364 81	
	Siphon, Charles River..........	26,532 35				
	Water-pipes, Wards 17 and 19	288,039 03				
	Additional Supply of Water........	783,613 49				2,460,419 11
1876-77	Additional Supply of Water........	1,924,060 24	Mystic, 66,934 60	255,134 08	747,624 77	
	Water-works, W. Roxbury and Brighton.............	160,487 71				3,154,241 40
1877-78	Water-works, W. Roxbury and Brighton.............	25,403 78	Mystic, 48,674 10	257,397 09	751,484 94	
	Additional Supply of Water.......	1,257,715 26				2,340,675 17
1878-79	Additional Supply of Water.......	635,658 08	Mystic, 48,851 11	237,054 35	617,378 20	1,538,941 74
1879-80	Additional Supply of Water.......	213,350 97	Mystic, 44,013 24	207,680 27	643,037 93	1,108,132 41
			Refunds, 50 00			
1880-81	Additional Supply of Water.......	35,677 98		316,456 56	619,476 52	
	New Main.............	267,778 80				
1881-82	New Main.............	2,398 24		325,846 41	598,974 76	1,239,389 86

APPENDIX — TABLE NO. 36.

1882-83	Additional Supply of Water	97,406 78				
	Additional Supply of Water	167,621 43				1,024,626 19
1883-84	New Main	336 18				
	New Main	71,189 06	Refunds, 15 00	317,462 16	630,018 30	1,115,438 07
	Additional Supply of Water	423,625 79				
1884-85	Introduction of Meters and Inspection	55,345 64			639,213 41	
	Introduction of Meters and Inspection	114,709 87	Refunds, 13,211 83	377,974 75		1,567,363 65
	Additional Supply of Water	276,292 13				
	New Main	8,297 72		418,368 97	668,658 07	
	Extension of Mains, etc.	1,050 90				
	High Service	5,332 72				
1885-86	Introduction of Meters and Inspection	84,455 69	Refunds, 416 00	283,920 78	681,758 78	1,505,922 21
	Additional Supply of Water	139,187 68				
	Extension of Mains, etc.	157,421 31				
1886-87	High Service	197,041 33		327,011 10	694,931 76	1,544,201 57
	Extension of Mains, etc.	131,272 11	Refunds, 706 75			
	Additional Supply of Water	167,905 54				
1887-88	Introduction of Meters and Inspection	128,109 32		351,238 38	729,380 46	1,460,039 82
	Extension of Mains, etc.	10,103 24	Refunds, 481 87			
	High Service	31,678 54				
	Additional Supply of Water	371,494 32				
1888-89	Improvement of Lake Cochituate	239,298 88		345,938 81	746,239 82	1,785,512 94
	Improvement of Lake Cochituate	30,332 77	Refunds, 452 03			
	High Service	31,607 72				
	Extension of Mains, etc.	28,576 29				
	Additional Supply of Water	150,618 59				
1889-90	Introduction of Meters and Inspection	294,118 79		367,582 45	760,385 33	1,582,585 03
	Introduction of Meters and Inspection	2,398 90	Refunds, 2,708 00			
		14,241 80				
		12,755 65				
	Carried forward	$14,200,621 20	$537,913 58	$13,325,193 14	$21,266,164 50	$48,186,460 99

COCHITUATE WATER-WORKS. — Concluded.

YEARS.	Special Appropriations.		Payments to Mystic Water, and Refunds.	Construction, Maintenance, etc.	Interest, Premiums, and Discount.	Totals.
	Brought forward	$14,200,621 20	$537,913 58	$13,325,193 14	$21,266,164 50	$48,186,460 99
	Additional Supply of Water	18,518 01				
	Shops, Albany St.	421 31				
	Extension of Mains, etc.	299,689 20				
	High Service	15,088 81				
	Improvement of Lake Cochituate	12,318 83				
1890–91	Shops, Albany St.	59,578 69	Refunds, 594 05	368,402 89	785,117 17	1,489,457 59
	Introduction of Meters and Inspection	6,709 57				
	Extension of Mains, etc.	267,977 67				
	High Service	27,433 51				
	Improvement of Lake Cochituate	6,131 20				
1891–92	Additional Supply of Water	233,710 59	Refunds, 365 39	312,481 86	466,347 78	1,755,715 34
	Extension of Mains, etc.	281,271 82				
	High Service	205,652 56				
		697 78				
1892–93	High Service	63,657 77	Refunds, 963 05	480,188 14	810,981 63	1,266,817 19
	Extension of Mains, etc.	134,689 71				
	Additional Supply of Water	313,844 53				
1893–94	Additional Supply of Water	190,655 62	Refunds, 1,479 18	719,129 38	826,077 88	1,804,324 83
	High Service	36,346 05				
	Totals	$16,375,014 43	$541,315 25	$15,205,455 41	$24,154,688 96	$56,276,474 05

Table No. 37.

COCHITUATE WATER-WORKS.

Expenditures from 1846 to January 31, 1894, according to the Sources from which the Money was Obtained.

	From Loans.	From Revenue.	From Taxes.	Totals.
Original cost of Works	$5,430,711 11			$5,430,711 11
Chestnut-Hill Reservoir	2,449,982 07			2,449,982 07
New Mains:				
From Brookline Reservoir	304,991 83			304,991 83
From Chestnut-Hill Reservoir	350,000 00			350,000 00
Additional Supply:				
Improvement of Lake Cochituate	78,634 04			78,634 04
Miscellaneous	7,190,305 68	¹ $355,386 80	$10,000 00	7,555,692 48
High Service:				
To South Boston	26,832 25			26,832 25
Parker-Hill Reservoir	161,000 00		67,246 17	228,246 17
Miscellaneous	866,787 55			866,787 55
Shops, Albany street	60,000 00			60,000 00
Extensions:				
Water to Deer Island	75,000 00			75,000 00
New Mains to East Boston			24,878 08	24,878 08
New Water-Pipes, East Boston			20,999 43	20,999 43
Water-Works, Wds. 13, 14, and 15	700,000 00	983 03		700,983 03
" Ward 16	375,000 00			375,000 00
" Wds. 13, 14, 15, and 16	415,000 00		4,885 15	419,885 15
" Wards 17 and 19	460,000 00	² 10,570 00	5,749 11	476,319 11
Water-Works, Wds. 13, 14, 15, and 16, and extensions to Wds. 17 and 19	60,000 00		44,250 89	104,250 89
Siphon, Charles River			26,532 35	26,532 35
Extension of Mains	1,900,000 00	³ 373,147 13		2,273,147 13
Water-Meters:				
Introduction of Meters and Inspection	330,000 00			330,000 00
General Account	215,175 92	32,327,954 73	1,554,470 73	34,097,601 38
Totals	$21,449,420 45	$33,068,041 69	$1,759,011 91	$56,276,474 05

¹ Includes $352,886.80 Premium on Loans.   ² Premium on Loan.
³ Includes $182,369.57 Mystic Water Revenue. This expenditure of $373,147.13 also includes $75,199.70 paid for Jamaica Pond Aqueduct Co.'s plant in 1893-94.

```
Total amount of Loans issued to January 31, 1894 . . . . . . . . . . . . . . . $21,563,711 11
    Payments as above . . . . . . . . . . . . . . . . . $21,449,420 45
    Payments to Sinking-Fund . . . . . . . . . . . . . . . . .       17 93
    Balances on hand January 31, 1894 . . . . . . . . . . . . .  114,272 73
                                                                 ─────────
                                                                             21,563,711 11
```

Wards 13, 14, and 15 comprised the city of Roxbury.
Ward 16 comprised the town of Dorchester.
" 17 " " " " West Roxbury.
" 19 " " " " Brighton.

Table No. 38.
COCHITUATE WATER-WORKS.
Receipts.

Years.	Total Water Rates, including Hydrants and Department Charges.	From other Sources.	Total.
1846–47		$22,263 39	$22,263 39
1847–48		10,517 54	10,517 54
1848–49	$15,933 01	4,691 66	20,624 67
1849–50	142,704 65	10,296 34	153,000 99
1850–51	136,290 75	12,734 34	149,025 09
1851–52	183,987 56	15,438 92	199,426 48
1852–53	193,941 81	9,362 31	203,304 12
1853–54	206,736 22	6,941 45	213,677 67
1854–55	250,429 82	12,728 81	263,158 63
1855–56	284,189 49	7,669 65	291,859 14
1856–57	292,181 89	21,060 76	313,242 65
1857–58	296,512 25	13,115 97	309,628 22
1858–59	313,694 60	40,516 72	354,211 32
1859–60	341,479 50	11,985 87	353,465 37
1860–61	363,561 08	8,729 59	372,290 67
1861–62	369,261 53	11,307 08	380,568 61
1862–63	391,588 85	9,219 51	400,808 36
1863–64	420,281 99	13,972 62	434,254 61
1864–65	439,834 21	24,076 70	463,910 91
1865–66	462,221 92	10,986 83	473,208 75
1866–67	517,101 95	13,424 85	530,526 80
1867–68	538,879 66	13,286 65	552,166 31
1868–69	593,150 49	16,863 03	610,013 52
1869–70	655,217 29	20,442 22	675,659 51
1870–71	795,718 92	32,336 63	828,055 55
1871–72	859,578 85	30,091 81	889,670 66
1872–73	933,464 67	20,896 37	954,361 04
1873–74	993,914 88	40,486 18	1,034,401 06
1874–75	1,039,201 10	45,779 68	1,084,980 78
1875–76	1,075,727 98	193,960 99	1,269,688 97
1876–77	1,073,593 39	244,609 42	1,318,202 81
1877–78	1,060,537 81	24,720 40	1,085,258 21
1878–79	1,059,067 21	31,286 57	1,090,353 78
1879–80	1,093,104 52	20,608 30	1,113,712 82
1880–81	1,113,028 79	20,335 23	1,133,364 02
1881–82	1,094,869 63	24,285 98	1,119,155 61
1882–83	1,140,020 88	25,282 34	1,165,303 22
1883–84	1,199,657 10	26,804 45	1,226,461 55
1884–85	1,195,946 03	24,421 96	1,220,367 99
1885–86	1,236,472 20	28,052 31	1,264,524 51
1886–87	1,217,274 87	34,075 97	1,251,350 84
1887–88	1,302,262 06	36,852 22	1,339,114 28
1888–89	1,360,444 09	[1] 197,935 77	1,558,379 86
1889–90	1,350,817 76	59,177 24	1,409,995 00
1890–91	1,405,537 67	63,528 09	1,469,065 76
1891–92	816,357 53	101,215 11	917,572 64
1892–93	1,433,413 78	40,936 09	1,474,349 87
1893–94	1,637,531 94	54,627 79	1,692,159 73
Totals	$34,896,724 18	$1,763,939 71	$36,660,663 89

[1] Including $150,000 from sale of the reservoir lot on Derne street. The money, however, was not credited to the Water Works, but was used for municipal purposes. See Doc. 123 of 1888, and Doc. 49 of 1889.

Table No. 39.
COCHITUATE WATER-RATES.

Assessments, Abatements, and Net Assessments, less Hydrant Charges, from January 1, 1880, to December 31, 1894.

Year.	Assessments.	Abatements.	Net Assessments.	Hydrant Charges.	Net Assessments exclusive of Hydrant Charges.
1880....	$1,086,456 37	$35,895 95	$1,050,560 42	$73,764 00	$976,796 42
1881....	1,129,547 69	28,334 91	1,101,212 78	83,080 00	1,018,132 78
1882....	1,157,840 03	25,654 31	1,132,185 72	84,460 00	1,047,725 72
1883....	1,213,310 06	18,247 82	1,195,062 24	85,760 00	1,109,302 24
1884....	1,224,265 89	13,683 89	1,210,582 00	86,180 00	1,124,402 00
1885....	1,372,756 86	111,360 40	1,261,396 46	90,720 00	1,170,676 46
1886....	1,282,322 47	89,353 33	1,192,969 14	86,837 20	1,106,131 94
1887....	1,279,892 12	47,443 64	1,232,448 48	83,610 00	1,148,838 48
1888....	1,342,381 35	26,069 04	1,316,312 31	86,976 00	1,229,336 31
1889....	1,403,736 71	42,227 07	1,361,509 64	74,250 00	1,287,259 64
1890...	1,484,767 08	83,413 22	1,401,353 86	71,368 20	1,329,985 66
1891....	1,575,233 49	125,539 69	1,449,693 80	71,401 50	1,378,292 30
1892....	1,580,757 97	25,480 17	1,555,277 80	11,072 00	1,544,205 80
1893....	1,672,059 21	23,141 18	1,648,918 03	11,724 00	1,637,194 03
1894....	1,704,465 08	21,845 68	1,682,619 40	12,084 00	1,670,535 40

Table No. 40.
AMOUNTS PAID BY THE DEPARTMENTS OF
FROM 1854 TO

Year	Fire Department.	Public Schools.	Police Department.	Health Department.	Public Buildings.	Public Institutions.
1854..	$315 00	$1,290 00	$80 00	$658 00	$232 00	$775 00
1855..	381 00	1,525 00	87 00	664 00	238 00	737 00
1856..	381 00	1,525 00	98 00	664 00	238 00	711 22
1857..	381 00	1,532 00	98 00	664 00	232 00	842 00
1858..	462 00	1,614 00	210 00	668 00	259 50	929 56
1859..	417 00	1,592 00	215 00	668 00	259 50	879 56
1860..	415 00	1,624 00	367 00	663 75	283 50	879 56
1861..	430 00	1,836 00	447 00	682 00	517 50	879 56
1862..	462 00	1,847 00	625 00	682 00	548 75	879 56
1863..	462 00	1,840 00	625 00	827 00	576 75	879 56
1864..	415 00	1,888 00	719 00	890 00	567 00	929 56
1865..	592 00	1,894 00	728 00	927 56	482 00	937 00
1866..	603 00	1,882 00	1,004 35	905 75	880 89	1,302 53
1867..	603 50	1,970 00	961 71	905 75	1,027 56	1,425 25
1868..	530 00	1,932 00	1,006 37	1,715 54	1,340 42	1,940 11
1869..	545 00	2,278 00	1,207 33	1,409 49	1,218 46	3,784 36
1870..	33,599 00	2,666 00	1,054 27	2,822 74	1,405 00	4,335 68
1871..	36,443 00	2,958 00	1,077 54	2,392 13	741 98	4,113 69
1872..	45,410 00	3,000 00	988 89	2,157 14	829 58	3,631 00
1873..	49,566 00	3,238 00	1,144 63	1,673 75	787 67	6,086 22
1874..	55,378 00	3,214 00	1,095 91	1,076 25	747 38	6,600 46
1875..	60,450 00	3,364 00	1,136 31	1,144 67	735 59	6,940 38
1876..	67,944 50	3,358 00	1,243 50	1,612 89	1,003 52	6,528 10
1877..	70,696 50	3,904 00	1,010 41	2,572 16	816 87	5,985 33
1878..	72,526 50	3,742 00	819 94	2,601 25	630 41	6,305 15
1879..	73,816 50	4.227 00	671 29	3,517 50	688 00	5,710 52
1880..	75,064 00	3,796 00	665 43	917 50	578 25	6,090 91
1881..	84,360 00	3,653 00	638 38	917 50	295 33	7,306 51
1882..	85,755 00	4,350 18	893 36	917 50	278 97	6,734 83
1883..	87,055 00	3,616 28	1,373 15	917 50	612 00	6,908 57
1884..	87,475 00	3,315 70	1,471 00	917 50	577 50	6,658 25
1885..	92,025 00	3,362 90	1,229 00	917 50	570 00	8,023 00
1886..	88,073 30	3,547 40	1,135 50	900 05	545 78	7,327 81
1887..	84,780 00	4,010 50	1,483 90	981 50	693 00	8,193 40
1888..	88,381 00	4,279 99	1,666 60	1,036 75	832 10	9,069 06
1889..	75,695 00	4,374 71	1,902 10	1,036 75	920 30	9,678 47
1890..	72,726 00	4,887 58	1,818 83	985 57	1,520 67	10,909 99
1891..	72,762 00	4,311 95	2,131 50	957 83	1,052 35	11,058 40
1892..	12,657 00	4,735 20	2,451 90	Consolidated Street Department.	1,263 10	11,582 40
1893..	13,359 00	5,630 97	2,488 30		1,705 80	11,053 20
1894..	13,858 60	4,440 50	2,334 30		1,413 40	10,049 10
	$1,607,250 40	$124,052 86	$42,404 70	$46,568 77	$30,145 88	$205,591 08

APPENDIX — TABLE NO. 40. 269

Table No. 40. — *Continued.*
THE CITY OF BOSTON, FOR USE OF WATER, OCTOBER 1, 1894.

City Hospital.	Public Library.	Lamp Department.	Urinals for Markets.	Park Department.	Commons and Squares.	Cemeteries.
....	$5 00	....	$70 00	....	....	....
....	6 00	....	70 00	....	....	....
....	6 00	....	70 00	....	....	....
....	6 00	....	76 00	....	....	....
....	50 00	....	76 00	....	....	....
....	50 00	....	70 00	....	....	....
....	50 00	....	70 00	....	....	....
....	50 00	....	70 00	....	....	....
....	50 00	....	70 00	....	....	....
....	50 00	....	70 00	....	....	....
....	50 00	....	....	....	....	....
....	50 00	....	....	....	$60 00	....
$1,048 63	50 00	....	....	....	60 00	....
1,924 00	50 00	....	....	....	60 00	....
2,607 37	50 00	....	....	....	160 00	....
2,264 20	50 00	....	....	....	160 00	....
2,700 50	50 00	....	....	....	335 00	....
3,105 00	58 50	....	....	....	335 00	....
2,963 40	69 50	....	....	....	335 00	....
2,482 69	78 00	....	....	....	335 00	....
2,384 14	93 50	....	....	....	335 00	....
1,983 35	93 50	$17 25	....	....	335 00	....
2,272 81	162 50	22 25	....	....	335 00	....
2,592 22	146 50	42 25	....	....	335 00	....
2,453 26	60 50	42 25	....	....	385 00	....
2,102 04	71 50	42 25	67 50	....	385 00	....
2,020 69	....	42 25	67 50	....	385 00	....
1,869 53	....	42 25	67 50	....	385 00	....
2,159 88	....	20 00	67 50	....	410 00	....
2,291 33	....	20 00	67 50	....	385 00	....
2,096 50	236 00	20 00	67 50	$150 00	390 00	$25 50
2,338 50	235 50	20 00	67 50	28 00	350 00	118 00
2,104 30	223 72	21 15	63 45	31 02	347 80	114 92
2,632 60	238 00	22 50	67 50	242 12	406 00	120 80
3,146 20	214 00	26 25	62 50	171 68	458 00	94 50
2,196 40	214 00	26 25	62 50	889 75	502 85	89 50
2,228 95	199 02	24 42	58 13	1,688 95	486 13	86 09
2,823 70	127 80	23 62	56 25	1,876 17	539 10	77 55
2,612 80	142 00	26 25	62 50	2,693 00	599 00	86 90
2,825 20	142 00	26 25	62 50	3,465 08	579 00	89 70
2,240 80	142 00	23 75	62 50	821 50	613 20	102 30
$68,470 99	$3,621 04	$551 19	$1,742 33	$12,057 27	$10,786 08	$1,006 16

AMOUNTS PAID BY THE DEPARTMENTS. — Continued.

Year.	Board of Health.	City Surveyor.	Ferries.	Paving Department.	Sewer Department.	Bridge Department.
1854					$75 00	
1855					75 00	
1856					75 00	
1857					75 00	
1858					75 00	
1859					75 00	
1860					75 00	
1861					75 00	
1862					75 00	
1863					75 00	
1864					50 00	
1865				$9 00	50 00	
1866				9 00	50 00	
1867				9 00	56 00	
1868				9 00	56 00	
1869				6 00	56 00	
1870			$3,585 13	167 00	225 00	
1871			3,794 87	228 00	250 00	
1872			4,860 98	227 00	250 00	
1873	$943 91		4,797 23	202 00	250 00	
1874	933 04	$12 00	4,679 95	271 50	250 00	
1875	1,336 50	12 00	5,381 53	327 75	250 00	
1876	1,382 41	16 00	4,752 39	377 75	250 00	
1877	582 72	16 00	4,278 03	442 75	250 00	$82 00
1878	808 08		4,236 27	431 50	250 00	82 00
1879	588 21		3,296 30	423 75	200 00	82 00
1880	775 38		2,755 89	3,523 75	200 00	82 00
1881	750 75		2,760 76	4,170 51	200 00	82 00
1882	841 56		2,753 20	5,410 80	200 00	80 00
1883	1,176 25	12 50	3,805 50	6,761 11	256 00	80 00
1884	1,335 25	12 50	3,473 34	5,767 00	256 00	80 00
1885	1,013 00	12 50	3,807 96	7,008 07	1,297 00	95 00
1886	915'85	11 75	3,451 81	4,393 57	976 60	98 70
1887	968 60	12 50	3,516 30	4,126 03	1,326 40	120 00
1888	936 75	15 00	3,446 00	3,639 15	3,867 02	170 00
1889	950 00	15 00	3,232 70	6,442 29	4,951 80	175 00
1890	839 23	13 95	3,373 30	7,538 97	6,522 18	162 75
1891	926 63	13 50	3,345 00	7,768 95	5,165 24	144 00
1892	1,069 40	15 00	3,334 00	Consoli	dated	Street De-
1893	-1,005 40		2,947 20	Street De	partment.	partment.
1894	974 20		2,703 60			
	$21,053 12	$190 20	$92,369 24	$69,691 20	$28,711 24	$1,615 45

APPENDIX — TABLE No. 40.

AMOUNTS PAID BY THE DEPARTMENTS. — *Concluded.*

Consolidat'd Street Department.	Weights and Measures.	Suffolk County.	Suffolk Street District.	Northampton Street District.	Mystic Water-Works.	Total by Year.
....	$9 00	$225 00	....	....	....	$3,734 00
....	9 00	225 00	....	....	....	4,017 00
....	9 00	225 00	....	....	....	4,002 22
....	9 00	243 00	....	....	....	4,158 00
....	9 00	243 00	....	....	....	4,596 06
....	9 00	243 00	....	....	....	4,478 06
....	9 00	243 00	....	....	....	4,679 81
....	9 00	243 00	....	....	....	5,239 06
....	9 00	243 00	....	....	....	5,491 31
....	9 00	243 00	....	....	....	5,657 31
....	9 00	243 00	....	....	....	5,760 56
....	9 00	243 00	....	....	....	5,981 56
....	9 00	659 24	....	....	....	8,464 39
....	9 00	874 34	....	....	....	9,876 11
....	9 00	644 89	....	....	....	12,000 70
....	9 00	489 18	....	....	....	13,477 02
....	11 00	526 25	....	....	....	53,482 57
....	11 00	468 36	....	....	....	55,977 05
....	11 00	1,836 79	$227 40	....	....	66,797 68
....	11 00	1,777 22	....	....	....	73,373 32
....	11 00	2,025 97	....	$108 50	....	79,216 60
....	11 00	2,219 68	....	....	....	85,738 51
....	11 00	1,429 64	....	....	....	92,702 26
....	11 00	1,716 11	....	....	....	95,479 85
....	....	835 27	....	....	....	96,209 38
....	....	761 56	....	....	$19,172 70	115,823 62
....	....	874 39	....	....	....	97,838 94
....	....	1,033 29	....	....	....	108,532 31
....	....	997 93	....	....	....	111,870 71
....	....	601 50	....	....	....	115,939 19
....	....	811 50	....	....	....	115,136 04
....	....	1,022 00	....	....	....	123,540 43
....	....	858 10	....	....	....	115,142 58
....	....	1,006 40	....	....	....	114,948 05
....	....	1,028 70	....	....	....	122,541 65
....	....	1,225 60	....	....	....	114,580 97
....	....	1,330 00	....	....	....	117,400 71
....	....	1,733 60	....	....	....	116,895 14
$10,183 47	....	1,447 60	....	....	....	54,961 52
8,956 25	....	1,456 90	....	....	....	55,792 25
4,211 20	....	1,105 20	....	....	....	45,096 15
$23,350 92	$232 00	$35,659 21	$227 40	$108 50	$19,172 70	$2,446,630 65

Table No. 41.

AMOUNTS PAID BY FIRE DEPARTMENT
For use of Water for Hydrants and Reservoirs from 1870 to 1894, inclusive.

Date.	Number.	Rate.	Amount.
1870	1833	$18 00	$32,994 00
1871	1991	18 00	35,838 00
1872	2485	18 00	44,730 00
1873	2702	18 00	48,636 00
1874	3016	18 00	54,288 00
1875	3295	18 00	59,310 00
1876	5707	18 00	66,726 00
1877	3851	18 00	69,318 00
1878	3951	18 00	71,118 00
1879	4027	18 00	72,486 00
1880	4098	18 00	73,764 00
1881	4154	20 00	83,080 00
1882	4223	20 00	84,460 00
1883	4288	20 00	85,760 00
1884	4309	20 00	86,180 00
1885	4536	20 00	90,720 00
1886	4619	20 00	[1]92,380 00
1887	4615	18 00	83,610 00
1888	4832	18 00	86,976 00
1889	4950	15 00	74,250 00
1890	5116	15 00	[2]76,740 00
1891	5289	15 00	[3]79,335 00
1892	5536	2 00	11,072 00
1893	5862	2 00	11,724 00
1894	6042	2 00	12,084 00

[1] $5,542.80 refunded.   [2] $5,371.80 refunded.   [3] $7,933.50 refunded.

N.B. — The payments in this table are also included in Table 40.

Table No. 42.
COCHITUATE WATER-WORKS.
Net Result of Expenditures and Receipts.

Year.	Total Payments.	Total Receipts.	Net Payments.	Net Receipts.	Cost at close of Year.
1846-47..	$421,174 78	$22,263 39	$398,911 39		$398,911 39
1847-48..	1,668,386 43	10,517 54	1,657,868 89		2,056,780 28
1848-49..	1,754,930 77	20,624 67	1,734,306 10		3,791,086 38
1849-50..	814,784 12	153,000 99	661,783 13		4,452,869 51
1850-51..	644,519 55	149,025 09	495,494 46		4,948,363 97
1851-52..	436,046 95	199,426 48	236,620 47		5,184,984 44
1852-53..	413,122 82	203,304 12	209,818 70		5,394,803 14
1853-54..	344,718 21	213,677 67	131,040 54		5,525,843 68
1854-55..	344,475 66	263,158 63	81,317 03		5,607,160 71
1855-56..	329,319 17	291,859 14	37,460 03		5,644,620 74
1856-57..	355,300 98	313,242 65	42,058 33		5,686,679 07
1857-58..	376,213 98	309,628 22	66,585 76		5,753,264 83
1858-59..	394,340 86	354,211 32	40,129 54		5,793,394 37
1859-60..	675,368 60	353,465 37	321,903 23		6,115,297 60
1860-61..	404,970 78	372,290 67	32,680 11		6,147,977 71
1861-62..	378,436 26	380,568 61		$2,132 35	6,145,845 36
1862-63..	413,483 11	400,808 36	12,674 75		6,158,520 11
1863-64..	530,607 47	434,254 61	96,352 86		6,254,872 97
1864-65..	765,556 81	463,910 91	301,645 90		6,556,518 87
1865-66..	688,665 03	473,208 75	215,456 28		6,771,975 15
1866-67..	873,260 79	530,526 80	342,733 99		7,114,709 14
1867-68..	1,114,832 77	552,166 31	562,666 46		7,677,375 60
1868-69..	1,788,015 65	610,013 52	1,178,002 13		8,855,377 73
1869-70..	1,588,368 03	675,659 51	912,708 52		9,768,086 25
1870-71..	1,666,500 83	828,055 55	838,445 28		10,606,531 53
1871-72..	1,312,750 77	889,670 66	423,080 11		11,029,611 64
1872-73..	1,215,655 85	954,361 04	261,294 81		11,290,906 45
1873-74..	1,314,505 15	1,034,401 06	280,104 09		11,571,010 54
1874-75..	1,730,659 64	1,084,980 78	645,678 86		12,216,689 40
1875-76..	2,460,419 11	1,269,688 97	1,190,730 14		13,407,419 54
1876-77..	3,154,241 40	1,318,202 81	1,836,038 59		15,243,458 13
1877-78..	2,340,675 17	1,085,258 21	1,255,416 96		16,498,875 09
1878-79..	1,538,941 74	1,090,353 78	448,587 96		16,947,463 05
1879-80..	1,108,132 41	1,113,712 82		5,580 41	16,941,882 64
1880-81..	1,239,389 86	1,133,364 02	106,025 84		17,047,908 48
1881-82..	1,024,626 19	1,119,155 61		94,529 42	16,953,379 06
1882-83..	1,115,438 07	1,165,303 22		49,865 15	16,903,513 91
1883-84..	1,567,363 65	1,226,461 55	340,902 10		17,244,416 01
1884-85..	1,505,922 21	1,220,367 99	285,554 22		17,529,970 23
1885-86..	1,544,201 57	1,264,524 51	279,677 06		17,809,647 29
1886-87..	1,460,039 82	1,251,350 84	208,688 98		18,018,336 27
1887-88..	1,785,512 94	1,339,114 28	446,398 66		18,464,734 93
1888-89..	1,582,585 03	1,558,379 86	24,205 17		18,488,940 10
1889-90..	1,489,467 59	1,409,995 00	79,472 59		18,568,412 69
1890-91..	1,755,715 34	1,469,065 76	286,649 58		18,855,062 27
1891-92..	1,266,817 19	917,572 64	349,244 55		19,204,306 82
1892-93..	1,804,324 43	1,474,349 87	329,974 96		19,534,281 78
1893-94..	1,773,688 11	1,692,159 73	81,528 38		19,615,810 16
Totals...	$56,276,474 05	$36,660,663 89	$19,767,917 49	$152,107 33	

Table No. 43.
COCHITUATE WATER LOANS,
Authorized, Issued, and Expended to January 31, 1894.

PURPOSE OF LOAN SPECIFIED IN THE ORDER.	Date of Order.	Amount authorized by the Order.	Actual amount issued for the purpose specified in the first column.	Amount expended for the purpose specified in the first column.	Unexpended balance, Feb. 1, 1894.
Original Cost of Works. (Including deficit in interest and current expense accounts to Apr. 30, 1853, under the authority of St. 1846, ch.16; and St.1849, ch.187.)	June 8, 1840 (temporary) June 22, 1846 May 3, 1852	$2,500,000 00 balance authorized			
Chestnut-Hill Reservoir.	Dec. 13, 1864 Sept. 9, 1865 Nov. 10, 1865 Nov. 17, 1865 May 28, 1867 May 28, 1867 April 21, 1868 June 29, 1868 July 2, 1869 July 2, 1870	$50,000 00 30,000 00 30,000 00 300,000 00 300,000 00 200,000 00 250,000 00 540,000 00 500,000 00 250,000 00	$5,430,711 11	$50,000 00 30,000 00 30,000 00 300,000 00 300,000 00 200,000 00 250,000 00 540,000 00 500,000 00 250,000 00	$5,430,711 11
			$2,450,000 00 17 93		
Paid into the Sinking-Funds.			2,449,982 07		2,449,982 07
New Mains. From Brookline Reservoir. Transferred to "General Purposes".	June 30, 1858	$400,000 00	$305,000 00 8 17		
From Chestnut-Hill Reserv'r. From Chestnut-Hill Reserv'r.	Mar. 20, 1850 Mar. 3, 1885	280,000 00 70,000 00	$304,991 83 280,000 00 70,000 00		
			654,991 83		654,991 83

APPENDIX — TABLE NO. 43.

"*Additional Supply,*" Under St. 1872, ch. 177, and amendments						
	Apr. 12, 1872	$100,000 00		$100,000 00	$100,000 00	
	Apr. 11, 1873	500,000 00		500,000 00	500,000 00	
	Feb. 28, 1875	1,500,000 00		1,500,000 00	1,500,000 00	
	July 18, 1876	2,000,000 00		2,000,000 00	2,000,000 00	
	Apr. 20, 1878	600,000 00		600,000 00	600,000 00	
	Apr. 11, 1879	350,000 00		350,000 00	350,000 00	
	Aug. 17, 1881	324,000 00		324,000 00	324,000 00	
	June 2, 1883	621,000 00		621,000 00	621,000 00	
	Oct. 14, 1884	150,000 00		150,000 00	150,000 00	
	May 29, 1887	35,000 00		35,000 00	35,000 00	
	May 28, 1887	40,000 00		40,000 00	40,000 00	
	Nov. 13, 1889	50,000 00		50,000 00	20,000 00	$30,000 00
	Apr. 28, 1890	1,045,000 00		1,039,000 00	1,003,252 16	35,747 84
		2,500,000 00				
Transferred from "High Service" net			9,815,000 00	25,687 56	25,687 56	
"*High Service,*" "To South Boston"	June 27, 1871	$30,000 00		$30,000 00		
Transferred to "General Purposes"				3,167 75		
Parker Hill	June 6, 1873	161,000 00		$26,532 25		
Miscellaneous	Dec. 23, 1884	766,000 00		161,000 00		
	Jan. 3, 1890	100,000 00		766,000 00		
	Mar. 1, 1890	100,000 00		100,000 00		
	June 1, 1892	75,000 00		100,000 00		
				75,000 00		
				$1,228,832 25		
Transferred to "Additional Supply" net				25,687 56		
				$1,203,144 69	1,103,144 69	
Transferred to "Extension of Maine"				100,000 00	60,000 00	
Shops on Albany st.	June 8, 1899		1,232,000 00		1,054,519 80	45,524 80
			60,000 00		60,000 00	
Amounts carried forward			$19,737,711 11	$17,083,517 26	$16,919,244 53	$114,272 73

COCHITUATE WATER LOANS. — Concluded.

Purpose of Loan specified in the Order.	Date of Order.	Amount authorized by the Order.	Actual amount issued for the purpose specified in the first column.	Amount expended for the purpose specified in the first column.	Unexpended balance, Feb. 1, 1894.
Amounts brought forward,		$19,737,711 11	$17,033,517 26	$16,919,244 53	$114,272 73
Extensions: in annexed districts - Roxbury and Dorchester.	Apr. 21, 1868	$200,000 00	$200,000 00		
	Dec. 15, 1868	250,000 00	250,000 00		
	Oct. 2, 1869	125,000 00	125,000 00		
	Apr. 15, 1870	125,000 00	125,000 00		
	July 19, 1870	375,000 00	375,000 00		
	June 27, 1871	300,000 00	300,000 00		
	June 6, 1873	115,000 00	115,000 00		
	June 6, 1874	50,000 00	50,000 00		
Brighton and W. Roxb'y,	June 6, 1874	10,000 00	10,000 00		
	Dec. 24, 1874	200,000 00	200,000 00		
	Apr. 30, 1875	100,000 00	100,000 00		
	Dec. 31, 1875	160,000 00	160,000 00		
To *Deer Island*	Sept. 1, 1869	54,000 00	64,000 00		
	Apr. 22, 1870	21,000 00	21,000 00		
"*Extension of Mains*"	Mar. 6, 1885	200,000 00	200,000 00		
	Apr. 17, 1886	100,000 00	100,000 00		
	Jan. 1, 1887	200,000 00	200,000 00		
	May 28, 1887	150,000 00	150,000 00		
	Oct. 15, 1887	150,000 00	150,000 00		
	June 4, 1888	100,000 00	100,000 00		
	Sept. 29, 1888	100,000 00	100,000 00		
	Apr. 15, 1889	200,000 00	200,000 00		
	Nov. 13, 1889	150,000 00	150,000 00		
	Oct. 13, 1890	250,000 00	250,000 00		
	June 27, 1891	100,000 00	100,000 00		
	June 23, 1892	100,000 00	100,000 00		
		$3,885,000 00	$3,985,000 00	3,985,000 00	
Transferred from "High Service"					
"*Introduction of Meters*"	June 2, 1883	$80,000 00	$80,000 00		
	Jan. 4, 1884	250,000 00	250,000 00		
		330,000 00	330,000 00	330,000 00	

APPENDIX — TABLE No. 43.

"*General Purposes*"	Feb. 17, 1854	¹ $16,000 00		$16,000 00		
	July 14, 1860	¹ 16,000 00		16,000 00		
	Dec. 8, 1860	¹ 5,000 00		5,000 00		
	Dec. 20, 1873	175,000 00		175,000 00		
Transferred from "New Maine"				$212,000 00		
				8 17		
Transferred from "High Service"				$212,008 17		
				3,167 75		
			212,000 00		215,175 92	215,175 92
Totals			$24,164,711 11		$21,563,693 18	$21,449,420 45
Issued and paid to sink'g funds					17 93	
Total amount issued					$21,563,711 11	$114,272 73

¹ Issued as City Debt.

Table No. 44.
COCHITUATE WATER SINKING-FUND RECEIPTS
[SINCE THE ESTABLISHMENT OF THE BOARD OF SINKING-FUND COMMISSIONERS IN 1871].

YEAR.	From Tax Levy or City Income.		Interest on Investments.	Interest on Bank Deposits.	Water Rates, etc.	Premiums on Loans.	Other Sources.	TOTALS.
1871, April 30, received from Committee on Reduction of Debt	$1,100,000 00							$1,100,000 00
1871-72	14,325 00	Taxes,	$61,000 00	$349 67				85,049 67
1872-73	9,375 00		70,137 50	1,017 80				80,155 30
1873-74	9,000 00		76,799 60	2,072 65				106,962 25
1874-75	30,090 00		82,842 25	2,121 18				160,936 66
1875-76	75,973 28		85,470 00	3,617 55				155,027 55
1876-77	65,554 00		86,245 66	4,119 47				352,574 77
1876-77	234,814 00		85,830 85	10,809 31	$26,480 18			338,240 08
1877-78	214,500 00	Taxes,	93,264 49	6,181 26	27,099 92			493,971 87
1878-79	207,456 00	Taxes,	90,472 42	5,687 62	177,195 91		$9,874 21	315,278 92
1879-80			86,460 00	167 32	214,707 24		4,411 64	284,058 26
1880-81			96,546 35	2,767 90	195,668 90		1,762 04	293,648 69
1881-82			105,129 51	8,486 33	193,840 36		494 08	331,438 60
1882-83	973 00	Taxes,	138,120 90	2,266 22	216,581 72		1,241 04	141,362 12
1883-84			143,049 45	7,510 40	209,258 39			350,818 24
1884-85			156,694 01	5,804 31	120,129 12		442 27	283,069 71
1885-86			181,264 89	2,644 70	297,928 95		5,081 12	562,415 66
1886-87	75,496 00	Taxes,	193,883 90	4,178 16	221,620 11			425,682 17
1887-88			213,048 22	8,958 69	256,013 57	$11,552 50		489,572 98
1888-89			228,000 83	11,730 60	300,903 00	36,092 50		576,726 93
1889-90			229,509 17	29,763 94	242,675 22	36,530 00		538,478 33
1890-91			175,808 33	22,560 16	275,014 05			562,247 54
1891-92			260,506 20	30,148 34	240,436 00	16,413 50	78,865 00	547,503 04
1892-93			298,224 44	18,133 03	299,467 27	14,621 75		630,446 49
1893-94	$2,037,656 28		$3,244,308 97	$191,098 56	$3,515,018 91	$115,210 25	$103,472 86	$9,206,665 83

APPENDIX — TABLE NO. 45. 279

Table No. 45.
COCHITUATE WATER DEBT, GROSS AND NET,
At the Close of Each Fiscal Year.

Fiscal Year.	Gross Debt.	Sinking-Funds.	Net Debt.
1847–48....	$2,129,056 32 [1]	....	$2,129,056 32
1848–49....	3,787,328 98	....	3,787,328 98
1849–50....	4,463,205 56	....	4,463,205 56
1850–51....	4,955,613 51	....	4,955,613 51
1851–52....	5,209,223 26	....	5,209,223 26
1852–53....	5,972,976 11	....	5,972,976 11
1853–54....	5,432,261 11	....	5,432,261 11
1854–55....	5,403,961 11	....	5,403,961 11
1855–56....	5,230,961 11	....	5,230,961 11
1856–57....	5,031,961 11	....	5,031,961 11
1857–58....	4,724,961 11	....	4,724,961 11
1858–59....	4,754,461 11	....	4,754,461 11
1859–60....	3,846,211 11	....	3,846,211 11
1860–61....	3,455,211 11	....	3,455,211 11
1861–62....	3,012,711 11	....	3,012,711 11
1862–63....	2,992,711 11	....	2,992,711 11
1863–64....	2,992,711 11	....	2,992,711 11
1864–65....	2,942,711 11	....	2,942,711 11
1865–66....	3,152,711 11	....	3,152,711 11
1866–67....	3,370,711 11	....	3,370,711 11
1867–68....	3,867,711 11	....	3,867,711 11
1868–69....	5,107,711 11	....	5,107,711 11
1869–70....	5,731,711 11	....	5,731,711 11
1870–71....	6,482,711 11	$1,100,000 00	5,382,711 11
1871–72....	6,812,711 11	1,185,049 67	5,627,661 44
1872–73....	6,912,711 11	1,268,234 97	5,644,476 14
1873–74....	7,863,711 11	1,372,953 62	6,490,757 49
1874–75....	8,123,711 11	1,533,890 28	6,589,820 83
1875–76....	9,735,711 11	1,560,917 83	8,174,793 28
1876–77....	11,548,711 11	1,709,492 60	9,839,218 51
1877–78....	11,545,273 98	2,043,764 73	9,501,509 25
1878–79....	11,753,273 98	2,143,847 85	9,609,426 13
1879–80....	11,697,273 98	1,771,692 92	9,925,581 06
1880–81....	11,631,273 98	1,989,300 88	9,641,973 10
1881–82....	11,631,273 98	2,281,857 89	9,349,416 09
1882–83....	11,955,273 98	2,607,768 46	9,347,505 52
1883–84....	12,882,273 98	2,746,505 58	10,135,768 40
1884–85....	13,045,473 98	3,106,323 82	9,939,150 16
1885–86....	13,491,473 98	3,385,201 26	10,106,272 72
1886–87....	14,142,273 98	3,947,616 92	10,194,657 06
1887–88....	14,741,273 98	4,373,304 09	10,367,969 89
1888–89....	14,941,273 98	4,864,092 54	10,077,181 44
1889–90....	15,696,273 98	5,440,819 47	10,255,454 51
1890–91....	16,267,773 98	5,979,297 80	10,288,476 18
1891–92....	16,423,773 98	6,471,545 34	9,952,228 64
1892–93....	16,758,773 98	7,019,058 38	9,739,715 60
1893–94....	17,055,273 98	7,649 504 87	9,405,769 11

[1] No account taken of amounts borrowed temporarily from 1846 to 1852 and afterwards funded by the issue of the water bonds that figure in this statement.

Table No. 46.
PARK APPROPRIATIONS.
To December 31, 1894.

Name.	Date.	Special Statutes.	Amount.	Object.	Amount expended.	Balance.
Park Department	Oct. 6, 1876,		Appropriation, $6,900 00	Dept. Expenses,	$5,409 38	Merged, $1,490 62
"	May 1, 1876,		5,000 00	"	5,000 00	
Public Park, Back Bay	July 23, 1877,	Chap. 185, Acts 1875	Loan, 450,000 00	Land	450,000 00	
Park Department	Dec. 24, 1877,		Appropriation, 3,000 00	Dept. Expenses,	2,992 63	Merged, 7 37
Public Park, Back Bay	Feb. 12, 1878,		25,000 00	Construction	25,000 00	
"	26, 1878,		16,000 00	Land	16,000 00	
Park Department	Apr. 16, 1878,		6,000 00	Dept. Expenses,	4,300 00	Transferred to Back Bay, 1,700 00
Public Park, Back Bay	July 3, 1878,		25,000 00	Construction	25,000 00	
Park Nursery	July 31, 1878,		2,000 00	"	1,911 09	88 91
Public Park, Back Bay	Mar. 15, 1879,	Transferred from Park Department				
Park Department	Apr. 29, 1879,		1,700 00	Dept. Expenses,	1,700 00	
Public Park, Back Bay	" 29, 1879,		5,000 00	Construction	5,000 00	
"	" 10, 1880,		120,000 00	"	120,000 00	
Park Department	" 10, 1880,		214,000 00	Dept. Expenses,	214,400 00	
Park Nursery	6, 1881,		5,000 00	Construction	4,767 97	Merged, 232 03
Public Park, Back Bay	" 6, 1881,		1,000 00	"	1,000 00	
Park Department	" 6, 1881,		202,000 00	Dept. Expenses,	202,000 00	
Muddy River Improvement	" 6, 1881,		5,000 00	Construction	4,950 53	Merged, 49 47
West Roxbury Park (Franklin Park)			4,000 00	"	4,000 00	Transferred to Arboretum, 1,000 00
Charles River Embankment	Dec. 10, 1881,	Chap. 185, Acts 1875	Loan, 600,000 00	Land	600,000 00	
Muddy River Improvement	" 24, 1881,	"	300,000 00	"	300,000 00	
City Point Park (Marine Park)	" 24, 1881,	"	200,000 00	"	200,000 00	
East Boston Park (Wood Island Park)	" 24, 1881,	"	100,000 00	"	100,000 00	
Arnold Arboretum	" 24, 1881,		50,000 00	Construction	50,000 00	
Public Park, Back Bay	" 28, 1881,		60,000 00	"	60,000 00	
Park Department	Apr. 20, 1882,		Appropriation, 200,000 00	Dept. Expenses,	200,000 00	
"	" 20, 1882,		5,000 00	"	4,392 07	Merged, 607 93
Park Nursery	" 6, 1883,		1,000 00	Construction	1,000 00	
Public Park, Back Bay	" 6, 1883,		100,000 00	"	100,000 00	
Arnold Arboretum	" 6, 1883,		15,000 00	Dept. Expenses,	15,000 00	Transferred to Arboretum, 1,000 00
West Roxbury Park (Franklin Park)	" 6, 1883,		5,000 00	Construction	5,000 00	

APPENDIX — TABLE No. 46.

Wood Island Park	" 6, 1883,	Chap. 185, Acts 1875	Loan,	5,000 00	1,000 00
City Point Park (Marine Park)	" 17, 1883,	"	Appropriation,	120,000 00 Land	120,000 00
Marine Park	June 21, 1883,	"	"	3,000 00 Construction	3,000 00
Charles River Embankment	" 21, 1884,	"	"	1,000 00 "	1,000 00 Transferred to Arboretum, 4,000 00
Arnold Arboretum	Jan. 1, 1884,	Transfer'd from Wood Island Park		4,000 00	4,000 00
"	" 1, 1884,	Transfe'd from Muddy River Improvement,		1,000 00	1,000 00
"	" 1, 1884,	Transferred from Park Nursery		1,000 00	1,000 00
West Roxbury Park (Franklin Park)	" 4, 1884,	Chap. 185, Acts 1875	Loan,	500,000 00	500,000 00
Public Park, Back Bay	Apr. 30, 1884,	"	Appropriation,	150,000 00 Land	150,000 00
Charles River Embankment	" 30, 1884,	"	"	126,000 00 Construction	126,000 00
Wood Island Park	" 30, 1884,	"	"	25,000 00 "	25,000 00
West Roxbury Park (Franklin Park)	" 30, 1884,	Transferred from West Roxbury Park		24,000 00 "	16,000 00
Marine Park	" 30, 1884,	"		24,000 00 "	24,000 00 Transferred to Arboretum, 8,000 00
Arnold Arboretum	" 30, 1884,	"		20,000 00 "	20,000 00
Park Department	" 30, 1884,	"		5,000 00 Dept. Expenses,	5,000 00
Arnold Arboretum	Nov. 22, 1884,	"			
Public Park, Back Bay	Apr. 30, 1885,	"	"	8,000 00 Construction	8,000 00
Marine Park	" 30, 1885,	"	"	45,000 00 "	45,000 00
Arnold Arboretum	" 30, 1885,	"	"	10,000 00 "	15,000 00
Franklin Park	" 30, 1885,	"	"	10,000 00 "	10,000 00
Wood Island Park	" 30, 1885,	"	"	5,000 00 "	5,000 00
Park Department	" 30, 1885,	"	"	5,000 00 Dept. Expenses,	6,000 00
Park Nursery	" 30, 1885,	"	"	4,000 00 Construction	4,000 00
Franklin Park	June 29, 1885,	"	"	3,000 00 "	3,000 00
Wood Island Park	Sept. 26, 1885,	"	"	10,000 00 "	10,000 00
Park Nursery	Nov. 14, 1885,	"		2,800 00 "	2,000 00
Charles River Embankment	" 14, 1885,	"	Loan,	2,000 00 Land	16,000 00
"	Dec. 28, 1885,	Chap. 185, Acts 1875	"	16,000 00 Construction	50,000 00 Transferred to City Account, 27 43
Marine Park		"	"	60,000 00 Land	
Public Park, Back Bay		"	"	13,000 00 "	12,972 57
Park Department	May 6, 1886,	Transferred from Coveredered Channel, Muddy River	Appropriation,	2,300 00 Construction	2,300 00
Park Nursery	" 6, 1886,	"	"	6,500 00 Dept. Expenses,	6,500 00
Arnold Arboretum	Apr. 24, 1886,	Chap. 185, Acts 1875	Loan,	5,000 00 Construction	5,000 00
"	June 12, 1886,	"	"	4,000 00 Land	4,000 00
Charles River Embankment	Oct. 22, 1886,	"	"	16,000 00 "	15,932 71 Transferred to Sinking-Fund, 67 29
Public Park Construction	Jan. 4, Feb. 10, Dec. 31, 1887	Chap. 304, Acts 1886	"	55,000 00 "	54,886 45 Transf'red to Sinking-Fund, 113 55
				2,500,000 00 Construction	2,500,00 00

Public Parks. — Table of Appropriations. — *Concluded.*

Name.	Date.	Special Statutes.		Amount.	Object.	Amount expended.	Balance.
Park Department	Apr. 30, 1887,	. . .	Appropriation,	$6,500 00	Dept. Expenses,	$6,500 00	
Park Nursery	" 30, 1887,	. . .	"	5,000 00	Construction	5,000 00	
Park Maintenance	" 30, 1887,	. . .	"	15,000 00	Maintenance	14,965 44	$34 56
Public Park Lands	June 4, 1887,	Chap. 312, Acts 1887	Loan,	400,000 00	Land	400,000 00	
Park Department	" 2, 1888,	. . .	Appropriation,	6,500 00	Dept. Expenses,	6,500 00	
Park Nursery	" 2, 1888,	. . .	"	5,000 00	Construction	5,000 00	
Park Maintenance	Apr. 29, 1889,	. . .	"	20,000 00	Maintenance	20,000 00	
Park Department	" 29, 1889,	. . .	"	7,500 00	Dept. Expenses,	5,969 46	Merged,
Park Nursery	" 29, 1889,	. . .	"	6,000 00	Construction	6,000 00	
Park Maintenance	" 29, 1889,	. . .	"	35,000 00	Maintenance	35,000 00	30 56
Public Park Lands " received from town of Brookline	Feb. 11, 1890,	Chap. 392, Acts 1889	Loan,	600,000 00	Land	600,000 00	
Park Maintenance	" 11, 1890,	" 339, " 1890	"	20,000 00	Maintenance	20,000 00	
"	Mar. 8, 1890,	Transferred by City Auditor		2,856 52	"	2,836 52	
"	May 9, 1890,	Chap. 271 and 444, Acts 1890	Appropriation,	56,500 00	"	56,500 00	
Public Parks, Charlestown	Oct. 13, 1890,	Chap. 185, Acts 1875	Loan,	200,000 00	Land and Cons.	200,000 00	
Franklin Park	" 17, 1890,	Transferred from sale of city property	"	14,000 00	Land	14,000 00	
Charlesbank	Apr. 15, 1891,	Chap. 301, Acts 1891	"	2,869 02	"	2,869 02	
Park Maintenance	May 7, 1891,	. . .	Appropriation,	60,000 00	Maintenance	60,000 00	
Public Parks	May 20, 1891,	. . .	Loan,	3,500,000 00	Land and Cons.	3,451,785 01	48,214 99
Park Department	Jan. 30, 1892,	. . .	Appropriation,	60,000 00	Maintenance	60,000 00	
"	May 18, 1892,	Transferred from Reserved Fund by Mayor and Committee on Finance		5,000 00	"	6,000 00	Balance,
"	June 9 1892,			8,000 00	"	8,000 00	
"	Jan. 31, 1893,	Transferred by City Auditor		3,626 07	"	3,626 07	
"	Feb. 10, 1893,	Transferred by City Auditor	Appropriation,	80,000 00	"	80,000 00	
"	Dec. 6, 1893,	Transferred by City Auditor		20,000 00	"	20,000 00	
"	Jan. 31, 1894,	Chap. 282, Acts 1893		6,431 80	"	6,431 80	
Public Parks, Wards 6 and 7	May 17, 1893,		Appropriation,	350,000 00	Land and Cons.	199,540 88	Balance, 150,459 12
Playstead, No. Brighton	July 10, 1893,		"	25,000 00	Land	21,114 83	Balance, 3,885 17

APPENDIX — TABLE No. 46.

Public Parks	Feb. 1, 1894,			500,000 00	Construction	500,000 00
"	" 1, 1894,	Transferred from Crushed Stone Appropriation for Street Improvements		50,000 00	Street Improv'ts,	50,000 00
Park Department	" 12, 1894,			100,000 00	Maintenance	93,618 24 Balance, 6,381 76
"	May 10, 1894,			7,000 00	"	7,000 00
"	June 11, 1894,			5,000 00	"	5,000 00
"	Dec. 31, 1894,	Transferred by City Auditor		3,898 61		3,898 61
				$12,711,662 02		$12,484,271 27 $227,390 75
Income appropriated to Maintenance by City Council orders approved December 18, 1883, June 15 and October 23, 1896 1883				1,772 28		
Income appropriated to Maintenance by City Council orders approved December 18, 1883, June 15 and October 23, 1886 1884				13,996 08		
Income appropriated to Maintenance by City Council orders approved December 18, 1883, June 15 and October 23, 1886 1885				12,999 80		
Income appropriated to Maintenance by City Council orders approved December 18, 1883, June 15 and October 23, 1886 1886				15,900 93		
Income appropriated to Maintenance by City Council orders approved December 18, 1883, June 15 and October 23, 1886 1887				7,415 54		
Income appropriated to Maintenance by City Council orders approved December 18, 1883, June 15 and October 23, 1886 1888				3,950 06		
Income appropriated to Maintenance by City Council orders approved December 18, 1883, June 15 and October 23, 1886 1889				4,421 12		
Income appropriated to Maintenance by City Council orders approved December 18, 1883, June 15 and October 23, 1886 1890				6,452 97		
				$12,778,470 80		$12,551,080 05 66,806 78 $12,551,080 05 $227,390 75

Summary.

Appropriations for Construction	$4,529,600 00	
" Land and Construction	4,040,000 00	
" Land	3,561,869 02	
" Maintenance, including Income	655,101 78	
" Department expenses	61,900 00	
	$12,778,470 80	
Less expenditures as above	12,551,080 05	
	$227,390 75	
Less transfers and merged balances	18,449 71	
Balances on hand January 1, 1895	$208,841 04	

Expenditures, as above $12,551,080 05
Expenditures, as per City Auditor's account 12,547,853 94

Difference $3,226 11

NOTE.

The difference between the total cost of land, construction, and maintenance as given in the Auditor's statements and that given above is due to special drafts, amounting to $3,226.11 drawn by the Park Department, but not yet paid.

Table No. 47.

PUBLIC PARKS.—Table of Annual Expenditures under certain heads from 1875 to January 1, 1895.

	1875-76.	1876-77.	1877-78.	1878-79.	1879-80.	1880-81.	1881-82.	1882-83.	1883-84.	1884-85.
Payments for land			$295,445 40	$134,946 80	$9,298 70	$4,383 89		$478,106 51	$468,488 47	$276,837 97
Payments for construction:										
Excavating, filling, grading, sea-walls, etc., other than done by Department				37,629 36	107,709 02	87,875 91	$67,493 43	17,861 62	64,492 62	69,331 93
Materials			43 75	143 32	1,431 60		41,528 30	62,128 42	37,479 57	22,466 58
Labor			111 72	6,763 03	3,818 12	1,622 01	31,965 72	72,570 91	82,171 11	80,937 54
Teaming and freight					19 00		4,943 79	7,784 29	33,762 84	59,875 41
Bridge constructions, other than done by Department				592 80		9,118 41	72,962 36	11,526 61	547 16	828 03
Buildings, other than done by Department	$2,449 69		3,503 52	4,884 57	2,296 45	2,556 00	4,164 50	5,901 81	5,620 55	5,866 51
Professional services, etc.	2,059 09		2,135 36	2,916 44	7,603 44	5,013 99	6,284 63	5,109 66	6,060 31	8,439 03
Miscellaneous expenses										11,365 02
Total construction account	$5,409 38		$5,816 15	$52,929 52	$122,877 63	$106,186 32	$229,322 74	$183,453 32	$228,734 46	$259,110 05
Total cost	$5,409 38	$2,840 08	$301,261 55	$187,876 32	$132,176 33	$110,570 21	$229,322 74	$661,588 83	$697,222 93	$535,948 02
Maintenance account:										
Franklin Park									$2,944 74	$5,055 84
Parkway									829 66	205 50
Charlesbank Park										1,120 26
Marino Park										
Arnold Arboretum										66 95
Charlestown										
Wood Island										
Dorchester Park										
Franklin Field										
Total									$3,774 40	$6,468 55
Total land, construction, and maintenance	$5,409 38	$2,840 08	$301,261 55	$187,876 32	$132,176 33	$110,570 21	$229,322 74	$661,588 83	$700,997 33	$542,416 57
Covered channel, Stony Brook						$46,731 85	$62,036 10	$13,539 55	$2,014 06	
Covered channel, Muddy River								55,712 12	47,213 03	$27,000 25
	$5,409 38	$2,840 08	$301,261 55	$187,876 32	$132,176 33	$157,302 06	$291,358 84	$730,840 50	$750,225 04	$569,416 82

APPENDIX — TABLE NO. 47. 285

PUBLIC PARKS. — Table of Annual Expenditures. — Continued.

	1885-86.	1886-87.	1887-88.	1888-89.	1889-90.	1890-91.	1891-92.	1892-93.	1893-94.	Feb. 1, 1894, to Jan. 1, 1895.
Payments for land	$488,105 27	$147,046 43	$471,458 18	$55,684 82	$1,029 48	$307,673 70	$304,742 73	$402,219 45	$391,401 37	$330,580 81
Payments for construction:										
Excavating, filling, grading, seawalls, etc., other than done by Department	116,992 58	65,858 16	26,643 57	55,837 15	36,142 37	192,046 26	298,459 86	279,965 27	235,458 69	320,269 48
Materials	19,109 98	1,553 81	77,568 73	60,189 51	58,001 64	35,244 65	44,637 10	42,345 28	76,744 11	221,274 39
Labor	50,979 39	10,814 97	226,881 57	232,107 39	247,351 69	217,010 73	187,125 64	202,408 39	223,249 39	107,949 02
Teaming and freights	5,560 48	294 95	74,216 41	66,999 93	46,388 08	43,457 45	41,095 14	50,180 99	72,320 02	88,061 26
Bridge construction, other than done by Department	11,633 44	765 04	99,393 62	102,756 57	73,409 67	22,026 44	72,171 53	41,948 49	82,534 07	76,915 21
Buildings, other than done by Department			324 07	28,881 16	8,628 12	3,000 00	4,752 70	10,433 45	29,011 34	61,037 01
Professional services, etc.	12,119 05	2,800 00	6,664 03	9,395 73	9,820 32	11,537 02	13,834 87	14,905 25	18,233 46	20,788 44
Miscellaneous expenses	13,007 30	14,023 39	14,007 19	14,906 30	15,155 33	13,424 33	12,843 76	18,469 25	18,393 78	13,385 15
Total construction account	$229,402 22	$104,337 93	$325,699 21	$371,074 74	$493,897 22	$530,746 88	$674,952 60	$690,676 37	$755,930 06	$1,019,679 99
Total cost	$717,507 49	$251,384 36	$997,157 39	$626,759 56	$497,926 70	$838,420 58	$979,695 33	$1,062,895 82	$1,347,351 43	$1,350,560 80
Maintenance account:										
Franklin Park	$7,986 27	$5,791 92	$8,270 94	$10,477 18	$17,568 15	$22,091 89	$24,122 93	$24,973 46	$27,711 33	$31,657 91
Parkway	2,395 45	3,701 66	937 26	7,193 91	11,923 71	13,430 94	14,238 29	17,225 21	28,702 05	33,469 72
Charlesbank Park	1,907 47	1,834 15	1,237 64	2,241 27	6,107 65	8,885 37	10,225 65	12,819 52	15,952 37	12,430 21
Marine Park	1,385 88	2,003 42	2,737 75	3,726 43	4,030 93	4,348 84	4,221 14	8,365 77	12,619 33	11,238 61
Arnold Arboretum	1,193 37	2,027 98	1,600 46	3,659 36	3,414 30	3,806 64	3,745 76	5,178 83	6,191 45	7,250 24
Charlestown							192 50	49 00	3,310 36	1,834 87
Wood Island					1 50		3 50	1,197 00	1,346 12	190 00
Dorchester Park								1,077 28	77	6 30 24
Franklin Field								61 25	390 25	916 89
Commonwealth avenue						5 75				8,307 19
Office Expenses										
Total	$14,868 44	$15,379 13	$14,784 05	$27,303 15	$43,056 24	$52,569 43	$56,749 77	$70,997 32	$98,500 76	$109,516 85
Total land, construction, and maintenance	$732,375 93	$266,763 49	$1,011,941 44	$654,072 71	$540,982 94	$890,990 01	$1,036,445 10	$1,133,893 14	$1,445,852 19	$1,960,077 65
Covered channel, Stony Brook	$17,500 12	$1,021 04	$25 00	$7 99						
Covered channel, Muddy River	$749,876 05	$267,784 53	$1,011,966 44	$654,080 70	$540,982 94	$890,990 01	$1,036,445 10	$1,133,893 14	$1,445,852 19	$1,960,077 65

PUBLIC PARKS. — Concluded.

Summary.

	Totals.
Payments for land	$5,270,758 98
Payments for construction:	
Excavating, filling, grading, sea-walls, etc., other than done by Department	2,066,097 48
Materials	804,847 30
Labor	2,075,772 37
Teaming and freights	593,071 76
Bridge construction, other than done by Department	679,129 45
Buildings, other than done by Department	174,734 36
Professional services, etc.	171,150 50
Miscellaneous expenses	198,323 05
Total construction account	$6,763,126 87
Total cost	$12,033,885 85
Maintenance account:	
Franklin Park	$188,652 56
Parkway	133,468 70
Charlesbank Park	75,611 22
Marine Park	54,678 10
Arnold Arboretum	40,155 34
Charlestown	5,152 73
Wood Island	4,588 84
Dorchester Park	1,344 78
Franklin Field	1,091 74
Commonwealth Avenue	916 89
Office expenses	8,307 19
Total	$513,968 09
Total land, construction, and maintenance	$12,547,853 94
Covered channel, Stony Brook	$124,332 16
Covered channel, Muddy River	148,479 57
	$12,820,655 67

Table No. 48.
PARK STATISTICS TO JANUARY 1, 1895.

Parks.	Year of Taking.	Cost to Date. Land.	Cost to Date. Construction.	Total.	Area.	Length of Driveways.	Length of Walks.	Length of Rides.	Area of Ponds and Rivers.
MAIN PARK SYSTEM:									
*Commonwealth Avenue	1894				30 acres	2.8 miles	4.13 miles		
*Fens	1879	$580,764 49	$85,384 98	$85,384 98	115 "	4 "	6.7 "	1.1 miles	28 acres.
†Riverway	1880	432,457 53	2,033,539 44	2,614,303 93	40 "	1.4 "	2.8 "	1.2 "	8 "
*Leverett Park	1890 and 1892	153,008 77	531,963 24	984,420 77	60 "	1.2 "	3.4 "	0.9 mile	14 "
Jamaica Park	1892	645,862 69	314,621 43	467,630 20	120 "	1.5 "	5.6 "	0.7 "	64.5 "
Arborway	1892	84,679 01	117,707 66	763,570 35	38 "	3.4 "	1.25 "	1.4 miles	
*Arnold Arboretum	1882	74,043 38	174,018 28	258,697 29	155 "	2 "	5.6 "		
West Roxburywy.	1894	3,561 75	225,228 18	299,271 56	150 "	1 "	4.2 "		0.5 acre.
*Franklin Park	1883 and 1884	1,551,120 01	434 31	3,996 06	527 "	4.1 "	19.1 "	2.5 "	7.4 acres.
			1,593,688 33	3,144,808 34		10.0 "			
MARINE PARK SYSTEM:									
Dorchesterway	1892	69,887 89	44,496 30	104,384 19	6 "	0.75 mile	1.6 "		
Strandway	1890 and 1892	356,830 97	22,246 87	379,077 84	20 land	1.7 miles	3.1 "		
					174 flats				
*Marine Park	1893	232,972 57	336,057 77	836,057 77	32 land	0.9 mile	2.6 "		4.4 "
					235 flats				
Castle Island	1890		31,960 83	31,960 83	21 "	0.4 "	1.6 "		
*CHARLESBANK	1881	373,916 99	282,181 78	656,093 77	10 "		1.5 "		
*WOOD ISLAND PARK	1882 and 1891	132,900 00	184,238 36	317,083 36	46 "		2.9 "		
					165 land				
*CHARLESTOWN HEIGHTS	1891	50,538 02	87,902 27	138,340 29	4 "	1.1 miles	0.4 mile		
CHARLESTOWN PLAY-GROUND	1891	149,554 98	5,631 53	155,186 51	6 land				
					11 flats				
NORTH END PARK	1893	194,407 04	5,133 24	199,540 28	4 "		0.9 "		
DORCHESTER PARK	1891	31,401 13	2,789 37	34,190 50	3 "				
FRANKLIN FIELD	1892	119,093 59	64,204 32	183,297 91	26 "				
*PLAYSTEAD, No. Brighton	1894	132,900 00		21,114 83	57 land		0.43 "		
					14 flats				
Sundry surveys		$5,268,016 24	$5,643,378 49	$11,911,394 73	2,094 acres.	35.35 miles.	62.21 miles.	7.8 miles.	126.9 acres.
General account		2,919 19		2,919 19					
Park Nursery			73,987 50	73,987 50					
Betterment expenses			29,947 07	29,947 07					
			11,669 89	11,669 89					
		$5,269,935 43	$6,758,982 95	$12,029,918 38					

* The land in these parks has been paid for in full. † An additional area of 34 acres is within the limits of the town of Brookline.
Of the above total lengths of Driveways, Walks, and Rides there have been completed to date respectively 20.4 miles, 27.8 miles, and 5.6 miles.
The difference between the total cost of land and construction as given in the Auditor's statements and that given above, is accounted for by drafts drawn and not paid amounting to $3,226.11, and by the Auditor's maintenance account being $7,193.53 less than the maintenance account of this department.

Table No. 49.

PARK BETTERMENTS COLLECTED TO FEBRUARY 1, 1894.

	Assessm'ts committed to Collector.	Abated.	Net Assessm'ts.	Collected.	Outstand'g February 1, 1894.
Public Park, Back Bay ..	$434,600 00	$143,126 73	$291,473 27	$290,404 27	$1,069 00
Marine Park, City Point ..	23,543 00	12,616 80	10,926 20	10,926 20	
Franklin Park	135,029 00	122,000 66	13,028 34	13,028 34	
Parkway, Old Harbor .	60,789 00	38,042 30	22,746 70	7,250 70	15,496 00
Parkway, Muddy River ..	108,972 00	6,349 00	102,623 00	17,620 00	85,003 00
Totals	$762,933 00	$322,135 49	$440,797 51	$339,229 51	$101,568 00

Table No. 50.
THE PARK DEBT
December 31, 1894.

Total loans outstanding		$9,849,000 00
Means of Redemption:		
Sinking-Funds	$1,573,948 68	
Betterments outstanding	154,663 00	
Total		1,728,611 68
Net Park debt December 31, 1894		8,120,388 32
Right to borrow January 1, 1895, under St. 1894, ch. 396 *		$1,000,000 00

* Issued January 4, 1895.

www.ingramcontent.com/pod-product-compliance
Lightning Source LLC
Chambersburg PA
CBHW032054230426
43672CB00009B/1587